On High Ground

A History of the Olivetan Benedictine Sisters

Jonesboro, Arkansas

1887-2003

Sr. Henrietta Hockle, OSB

Published by Pinpoint Printing.

ISBN 0-9702324-0-3 Paperback Edition

ISBN 0-9702324-3-8 Hardbound Edition

Cover design by Jennifer Shane and Dana Kelley.
Text design by Jennifer Shane.
Set in 10-point Centennial Text.

Printed in the United States of America.
FIRST EDITION

For information, contact

5115 East Highland Drive
Jonesboro, Arkansas 72401
www.pinpointprinting.com

Coat of Arms

Congregation of the Olivetan Benedictines

Symbolism

The Coat of Arms of the Olivetan Benedictines reveals peaks of three snow-covered mountains, which symbolize Mary's purity. The crimson cross surmounting the highest peak, symbolizes Christ's love for us by His sufferings and death on the cross. The olive branches between the mountains symbolize peace.

The white mountain peaks inspire the religious to imitate Mary's virtues and her love for Jesus. The crimson cross reminds one, in gratitude, to develop a devotion to the passion of Christ. The olive branches call one to live and witness to a life in peace.

Contents

Appendix Contents

Prologue

Benedictines, men and women, were late-comers onto the America Catholic scene. Monks and Nuns of the Benedictine family only came to the United States in the mid-1840s. They came from Bavaria to Pennsylvania. Once arrived, though, Benedictines expanded rapidly.

The Benedictine Sisters of Jonesboro, Arkansas stem, not from this Bavarian "family root," but from a slightly later arrival of Swiss Benedictines in the 1870s. The coming of these Swiss Monastics was also somewhat different from that of their Bavarian sisters and brothers. The Swiss Benedictines were motivated by missionary zeal, so common in the 1880s, but also because the Swiss government, at the time, was anti-clerical and was harassing or closing religious houses. The Benedictines there thought rather seriously that they might need a place of refuge in another land.

Also, the Jonesboro Community descended from a convent of Benedictine Women, newly organized for the purpose of Perpetual Adoration of the Blessed Sacrament. This devotion was very popular in Europe at this time and was spreading rapidly. The first Swiss Sisters from this fairly new convent of Maria Rickenbach came to Missouri to help Monks from their Swiss neighbor, the Abbey of Engelberg, who were starting a new mission in northwest Missouri. Upon arrival on the American "frontier" in Missouri in the late 1870s, these Swiss Nuns found that they were desperately needed as teachers in parochial schools and their aim for Perpetual Adoration was not at all possible. But the communities that stem from this Swiss "shoot" retained a strong Eucharistic orientation and have kept it to the present day.

A whole list of "what ifs" for the Jonesboro Benedictine Sisters in northeastern Arkansas could be drawn up:

—*What if* the Benedictine Sisters of the Swiss Convent Maria Rickenbach had not gone to Missouri? Would Holy Angels Convent in Jonesboro have come into existence?

—*What if* German-speaking immigrants were not coming to Arkansas in such numbers in the 1870s and 1880s? Would these Benedictine women have come to what was then a rather God-forsaken part of the state?

—*What if* the monks' Abbey of Maria Stein in Switzerland had not been closed by the Swiss government and the Monks dispersed? Would Fr. Eugene Weibel, a monk of this Abbey, and chief instigator of the Jonesboro Benedictines, have come to the United States, to Arkansas, and to Pocahontas and needed Sisters? Would the Convent of Maria Stein, later becoming Holy Angels Convent have started?

—*What if* a pressing need for a hospital in Jonesboro not arisen? Would these Benedictine women have gone into the hospital ministry anyhow and would St. Bernards Medical Center become such a part of the life of this Community?

This list could go on. Over the doors of the National Archives Building in Washington, D.C. are the words: "The Past is Prologue." These words could apply to all the "what ifs" that could be catalogued and which contributed to the foundation of a new Benedictine Community. Thus a new chapter in the Catholic Diocese of Little Rock was written and a new shoot of the great tree that is the Order of St. Benedict sprouted. And most importantly, since the founding of this Benedictine house, many lives have been lived there and many more lives of others have been touched "that in all things God may be glorified."

Fr. Hugh Assenmacher, OSB
Feast of Christ the King
November 23, 2003

Dedication

Lovingly dedicated to all my Sisters, past and present, whose story this is, and to our families who made the story possible.

Throughout the 116 year history of this Community, many generous women have responded to the challenge to seek God by following the Benedictine way of life as lived at Holy Angels Convent. By their indomitable faith and courage these Sisters have responded to the needs of the Church and the needs of the times from the late 1880s to the present Twenty-first Century.

May this story inspire others to seek God through prayer and work in the Olivetan Benedictine Tradition.

Sister Henrietta Hockle, OSB
Feast of the Holy Family
December 28, 2003

Foreword

History of the First 116 Years of the Olivetan Benedictine Sisters in Arkansas 1887-2003

High ground is a distinguishing characteristic of the Olivetan Benedictine Community throughout its 116 year history in Arkansas. The Community had its roots in Kloster Maria Rickenbach, located high in the Swiss Alps. To replicate this location the "Jonesboro Benedictines," as the Community is often referred to, consistently chose high ground on which to build their foundation.

After a 13 year stay in the hills of northwest Missouri, four founding Sisters came to Arkansas in 1887 to settle in Pocahontas on "Catholic Hill," one of the highest points in Randolph County. In 1898, after 11 years in Pocahontas, the fledgling community relocated their Motherhouse to Jonesboro, on Crowley's Ridge. This Ridge separates the Delta flat land from the northeast Arkansas hills, and at points reaches an altitude of 550 feet.

Dr. John Branner, a state geologist, believes the Ridge resulted from two massive shifts in the channel of the Mississippi River during the years of 1811-1812. The Ridge was formed of the original strip between the two old channels of the River. In 1974, when the Community again relocated the Motherhouse, the Sisters chose a higher elevation, along Crowley's Ridge just north of the city limits of Jonesboro.

Throughout the history of this Community, the Sisters consistently chose high ground, not only for the physical location of their Motherhouse, but also, by choosing the high road—the road less traveled by—in following the Gospel precepts, to seek God through "Ora et Labora," prayer and work, in the Benedictine Tradition. The Community has maintained the monastic recitation of the Liturgy of the Hours, devotion to the Eucharist, continued a community life-style, and retained a recognizable "habit" or religious garb. Their ministries have touched thousands of lives through education, health care and a number of other apostolic works.

This is more of a documentary than just a story of the first 116 years of the Jonesboro Benedictines, as I have drawn information from the following sources: In Your Midst, by Sr. Dolores Dowling, OSB, of the Clyde Benedictine Community; Green Olive Branch, by Sr. Agnes Voth, OSB, Jonesboro Olivetan Benedictine Community; unpublished articles and letters by Mother Beatrice Renggli, OSB; articles by Sr. Felicitas Hunkler, OSB and Sr. Alexia Suter, OSB, of the Jonesboro Benedictine Community; personal interviews with Sisters; and materials found in the Archives of the Perpetual Adoration Monastery, Clyde, Missouri and Holy Angels Convent, Jonesboro, Arkansas.

I also did research in the Craighead County Jonesboro Public Library and the Dean B. Ellis Library of Arkansas State University, Jonesboro. References are noted at the end of each chapter and wherever appropriate, the source is credited in the narrative. A Necrology, a list of parishes or missions served, and pictures of all living Sisters and an Index are included in the Appendix.

Needless to say, I could not include all the names and happenings of these past 116 years, but I have tried to select significant information from each decade to document the history of the Jonesboro Benedictine Community. This book is meant to be an overview of the wonders and goodness of God manifested in northeast Arkansas.

Sister Henrietta Hockle, OSB

Acknowledgements

This book would not be possible without the many persons who assisted me in numerous ways in telling the story of the Jonesboro Benedictines. First, I express sincere gratitude to God for His assistance in the research and writing the manuscript. Secondly, I thank Sister Eileen Schneider, Prioress for commissioning me to write an updated version of the history of the Olivetan Benedictine Sisters in Arkansas, and for her encouragement along the way.

I express sincere appreciation to Father Hugh Assenmacher, OSB, Monk of Subiaco Abbey, for editing the book and for his insightful suggestions and advice. To Sister Mary Anne Nuce, I express thanks for faithfully proofreading the manuscript, to Dana Kelley, Managing Partner of McNabb Kelley & Barré, for directing production, and to Richard Bishop of Bishop's Photography for the cover photo, and all Sisters' photos. Special thanks to Sister Beatrice Schneider for preservation of materials in the archives over the years. I am truly grateful to all my Sisters for their words of encouragement and support throughout the two years I have worked on this project.

While I have received input and assistance from many people, interpretation of material reflects my own judgement and responsibility for any factual errors rests solely with me.

Sister Henrietta Hockle, OSB

Pre-Arkansas Foundation

CHAPTER I

1528-1874

Origins

The history of the Olivetan Benedictine Sisters of Jonesboro begins at a place of pilgrimage, the shrine of Maria Rickenbach. This shrine in the mountainous Canton of Unterwalden, Switzerland, sits on a green plateau with the towering Musenalp behind it. It looks over the valley of Engelberg and up to the Nidwalden Alps, the Stanzerhorn and the cloud-encircled Mount Pilatus. This shrine became a place of pilgrimage early in the 16th century, due to tensions and the persecutions of churches and monasteries. Zwingli was the chief reformation figure in Switzerland in the early years of the 16th century. Wherever he went, a wholesale destruction of altars, sacred vessels, pictures and images followed.

Kloster Maria Rickenbach when first group of Sisters left for America in 1874.

Legend of the Shrine

According to legend, in 1528 a shepherd lad named Zumbuel was grazing his sheep on the shoulder of Mount Rickenbach, when suddenly he spied a column of black smoke arising within a short distance from where he sat. Curiosity overcame him and he went near to see what was burning. Men were destroying pictures, and statues of saints, which according to Zwingli's teachings they considered superstitious practices. He saw a wooden statue of the Virgin and Child that had been consigned to the flames. He stretched out his arms and snatched the statue from the flames and made off with it. (He later claimed that the statue rose toward him out of the flames.) In the spring, he brought his treasure with him to the mountains at the foot of the Musenalp. There he placed it in a hollow of a tree, saying his prayers before it as he watched his sheep.

When fall came and it was time to return to his own village, Zumbuel could not budge the statue from the tree. Some of his friends came to help him, but to no avail. Then Zumbuel called the pastor, Curate Spanzig, of the neighboring church in Stans, to come and help. He came with several men, but their luck was no better. Only after the people agreed to build a small chapel there, did the Madonna allow herself to be removed from the tree. First a little wayside shrine of local stones was made for the miraculous statue. Later, in 1565, a chapel was built to accommodate the pilgrims who came to pray in ever larger numbers. By 1688, a still larger chapel was needed.[1]

Wooden statue of Mary and Child Jesus at shrine on Mount Rickenbach.

A Dream Realized

It was to Maria Rickenbach that two young courageous Swiss women came for the first time 1853. Both belonged to a diocesan religious institute in Baldegg, Canton Lucerne. Both wished to belong to a community devoted to perpetual adoration of the Blessed Sacrament and were disappointed that their institute continued only to teach, along with looking after orphans and old folks.

Sr. Vincentia Gretner, the older of the two, had come to Maria Rickenbach for her health, with Sr. Gertrude Leupi as companion. While the former's health improved in the fresh air and sunshine, the latter was fascinated by the story of the miraculous statue in the small church of Maria Rickenbach. Praying before this treasured image in the little church, they felt renewed in their desire to devote their lives to perpetual adoration of the Blessed Sacrament. Both Sr. Vincentia and Sr. Gertrude left Maria Rickenbach more determined than ever to find a religious life centered on the adoration of the Blessed Sacrament.[2]

Not far from Maria Rickenbach, at the head of the Nidwalden Valley of Canton Unterwalden, was the ancient Benedictine Abbey of Engelberg, founded in 1082. The Abbey had a commanding position and possessed influence over the surrounding areas. However, tensions were mounting between the church and state, due to increasing restrictions on religious institutions. It was to Engelberg Abbey that Sr. Vincentia and Sr. Gertrude turned for advice. With the help of Sr. Gertrude's confessor, Fr. Anselm Villiger, OSB, one of the monks of Engelberg Abbey, the Sisters were able to speak to Abbot Placidus Tanner, OSB.[3]

Abbot Placidus Tanner recognized that the two Sisters were deeply prayerful and intelligent women, attuned to the religious culture of their time. He allowed them to continue working at the orphanage at Engelberg, without renewing their annual vows with the Baldegg Institute. Not long after that, other young women were attracted to living a life the two Sisters hoped to live. They expressed an interest in living in a religious community dedicated to adoration of Jesus in the Blessed Sacrament. However, it was difficult for now, as the two Sisters were separated—Sr. Vincentia at Gauglera in Freiburg, and Sr. Gertrude at Engelberg. There was little time for any kind of religious training due to incessant work needed to care for the elderly at Gauglera. The director of the home was fearful of government interference if he allowed any time for novitiate instructions.[4]

Still the two Sisters persevered and on Holy Thursday, 1857, Abbot Placidus allowed Sr. Vincentia and Sr. Gertrude to make simple vows as Benedictines, though neither had a monastic novitiate. Sr. Vincentia, who had the larger group of novices at Gauglera, realized it was time to move and time to begin a community devoted to perpetual adoration, along with some form of active ministry. Sr. Gertrude, still at Engelberg, would have preferred perpetual adoration alone, as she did not feel the two could be successfully combined.

Through her brother, Sr. Vincentia was able to rent an old farmhouse, called Staefeli, about a three-minute walk from the Maria Rickenbach shrine. With her novices, she took possession of this house in 1857, despite its isolated location in a hamlet of less than twenty families which made any kind of caring for the sick or orphans rather unlikely. Within two weeks, the first six Sisters had begun perpetual adoration, kneeling at the shrine church from five in the morning until nine in the evening. At night they knelt in a room in the farmhouse whose window faced the church.

Old farmhouse, called "Staefleli"—first Kloster (Convent) Maria Rickenbach. (Chapel nearby houses Marian shrine).

Not everyone in the area appreciated the Sisters. The anti-clerical spirit of the times provoked a good deal of opposition. This combined with hard work and the severe winter, broke Sr. Vincentia's health. She wrote to Engelberg to ask for Sr. Gertrude as her assistant.Sr. Gertrude arrived at Maria Rickenbach in May 1858, and by August was elected Superior, as Sr. Vincentia wished to resign. Sr. Gertrude had an endearing personality, combined with firmness and tact. She also enjoyed the active interest and support of Fr. Anselm Villiger, then prior of Engelberg Abbey.[5]

Sr. Gertrude obtained permission from the civil authorities to establish a convent on Mount Maria Rickenbach on April 13, 1859. She also received ecclesiastical approbation through Abbot Placidus of Engelberg Abbey. In May 1859, Fr. Anselm directed an appeal to all the bishops, pastors, and religious institutes of Switzerland, asking for funds to help this young community at Maria Rickenbach to build a convent for the 13 Sisters, who were now very crowded in the old farmhouse. At this time the community also numbered two novices and three postulants. One of these was to be the future foundress of the Benedictines of Perpetual Adoration in America, Ann Elizabeth Felber.[6]

Through Prior Anselm's appeal for funds, the begging tours made by the Sisters from village to village and farm to farm, and a raffle, their resources began to grow. In addition, the Sisters began a spiritual Association of Perpetual Adoration in which a donor could be enrolled for the offering of five francs. All these efforts brought in enough money to start construction on the new convent in 1862. Every piece of equipment, every stone and pipe, had to be carried up the mountain on the backs of skilled mountaineers or patient mules.

The Abbess of Sarnen sent a gift to each of the Sisters—the traditional Benedictine habit, scapular and veil, with the white coif. "Now garbed in the black and white habit, the Sisters felt themselves to be real Benedictines."[7] Prior Anselm continued as spiritual director of the community. Although the Sisters were very poor, through careful economy, things gradually improved. To support themselves they did weaving, made church vestments, collected herbs from the mountains and had an Association of Perpetual Adoration.

The cornerstone of the new Benedictine Convent of Perpetual Adoration was laid on July 6, 1862, to house 13 Sisters, three Novices, and two Postulants. By September 1864, the Divine Office was begun in choir in the new convent chapel together with 24-hour adoration. Although the community added a boarding school for girls, with 40 students in 1865, they still considered adoration of the Blessed Sacrament their primary aim.

The following year, Prior Anselm was elected Abbot of Engelberg. It was he who witnessed the Sisters' annual vows, gave them their annual retreat, and who in 1886, drew up a set of statutes for them. He hoped that these statutes would explain the ancient rule of Benedict. According to Sr. Dolores Dowling, OSB, in In Your Midst, "A mixture of paternalism, genuine concern for the Sisters, good sense and unconscious humor, these statutes reveal much about the culture of the day." An example is given, "The Mother Prioress is to do nothing without the agreement and advice of the Father Confessor." At a time when weekly reception of Communion was considered advanced, he advocated few limits for Communion or the Sacrament of Penance. "The novices are not to be overwhelmed with work, and recreation is not to be used," said the Abbot sternly, "for gossip or womanish tattling."[8]

In these statutes, Abbot Anselm dealt only with the three vows of poverty, chastity, and obedience. There is no mention of the specifically Benedictine vows of stability and conversion. According to Sister Dolores, "This may have been due to the fact that he considered the Sisters to be Oblates of St. Benedict, in distinction from the cloistered Benedictine nuns. Whether this was to protect them from possible consequences at a time when the Swiss government was inimical to religious orders, or was owing to their lack of dowry and enclosure, is not clear."[9]

Responding to the Call

In 1868, the western half of Missouri had been separated from the Archdiocese of St. Louis, and became the Diocese of St. Joseph, with John Joseph Hogan as the first bishop. It was Bishop Hogan, who recognized the need for priests to minister to the colonists who were arriving in the northwest part of the state and he appealed to Abbot Martin Marty, OSB, at St. Meinrad's Abbey. Abbot Martin Marty did not feel he had enough monks to spare any for a Missouri foundation. He suggested that the Bishop apply to the Abbot of

Engelberg in Switzerland, whom he knew was considering just such a foundation.

In all its existence, the Abbey of Engelberg had never made a foundation. However, in December 1872, when Abbot Anselm received an offer of land to make a foundation in Missouri, USA, he was willing to give it serious consideration. A spirit of anti-clericalism and nationalism was very much abroad. The Swiss federal constitution was revised to prohibit the establishment of any new Catholic Dioceses or monasteries without the consent of the government. Jesuits and other religious orders were expelled.

It was time, thought the Abbot, to act. Swiss monasteries might well need a refuge elsewhere. In January 1873, the Monastic Chapter of Engelberg Abbey voted to accept Bishop Hogan's proposal. Engelberg would make its first foundation in America. The Abbot did not forget the Sisters at Maria Rickenbach. They too, might need a refuge. If Engelberg's foundation in Missouri would be successful, the monks would invite the Sisters to make a similar foundation there. The monk chosen to begin the American foundation was Frowin Conrad, OSB, who had been chaplain at Maria Rickenbach for a year.

The monk chosen by Abbot Anselm to cross the Atlantic with Frowin Conrad, OSB was Adelhelm Odermatt, OSB. Upon arriving at St. Meinrad Abbey in Indiana in May 1873, they found out that Abbot Martin had sent his prior, Fr. Fintan, ahead of them to Missouri to scout out the land. He had accepted, not the original offer of Bishop Hogan, but one from Fr. James Power of 260 acres of land in Nodaway County, near a small community at Conception, about 50 miles north of St. Joseph. Fr. Power, based in St. Joseph, had visited this area, about once a month during the past year, to serve the spiritual needs of the nearly 100 families who had built a small church and rectory.

Having learned something about frontier life in America from the veteran missionary, Abbot Martin Marty, Frs. Frowin and Adelhelm came to Missouri in September. Fr. Frowin moved into the rectory there, and set about learning his new parish, while Fr. Adelhelm was placed in charge of the parish in Maryville, about 17 miles away.

Maryville, named after the wife of the first county clerk, was regarded as one of the best business centers in northwest Missouri.

The two priests soon discovered that good Catholic schools were required in order to give solid Catholic instructions to the young in their respective parishes. It was clear from the beginning that Frowin Conrad, 40 years old at the time, was primarily a monk, and only secondarily a missionary. Twenty-nine year old Fr. Adelheim, was given to swift enthusiasm and action. However, by November 1873, Prior Frowin wrote to Mother Gertrude Leupi of Maria Rickenbach, asking her to furnish teachers and to send qualified Sisters from her convent to America. In a letter to his abbot at Engelberg he states, "I have asked the Sisters of Maria Rickenbach for help. I wish they could realize what their coming would mean for the people in this area." Fr. Adelhelm had also written to Mother Gertrude, "We always remember Maria Rickenbach and hope for a Maria Rickenbach in America. That shall be one of our first enterprises in Missouri, to find a place for you." With letters like this traveling back and forth from America, the Sisters were caught up in missionary fervor along with the monks.[10]

The chapter vote at Maria Rickenbach was nearly unanimous to send some Sisters to Conception, Missouri. The community had more candidates applying for entrance than it could accommodate so it was time to think of the church in other lands. Mother Gertrude, herself dreamed of going to the new foundation in America. However, she realized after talking it over with Abbot Anselm, whom she consulted on everything of importance to the small community, that her foundation was still too young to spare her. Not yet ten years old, Maria Rickenbach needed her guidance for some years to come.[11]

Finally, Mother Gertrude chose five Sisters to be pioneers on American soil. These five were: Sr. Anselma Felber, Sr. Agnes Dali, Sr. Augustine Kuendig, Sr. Adela Eugster, and Sr. Beatrice Renggli. At 35, Sr. Agnes was the oldest, Sr. Anselma was 30, and the rest were in their twenties.[12] Sr. Beatrice was 26 years old, and could not have known at the time, that she was destined to lead a group of Sisters to northeast Arkansas 13 years later. This is where they would eventually establish their Motherhouse in Jonesboro.

Initiatives in the New World

Travel between Europe and the United States was not easily undertaken in the late 1880s, especially for Sisters who had devoted their lives in religious communities. To aid in their travels, Abbot Anselm Villager of Engelberg was able to arrange for Mr. and Mrs. George Keel of Benziger Publishing Company, who were leaving for the United States in August 1884, to serve as a guide and chaperon for the Sisters. Mr. Keel agreed to take the Sisters under his protection and arranged to have their luggage picked up and shipped with his own to New York.

The next two months were spent busily packing what the Sisters would need. Prior Frowin had written in January 1874 that they would have to stay in Maryville for a while, but by April or May he hoped to have a place ready at Conception for at least two of them. "But they must not expect too much and I hope their zeal is greater than their expectations."[13]

Characteristic of Prior Frowin's attention to detail is his advice in a letter dated January 22, 1874: "The clothing they bring must be light for summer, but very warm for winter. They should also bring forks and knives, as well as sewing and embroidery needles. Here everything costs so much and often the simplest things cannot be procured. Some material for embroidery and simple vestments will also be useful, but most of the European school books should be left behind."[14] Prior Frowin was also negotiating with Abbot Martin Marty for a Benedictine Sister from the Ferdinand community who could teach the Rickenbach Sisters English and help them adapt to their American surroundings.

Kloster Maria Rickenbach when first group of Sisters left for America in 1874.

After a last visit to the pilgrim chapel of Maria Rickenbach and a farewell to the Sisters staying behind, the five pioneer Sisters set out with Abbot Anselm's blessing. The Engelberg carriage took the Sisters to Lucerne on August 17, 1874. From there they traveled to Basel by train with their chaperones, Mr. and Mrs. Keel. Having explored a few of the sights in this "Sea of Bishops," as Sr. Beatrice described it, they left their native Switzerland for a long hot, overnight trip to Paris.

According to Sr. Beatrice, "even nuns would be guilty of negligence if they had been in Paris without having seen the important and historic areas of that famous city." The five Sisters were taken on a hasty tour of the more illustrious churches, along with the Louvre and the Arc of Triumph, where they had a breath-taking view of the city. By 6:30 p.m. the evening of August 18th, they were again on the train which would take them to the port City of LeHarve. After a day there, on August 20th, they boarded the transatlantic steamer, "ODER," of the North-German Loyd Line, which was on its third voyage to America.

During the 11 days at sea, Sr. Beatrice kept a journal, as she was the only one not affected by sea-sickness, except for a short while. Writing in her journal, she described the cabins assigned to them and found them wanting in privacy, and she also commented that the insipid coffee in no way resembled Swiss coffee. She discovered there were 120 employees on the ship who gave them "friendly, courteous and respectful service." Most of the passengers were Catholic, although there were some who were not, including an agnostic who accosted Sr. Beatrice at one point to argue about the infallibility of the Pope.[15]

After exploring the ship, Sr. Beatrice observed the marine animals that followed their ship. She had promised her brother descriptions of all the animals she would see, but her opportunities were limited. By the fourth day, most of the passengers had recovered, but then a violent storm arose, which Sr Beatrice described, "The waves rose like mountains and crashed on deck…They forced themselves through the windows and inundated our beds. Painful cold accompanied the storm. Whatever we had, we put on, but nothing protected us from the cold and freezing weather."[16]

In calmer weather, Sr. Beatrice was again able to study the sea creatures as her brother in Switzerland had begged her to do. She wrote, "Above all, I enjoyed the dance maneuvers of the dolphins which accompany the vessel. They are companionable even though they tease each other greatly. Their small black eyes look so friendly and trusting. It appears they love people and wish to capture their attention with affectionate leaps. Among the birds, the most faithful escort is the three-toed sea gull, a dazzling white bird with black wings and feet, yellow bill and approximately the size of a duck."

But it was the sunset over the calm sea that most entranced the Swiss Sister, as she wrote, "Suddenly the azure blue disappeared and the water took on a light green shade. The sun sank, not gradually as at home. It disappeared suddenly, and suddenly the reflection of its rays painted both eastern and western horizon. The great sea lay framed in gold and the silent flood mirrored a 100 times over the fleeting gold of the firmament." In this sunset, Sr. Beatrice saw the beauty and grandeur of God. She wrote, "The oceanic voyage would truly be a grandiose pleasure and enjoyment if the weather would always be so pleasant."[17]

CHAPTER 2

1874-1884

Facing New Challenges

On August 31, 1874, the passengers aboard the ODER sighted land. The steamship docked at Hoboken, New Jersey, on the right bank of the Hudson River, and the Sisters stepped for the first time on American soil at noon. "After the quarantine, the physician on board our steamer had convinced himself of the well-being of the passengers, and so the landing took place," wrote Sr. Beatrice. Immediately the Sisters were overwhelmed at the rush, haste, and confusion of this new land. Later, Sr. Beatrice wrote, "They were loaded bag and baggage into a wagon with a team to take them at breakneck speed to New York." [1]

In New York they were lodged at Hotel Grutli managed by former Swiss immigrants. Sr. Beatrice wrote, "We soon felt at ease here because we found Swiss contentment, heard Swiss dialect, and were fed genuine Swiss food. The large amount of business at the customs house postponed our trip to the following day. The customs examinations are very comprehensive and not everyone's word of honor is respected. Even our Mother Prioress, who is as you know, honesty personified, was obliged to testify under oath that the trunks we claimed truly belonged to us." [2]

In another entry in her journal, Sr. Beatrice wrote, "In the afternoon, we visited the family Benziger, who welcomed us with great hospitality. They owned a stunning palace and their business is probably the largest in all of New York." [3] Mr. and Mrs. Benziger, under whose patronage the Sisters had traveled from Switzerland, procured their railroad tickets and provided for their departure. A representative from Benziger Company accompanied the Sisters to the depot. They boarded the train at 2 p.m. on September 2 for their eventual destination: Maryville, Missouri.

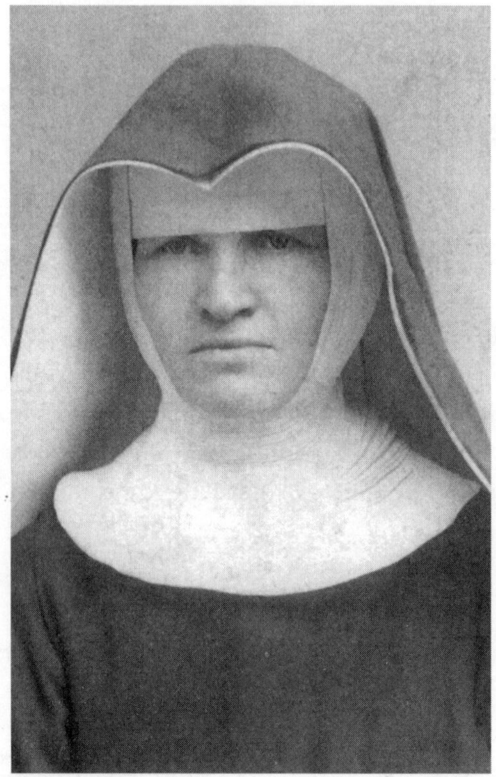

Sr. Beatrice Renggli, age 26, when she arrived in America — 1874.

In another entry in her journal, Sr. Beatrice wrote, "We were fortunate in having the coach to ourselves, because we were not to change coaches until we arrived in St. Louis." At 10:00 a.m. in the morning on September 3, they arrived in Pittsburgh, where they had a short stop, but the Sisters did not leave their salon, as they feared it may become occupied by others. At 1:20 p.m. on September 4, the Sisters arrived in St. Louis. They set out to look for a public eating place, as they were longing for some hot cooked food. "Their supply of ham sandwiches provided by Mrs. Benziger was exhausted." [3] They had a difficult time in ordering and paying for their food, as no one in that place could understand German. According to Sr. Beatrice, "Finally the proprietor wrote the bill on the wall and we were able to satisfy the manager."

That afternoon, "A kindly German accidentally met us and immediately offered to aid us strangers as our interpreter, guide, travel director and counselor. He stayed with us until 9:25 p.m. when we again boarded the train." [4] The destination of this train was St. Joseph, where the Sisters were to wait for three hours for the train to Maryville. Upon arrival in St. Joseph the next day, a man from Alsace-Lorraine was able to direct them to a priest. The priest accompanied them to the convent of the school Sisters, where they were able to rest for three hours until their train was due to leave for Maryville. At 4:00 p.m. that same afternoon, they left St. Joseph and reached Maryville at 6:00 p.m. that same evening, September 5, 1874.

Beginning of Disappointments

When they arrived in Maryville they were disappointed because no one was there to meet them. Fr. Adelhelm had forgotten the date of their arrival. A German speaking man, who happened to be at the station, took them to the Catholic Church where an astonished Fr. Adelhelm welcomed them. The Sisters first prayed before the Blessed Sacrament in thanksgiving for their safe arrival. Then, tired and hungry, they went over to the rectory where some ladies of the town hurriedly came and prepared supper and beds for the weary travelers.

The following morning, the ladies collected 350 francs for the Sisters, and brought them meat, milk, bread, etc. The Sisters never expected such a hearty welcome and friendly acceptance. At this time, Maryville, was regarded as one of the best business centers in northwest Missouri.[5] In letters back to Switzerland, Sr. Beatrice wrote, "The people are friendly, kind and courteous and are ever ready with good advice, and in charitable actions aid all in need, especially all newcomers. There are no high mountains here like those in Switzerland, only waving hillsides as far as the eye reaches." [6]

It was obvious from letters of Prior Frowin that he would have preferred that only three Sisters come in the beginning. Then they could have been housed at Conception, and he could have recalled Fr. Adelhelm to the monastery there. But five Sisters meant that all had to stay at the Maryville rectory with Fr. Adelhelm as guide and mentor. The rectory of the Maryville Parish was a flimsy wooden structure housing the pastor on the first floor and the five Sisters on the second, which was two rooms in an attic without windows or ventilation.

Gradually, the Sisters were settling into their new life, but were concerned about the school they were suppose to open. Since the

Americans wanted their children taught in English, it was obvious that the Sisters could not open even the most rudimentary kind of school until they learned the language. Many Catholic parents refused to send their children to public schools. At that era in Missouri, as in other States, the public school system was nothing to boast about. Only in 1875 did the State Constitution provide for the eventual establishment of free public schools. There was no college for teacher training until 1867 at the State University. The curriculum in those days was the three Rs: reading, writing and arithmetic. After the pupils mastered the alphabet, they went on to study spelling and reading. "Figuring" was taught, along with exercises, by means of charts and diagrams on rough blackboards. After the first reader the pupils received some instruction in plants and animals.

A letter from Mother Anselma to Abbot Anselm at Engelberg in September 1874, states, "Each day we get more and more into our conventual order. Fr. Adelhelm is teaching us English. Please pray that God may loose my tongue and make me hear right." The Daybook had endless entries about flour, butter, potatoes, corn, meat, fruit, lard, firewood, tables, lamps, bedding; all gifts from the people. [7]

In October, Abbot Martin Marty came with the Benedictine Sister he had promised to Prior Frowin, Sr. Rose Chapelle, OSB, of the Ferdinand, Indiana community. She was to live with the five Sisters from Maria Rickenbach, giving English lessons and preparing them to teach in English.

At this time the Swiss Sisters used the Exercises of St. Gertrude, divided into sections, as their choral prayer in German. Abbot Marty suggested that, like all other Sisters in America, they use the Latin 'Little Office of the Blessed Virgin Mary,' explaining that the Exercises were a private devotion never meant to replace the office.

Prior Frowin wrote to Abbot Anselm, "The Sisters would not lose their status as Sisters of Perpetual Adoration by adopting this Little Office, since it could become an integral part of their adoration." When this reached Abbot Anselm in Switzerland, it appears to have alarmed him. He wrote back, "Since the Sisters did not understand

Latin, this could harm their spiritual life. The Maria Rickenbach Sisters were Oblates of St. Benedict." Possibly he feared that Abbot Marty was assuming too much control of the fledgling community. In Abbot Anselm's mind the Sisters' chief work was to be perpetual adoration, not liturgical prayer. Prior Frowin pointed out in his reply that, this would mean difficulties when the first American postulants arrived who would not understand German. The Sisters could learn to understand Latin if properly taught. The essence of their perpetual adoration remains unchanged because the Divine Office is adoration by its very nature." [8]

Undaunted by the obstacles and unskilled teachers, Sr. Rose opened a small school in the church at Maryville for 32 children. The Rickenbach Sisters helped by teaching sewing and embroidery. Sr. Beatrice, the only one who had some previous teaching experience, was studying diligently to obtain a one-year teaching certificate, qualifying her to teach in public or private schools in Missouri. She also had to assist Sr. Rose with the baby class.

The Sisters were far too crowded in the rectory to accept postulants. Prior Frowin had drawn up plans for a small convent at Conception to house some of them and also to serve as a school. But it would not be finished until the following year. So far, the Sisters had not even seen Conception. Their first Christmas in America, however, was a peaceful one and Mother Anselma was able to report that many gifts were received from the people in the area.

Early Initiatives

Private schools were a necessity for Catholic education, according to a letter of Prior Frowin. "The school tax is quite high and is spent only to aid the public schools. To get state aid for our schools, the Sisters would have to pass an examination and oblige themselves not to teach religion during the legal school hours: that is, between nine and twelve in the morning and one and four in the afternoon." [9]

By April 1875, both Sr. Beatrice and Sr. Augustine could speak English fairly well. In June 1875, a letter from the Department of Education of Missouri arrived stating that if Sr. Beatrice wished to continue to teach in public schools in the state, she would have to be certified. This required passing a teacher's examination. An opportunity for this purpose would be offered in the Court House of Nodaway County in Maryville in July 1875. Sr. Rose helped her prepare for this dreaded examination, which she passed and thereby obtained the coveted license as a certified teacher.

Mother Anselma had hoped she could dispense with Sr. Rose's services by summer, but now it seemed she might need to stay longer. Prior Frowin wanted a small school at Conception also, and this was too much for the five Sisters to handle.

Due to the contributions of $300 from the people in the area, their little house and school at Conception was well under construction by November. The decision was made to leave Sr. Agnes and Sr. Augustine at the Maryville school to help Sr. Rose teach there, while Mother Anselma with Sr. Beatrice and Sr. Adela would go to Conception. Some young women had been asking to enter as Postulants and now at last there would be room to accept them. Mother Anselma began to dream of a novitiate and perpetual adoration. Up to then, they had only been able to have a few hours of adoration in the Maryville church.

On December 6, 1875, Mother Anselma, with Srs. Beatrice and Adela, in a carriage belonging to the monks, set out over the icy roads on the 18 mile drive to Conception. The three-hour drive passed quickly, as this was the day they were moving to their new convent in Conception. Their new convent, which was also to serve as a small school, had nine rooms. By the evening of December 6th, their beds and furniture were in place, the mattresses filled with fresh straw, the lamps with oil. On December 10th, the Sisters were able to open their school to 39 children, ages five to 20. The teachers' monthly salary was to be $40. Sr. Beatrice, with Sr. Adela's help would teach school, Mother Anselma would look after the house, the kitchen and the guests. [10]

The opening days of 1876, America's centennial year, brought three postulants to the new convent at Conception. Agnes Mayer and Angela Weber were German born, but had lived in the area with their families for quite some time. Mary Schrader had come to

America as a child with her parents from Bastogne, Belgium.

By the summer of 1876, Mother Anselma received word that three more Sisters were being sent from Maria Rickenbach to help with the American foundation. She prayed, "O Lord, let them be the right ones." According to the same notes, Prior Frowin was more blunt about it. Having experienced Sr. Beatrice and Sr. Adela's domineering ways, he asked for an experienced teacher or two and a good cook, but wanted no anarchists. [11]

With the arrival of the second group of Sisters from Maria Rickenbach—Sisters Bernadine Wachter, Scholastica von Matt, and Novice Anna Jann—in the Conception house that summer of 1886, there were five Sisters, three Novices, five candidates, and a boarder. Since Sr. Bernadine would be able to help Sr. Augustine teach in the Maryville school, Sr. Rose Chapelle could then return to her community in Ferdinand.

Mother Anselma's health was another concern as the affairs in the community and the schools pressed on the fragile superior. Conflicting accounts kept arriving from Maryville. Tensions were building between Fr. Adelhelm, the pastor, and the Sisters at the Maryville school, which weighed heavily on her. When the Sisters in Maryville were able to get a small house, she felt the separation from the rectory would alleviate the friction that had existed. Differences between Prior Frowin and Fr. Adelhelm only added to the stress experienced by the Sisters.

Another blow fell upon the community when Sr. Augustine succumbed to typhoid fever and died on October 27, 1879. Sr. Augustine was the youngest of the pioneers to come to America.

Mother Anselma was aware that Mother Gertrude was interested in coming to Maryville to open another novitiate after she was out of office in 1879. Her former longing to be a missionary in America had revived. All she needed was Abbot Anselm's consent and an invitation from Prior Frowin. Both hesitated. They could not approve two Motherhouses so close to each other as Maryville and Conception.

Expanding Horizons

The need for a larger convent was a growing concern for Mother Anselma. There was little money and the Sisters worked hard and prayed to St. Joseph for assistance. The Sisters went out on begging tours, as had been done decades before at Maria Rickenbach. Prior Frowin estimated the cost of the Sisters' Monastery at about $10,000. Although they had several offers of land around the area, they chose an offer of land only two miles from Conception Abbey and a half-mile from the railway station in the small town of Clyde, Missouri. It was established in 1880, when more than 50 townspeople came together to name their town. Since two residents, Frank Bellows and John Wirth, had recently bought some Clydesdale horses from Canada, the people decided to name the town after that famous breed. [12]

Besides the money the Sisters were able to raise, Mother Anselma had to borrow money three different times after construction began. On September 11, 1881, Abbot Frowin laid the cornerstone. He had been consecrated Abbot of Conception Abbey on June 29 of that year. By December 1881, the total cost of construction amounted to over $13,000. Mother Anselma wrote to Switzerland, "The days are so full of work that only a quiet night hour allows writing...We now have 15 Sisters and three Novices. Six of the Sisters are in schools... Besides the three public schools we have our perpetual adoration, a little Institute (boarding school) and our own school... Sewing for the church and the Father's convent and their laundry. Thanks be to God our new convent is up to the roof... besides a basement and a ground floor, there will be two stories." [13]

At Clyde, the Sisters engaged in various activities. Sister Beatrice Renggli (only one from this group who later came to Arkansas), is pictured first row on right with sewing machine.

One of the public schools mentioned above was the Wild Cat School about a mile east of Clyde. According to Sr. Julianna Bresson, retired librarian at Clyde, this school was near a creek on a Mr. Clever's property. The creek was called "Wild Cat" because, when heavy rains came, the creek would flow so rapidly that it seemed like a rushing wild cat. This school was funded by the State, at first paying $35, later $40 per month. The area farmers provided a horse or mule for the teacher to ride to school. Sr. Beatrice taught in this school for a time.

By early April 1882, the Sisters were often at Clyde working on their new land, planting trees and potatoes, as April 18th was moving day. Their chaplain was Fr. Pius, brother to Abbot Frowin. Besides his other duties, Fr. Pius also busied himself sowing oats in a large field for them. On May 3, Abbot Frowin, accompanied by all his monks, consecrated the convent and the little chapel. During these months Mother Anselma's health continued to decline and she was bedridden frequently. Undoubtedly, the strain over the problems with Maryville contributed to this.

By July 1880, Abbot Anselm of Engelberg wrote to Abbot Frowin at Conception that Mother Gertrude would be coming to Missouri, but would not interfere with the convent at Conception. By September, Abbot Frowin wrote that he would ask the Bishop to allow the Maryville convent to be separated from the one at Conception and to establish its own novitiate. Mother Anselma wrote rather wistfully, to Maria Rickenbach, "It is a great relief for me that now Maryville and Conception are to be separated. With my best of will I could not satisfy Maryville." [14]

Mother Gertrude with her five companions arrived in Maryville on November 2, but did not come to Conception to see Mother Anselma and her Sisters until November 11, 1880. The Daybook entry for that day states, "The meeting was not as joyful as we would have wished." On November 7, of that year, Mother Gertrude opened a novitiate at the Maryville convent, formally separating the two houses founded from Maria Rickenbach." [15]

Within a month, Mother Gertrude had an invitation from Bishop Marty to send some Sisters to teach at an Indian reservation in the

Dakotas, where the government would pay for house and salary. By December 11, Sr. Adela, one of the original group, asked to transfer to the Maryville house, as did a couple others. This was very hard for Mother Anselma to accept, as well as the news, that Mother Gertrude had requested Maria Rickenbach to send her ten to 15 more Sisters.

In May 1881, Mother Gertrude came to Conception, asking for two Sisters to teach in Dakota. Mother Anselma declined, however Sr. Agnes, of the pioneer group, decided to try out a missionary vocation and transferred to Maryville. According to documentation by Sr. Agnes Voth in *Green Olive Branch*, "Mother Gertrude also received requests for Sisters to conduct schools on the Grande Ronde Indian Reservation in North-Western Oregon from Bishop Charles Seghers, DD, Bishop of Vancouver Island and coadjutor to the Archbishop of Oregon City and from Fr. A.J. Croquet, who was in charge of the Indians. In response to these requests, Mother Gertrude sent Mother Agnes to Grande Ronde Indian Reservation, Oregon, with Sr. Monica and Sr. Radegundis as companions."

An account of the cumbersome journey the Sisters made to reach their destination is listed in the archives of Holy Angels Convent:

"As the North Pacific Railway was not built at the time, the itinerary was somewhat complicated. The Sisters traveled by rail from Omaha, Nebraska to San Francisco, California. Then they took an ocean liner from the City of the Golden Gate to Astoria. A smaller steamer carried them up the Columbia and the Willamette Rivers to Portland. From there they again took the railroad to Sheridan. Finally a coach conveyed the Sisters to their new sphere of activity, the Grande Ronde Indian Reservation." [16]

This Indian Reserve resulted from the united efforts of the Department of the Interior and an action of the President of the United States.

"Grande Ronde Reserve had been established when President James Buchannan on June 30, 1857 empowered the Department of the Interior to form a place for the needs of regional tribes. It occupied an area of 40 3/4 square miles or 59,759 acres. It was established by treaties of January 2, and January 31, 1855. Federal jurisdiction was lifted on August 13, 1954. Fifty-nine tribes claimed this reservation as their homeland." [17]

According to documents in the archives at Holy Angels Convent, the schools on the Indian Reservation were successful. The account from the agent states, "...I have to report the continued prosperity of the schools under the able supervision of the Benedictine Sisters. The progress of the pupils in their studies and industrial habits has been to a high degree satisfactory... During the year the agency has been visited by Inspector Gardner, Archbishop Seghers, and other persons of note, and all, I believe, express themselves as satisfied with the progress made by these Indians in the religious, social, and industrial habits of life..." [18]

According to these same records, Sr. Agnes worked energetically among the Indians for over three years. However, towards the end of 1884 she returned to her community in Maryville, where she served as Novice Mistress.

The enterprising Mother Gertrude asked the Conception Sisters to take over the Maryville convent, with its considerable debt, so she could move all her Sisters to South Dakota. Abbot Frowin wrote from Conception to Abbot Anselm in Engelberg on November 11, 1881, that he was uncomfortable with the Maryville convent and debt. He did not feel the Conception Sisters should take it on, unless they received more Sisters from Maria Rickenbach.

To impact the situation, Fr. Adelhelm along with Fr. Nicholas left Maryville to open a new mission in Oregon. He interested Mother Gertrude in this venture, so by December, Sr. Bernadine was sent to Oregon as superior and Sr. Benedicta as teacher of the Indians. [19]

Mother Anselma's health continued to deteriorate and when she contracted typhoid fever in August 1883, she became very ill. After receiving the last Sacraments, Mother Anselma died in the early hours of August 26, 1883. The Daybook states, "Because of the heat, it was necessary to have the funeral the very next day." It was the end of an era for the little community. The Sisters encouraged each other and prayed for the guidance of the Holy Spirit in choosing a new superior.

Transition

On September 3, 1883, Abbot Frowin gathered the community of Clyde around him, read Chapter 64 of the Rule of Benedict to those who were eligible to vote and proceeded to hold an election for a prioress to succeed Mother Anselma. "On the first ballot the 17 Sister-electors chose Sr. John Schrader as their second prioress." [20] Of the 17 Sisters, only two were in their thirties. Mother John was 29 and had been professed seven years. She was one of the first young women from the area to enter the new community, coming only six weeks after the Swiss Sisters had settled in Conception. After her profession she had taught in the Wild Cat school, often riding there on a horse or mule. She was also a skilled seamstress and had helped Mother Anselma with vestment making. Sr. John was frightened about the outcome of the Election but accepted it as the will of God. [21]

Poverty was one of Mother John's biggest problems, as the Sisters often ran out of staples, such as flour and fuel and could not always afford to buy more. There was still a debt on the convent building. The Sisters went out on begging tours and, gradually, conditions improved. It was still a common practice in the 1880s to be offered a cow in return for six-month's schooling. The Sisters placed their trust in God and spent their days planting fruit trees and garden produce so they would have their own food. However, the Sisters had the same worries of the neighboring farmers and the winters of the 1880s were bitter cold.

As more young ladies joined the community, they were able to undertake more sewing. Mother John taught her valuable skills in making vestments to others and this also brought in needed revenue. Another source of needed funds came from the schools. In 1885, the community had accepted a school in Clear Creek, Missouri and one in Booneville, Missouri, where Sr. Beatrice was now stationed. [22] In addition to accepting young ladies from the surrounding area, recruiting trips were made back to Switzerland, to interest others in coming to the mission field in Missouri. As the community grew in membership, Mother John continued to strive towards having perpetual adoration of Jesus in the Blessed Sacrament. She felt this should be the primary goal of the community, rather than teaching. However, as word spread about the thriving community of Benedictine Sisters at Clyde, Mother John received requests from other neighboring dioceses for Sisters to teach children of the immigrants.

Arkansas Foundation

CHAPTER 3

1885-1890

America Beckons

As railroad companies expanded the rails across the country, they frequently offered to donate land to build a church and school to attract settlers. German Catholic families preferred to settle in a community where they could find this support. As they continued to arrive in mid-America, the early missionaries actively sought Sisters to teach the children.

In the neighboring State of Arkansas, one such zealous priest, Fr. John Eugene Weibel, sought the assistance of Sisters to teach immigrant children in his parish.

A brief sketch of Fr. Weibel's early life is inserted at this time, as he was instrumental in securing the founders of the Benedictine Sisters for northeast Arkansas. This biography is taken in part from his autobiography, Forty Years Missionary in Arkansas, and The Catholic Missions of Northeast Arkansas.

Father John Eugene Weibel

John Eugene Weibel was born in Eschenbach, Canton Lucerne, Switzerland, May 27, 1853. His father was a blacksmith. His mother died some weeks after John's birth. John grew up under the loving care of a dear stepmother and his brothers played a large part in his education. After studying at the common school at Eschenbach, the district school at Rottenburg, he completed college education at Maria Einsiedeln. During the school year Fr. Martin Marty, then Prior of St. Meinrad, Indiana, later Abbot and Bishop, came to visit Einsiedeln. His purpose was to recruit both missionaries and students for the mission fields of America.[1]

John wanted to respond to his appeal, but his father refused, so he entered the Monastery of Maria Stein, Canton, Solothurn, 1873. This institution was dissolved in 1874 when Weibel was a Novice studying for the priesthood. In his autobiography Fr. Weibel describes the dissolution in a grim passage: "...on Wednesday in Holy Week, 1875, upon return from Compline, each monk found a policeman at the door of his cell. This man was ready to accompany the religious out of the monastery..."[2]

Abbot Carl Motschi sent his student monks to various monasteries to Switzerland to complete studies in preparation for ordination. Then he and some of the monks were able to cross the border into France, where the Abbot procured land for a foundation. John Eugene was sent to Einsiedeln, where he and his companions were to complete their studies in preparation for ordination to the priesthood, August 15, 1876. He later went to join his community in Delle, France where he taught Latin and Greek for three years.

When it was time to make solemn vows, he consulted with Bishop Eugene Lachat, who had ordained him. "Because of former contacts with Weibel, who had expressed the wish to go to America already as a college student, Bishop Lachat advised him to follow his inclination. The Bishop was particularly impressed by the young priest's hope to prepare a place in the United States for his Abbot Motschi and the community."[3]

Fr. Weibel left Europe in October 1878. He first went to St. Meinrad Abbey in Indiana to see Abbot Martin Marty and to determine whether or not he wished to enter this monastery. He soon discovered the climate was too cold for his constitution, so he became interested in a new daughter house in Arkansas that was being established from St. Meinrad. Prior Wolfgang Schlumpf and Fr. Boniface Lubermann were there in the act of founding what was then called, "St. Benedict" but which later became known as "Subiaco Abbey." It was located in the virgin forests of northwest Arkansas, where the Fathers were to care for all Catholics of the surrounding areas, including the Sisters at St. Scholastica at Shoal Creek.

Fr. John Eugene Weibel when he came to Arkansas.

After arrival at St. Benedict

in northwest Arkansas, Father Weibel's first assignment was Shoal Creek, where he was to build a small wooden church and instruct the confirmation class. On April 20, 1870, Bishop Edward Fitzgerald, the second Ordinary of the Diocese of Little Rock, came to bless the church and confirm the members of the class. While there, the Bishop offered Fr. Weibel membership in the diocesan clergy and the choice of two mission areas—one in northeast Arkansas with Pocahontas as its residential center—the other in the southwestern part of the state with Hope as it residential center. After visiting both locations, Fr. Weibel accepted the Bishop's offer and chose St. Paul's Church in Pocahontas that had not had a pastor for five years. St. Paul's Parish had been organized by Fr. James O'Kean in 1868, but had fallen into ruin after he was made pastor of the Cathedral parish three years later.[4]

Fr. Weibel arrived as pastor in Pocahontas on December 1, 1879 to care for 19 souls. During the first three months of his stay in Pocahontas, Fr. Weibel boarded with Dr. J. C. Esselmann, a great benefactor and friend of Catholics. Although not Catholic at the time, Dr. Esselmann became a Catholic on his deathbed. After three months, Fr. Weibel moved into an old house close to the church, which formerly belonged to Dr. Marvin.

"In January 1880, Fr. Weibel opened a school with 25 pupils in attendance, most of whom were non-Catholic. He conducted the school himself until March, when a new group of immigrants arrived, among whom was a Mr. Meir, who was a teacher. Mr. Meir assisted Fr. Weibel in teaching school and also played the organ. That same spring Bishop Fitzgerald assigned Fr. Weibel as missionary to the railroad workers from central Missouri to Wynne, Arkansas. This additional work forced him to engage other lay teachers who were unsatisfactory."[5]

When Meir died in 1881, Miss Catherine Weibel, sister to the pastor, taught 50 pupils by that time. By the summer of 1882, Fr. Weibel learned that three railroads, the Cotton Belt, the Kansas City & Memphis (later Frisco) and the Knobel-Helena (Missouri Pacific) would be built. It was forecast that they would pass through Jonesboro, because of all the hardwood mills in that area. Ambition seized him and he traveled to Jonesboro to purchase land to build a church. He procured 80 acres near the city for $500. Later he paid $1,000 for three-fourth of an acre, within the city limits, which consisted of four lots on Cate Street.

On returning to Pocahontas he was overcome by heat because

the conveyance had broken down and he had to ride the remaining 24 miles on horseback. By the time he reached Pocahontas, he was overcome with a serious illness and he lay in a coma for nearly three weeks. He had lockjaw and only the skill of Dr. Esselmann and the providence of God brought about his recovery.[6]

During the winter of 1882 and the spring of 1883, Fr. Weibel was again in a declining condition, with fever and severe cough and expectoration of blood. Everyone believed he had consumption. Dr. Esselmann, who attended him, notified the Bishop to send another priest to anoint Fr. Weibel, as he thought he was dying. However, when Fr. Benedict Brunet, pastor of Argenta (North Little Rock) arrived, Fr. Weibel, on feeling better, was away on one of his mission trips. Because high water had disrupted all postal communications, and Pocahontas had neither telegraph nor telephone, Fr. Weibel knew nothing of these arrangements. Upon his return, both laughed heartedly after the facts were known.

Although Fr. Weibel seemed to fully recover for a time, after a trip to his homeland, his health again declined toward the end of 1884. He planned a trip to Little Rock in order to obtain the Bishop's permission to leave the diocese and return to his homeland. By mistake he boarded the wrong train and when he realized it, he disembarked at Jonesboro.

The Jonesboro townspeople urged him to remain there until spring and they would care for him. Widow Foley offered to take him in as a boarder. Fr. Weibel consented to remain there, provided Bishop Fitzgerald approved it. Fr. Vincent Wehrli, OSB of St. Benedict's (now Subiaco Abbey) was sent to Pocahontas as pastor.

Fr. Weibel had offered Mass for the 18 members of the first congregation in Jonesboro in 1883, and now in 1884, decided to establish a parish. In order to have some type of employment for himself, he decided to erect a small church. Actual building began in February of 1885, and by the end of May the church stood completed with a small rectory. "On May 31, Bishop Fitzgerald blessed it for the greater honor of God, under the title and protection of the holy Abbot Roman, foster father of St. Benedict."[7]

During the building activities of the church, Father Weibel fully recovered his health. During the spring of 1886, Fr. Weibel opened the first Catholic school in Jonesboro with 20 pupils. He procured Miss Katie Esselmann, daughter of Dr. Esselmann, as the first teacher. She later married a Mr. Skinner from Pocahontas.

Since Fr. Vincent (pastor in Pocahontas) had been recalled to

St. Benedict's, the Bishop again appointed Fr. Weibel to the pastorate in Pocahontas, with Jonesboro as a mission. He was happy to return to his pastorate in Pocahontas and the parishioners were eager to welcome him back.

Fr. Weibel thought he had overcome all hindrances to the school in Pocahontas when he finally obtained four Dominican Sisters from Racine, Wisconsin in 1886. They concluded a successful school year at the end of May, but Fr. Weibel refused to allow them to return to their Motherhouse. He wished to establish a novitiate as a permanent source of teachers. However, the mother superior came to remove her Sisters in early June of 1887. Thus Fr. Weibel and his assistant Fr. Gleizner, (a priest who had been sent to help in the northeast Arkansas missions), completed the summer session according to the European plan, which ended the middle of July.[8]

The continuation of the biography of Fr. Weibel will be interwoven with the narrative of the Benedictine Sisters, the ones he sought for the schools.

Quest Continues

Fr. Weibel now turned his attention to Missouri, as he had heard of the community of Sisters at Clyde, near Conception Abbey. Word had spread about the good work Sr. Beatrice and her companion instructors were doing in the Missouri schools. Fr. Weibel wrote to Abbot Frowin to seek his support and then wrote directly to Mother John to request teachers. He persistently petitioned for some of the Sisters to devote themselves to work in his parish. In addition to his urgent requests, he enlisted the support of his Bishop, who sent an entreaty, dated August 23, 1887, from Little Rock, to give evidence of his support.

> "I beg to add my entreaties to his (Father Weibel's) and to implore you if at all possible for the good of religion to send three or at least two good Sisters to reopen the convent and school at Pocahontas... I am sure that the Sisters will be kindly received and kindly treated by him, and by his congregation, which is about three-fourths German speaking."
>
> Yours faithfully,
> (signed) Edward Fitzgerald
> Bishop of Little Rock.[9]

Neither Abbot Frowin Conrad nor Mother John Schrader wanted to found a Daughterhouse at that time, but they felt pressured into doing it by the insistence of the begging letters of the strong-willed Fr. Weibel. Bishop John Hogan, friend of Bishop Fitzgerald, also added his support for an Arkansas foundation. Abbot Frowin felt the Clyde Sisters had all they could do with their own schools. Finally he relented, but insisted that the new foundation remain under Mother John until it can stand on its own feet.[10]

Abbot Frowin, Spiritual Director of the Sisters at Clyde, and Mother John promised to send three Sisters from Clyde and one from the convent in Maryville. The Sisters appointed from Clyde were Sr. Beatrice Renggli, professed at Rickenbach; SEE PROFILE IN APPENDIX and Sr. Walburga McFadden from Donagel, Ireland, professed at Clyde December 15, 1886, and Sr. Frances Metzler from Switzerland, who had made first profession at Clyde on December 3, 1887, for the new foundation in Pocahontas. Sr. Agnes Dali, professed at Rickenbach, was appointed from the convent in Maryville. Because of her previous experience in teaching the Indians at the Reservation in Oregon, Sr. Agnes was considered a good choice for the Arkansas mission.

Sr. Beatrice had served as Assistant Superior at Clyde and played a prominent part in the foundation of that Convent. Sr. Agnes had been in charge of the church embroidery department at Maria Richenbach and was skilled in drawing and painting. She had also served as Novice Mistress for a time at Maryville. Sr. Frances Metzler had health problems and it was suggested to Mother John that the warmer climate in Arkansas would prove beneficial for her. According to the original plan, the Sisters were to arrive in Pocahontas in time for the opening of school in September 1887. However they could not leave until Sr. Beatrice had completed a three-month commitment at the Public School in Conception.[11]

Arkansas Bound

After fond farewells and Abbot Frowin's blessing, Mother

Beatrice, Sr. Walburga and Sr. Frances set out from Clyde on December 11, 1887, where they were to join Sr. Agnes at Maryville and the four were to journey to Pocahontas. At Maryville the Sisters met Redemptorist Fathers who were preaching a mission. One of them, Fr. Enright, cautioned the Sisters to take their coffins with them. He told the Sisters they would encounter intense heat and swarms of mosquitoes. He explained that even dogs were so emaciated that they leaned against rail fences to bark.[12]

The Sisters were undaunted by these negative remarks, as they were eager to go to their new foundation in Arkansas. From Maryville they traveled to Kansas City and at 6 p.m., boarded the Kansas City-Memphis-Birmingham train and reached the small town of Portia, Arkansas at noon on December 13. From there they rode a mule-drawn wagon to Pocahontas, the goal of their journey.

"At the steep bank of the Black River they boarded a wiggly poorly constructed ferryboat that was to carry them across the water. From their wagon seat the Sisters sat looking down into the black depth with fear that the vehicle might roll off into a premature watery grave. How happy they were to reach the opposite bank. The mules seemed equally relieved and required no urging to abandon the raft. After several climbs and descents, they stood before the little wooden St. Paul's Church built by Fr. James O'Kean, blessed by Bishop Fitzgerald on August 27, 1887."[13]

Convent Maria Stein

First Convent Maria Stein in Pocahontas, 1888 (line drawing by Fr. Eugene Weibel).

After welcome greetings, Fr. Weibel escorted the Sisters to church where he held Benediction and imparted the Lord's blessing to the new arrivals for the first time. Candles and coal oil lamps helped to dispel the gathering darkness as the pastor led the Sisters to their new home—Convent Maria Stein. The convent was a two-room log cabin flanked on two sides by an addition of one and a half stories. Ladies of the parish had prepared a delicious meal, which the Sisters heartily enjoyed. After this the ladies showed the Sisters their sleeping quarters furnished with four beds and some makeshift wash stands furnished with bowls and pitchers.

While the ladies acquainted three of the Sisters with the kitchen and cistern, and various other necessities, Mother Beatrice admired the replica of the reverse side of the medal of St. Benedict painted on the ceiling of the small hallway, as a special welcome gesture, by Mr. Henry Lesmeister, a local architect and builder.

Additions made to the original Convent Maria Stein to accommodate new members.

According to Mother Beatrice's notes, the total cash fund the Sisters had with them when they arrived from Clyde was 83 cents. She had hoped that Mother John would have given her the salary from her last three months' teaching in the public school in Conception. However, she was disappointed that she had been given only travel money to get to Pocahontas. They had to rely on the providence of God and the generosity of the people.

On the morning after their arrival, the four Sisters attended Mass, after which Fr. Weibel outlined the work he wished to accomplish in his parishes of northeast Arkansas. He reminded them of the agreements made with Abbot Frowin and Mother John

Schrader of Clyde. The Sisters themselves spent the day unpacking and planning their daily order of prayer, work and relaxation. They wanted to harmonize it as much as possible to the Rule of St. Benedict and the Constitution they had brought with them from Switzerland.

On the first Saturday after their arrival at Pocahontas, the Sisters had a surprise, Brother Gall Graf, who had once belonged to the Abbey of St. Meinrad, Indiana, but had followed Fr. Weibel to Arkansas, arrived with a bag of genuine Irish potatoes. A few days later he bought a cow and hay and constructed a makeshift barn near the kitchen.

Finally he decided to rent out his farm and live with the pastor so that he might be of service to the Sisters. Fr. Weibel procured lumber and Brother Gall constructed necessary furniture for the Sisters and did all the field work. He constructed fences, dug holes for planting trees, erected poles for a grape arbor and helped wherever needed.

Many generous people periodically brought vegetables from their gardens and fields. Sweet potatoes were not familiar to the Sisters, but they soon learned to eat them, as well as tomatoes and other produce not used in Switzerland. The prominent local physician, Dr. Esselmann, befriended the Sisters as he had done for Fr. O'Kean and Fr. Weibel when they first came to Pocahontas. Dr. Esselmann, frequently brought the Sisters rabbits and squirrels

Mother Beatrice Renggli and Sr. Felicitas Hunkler — in black habits when they first came to Arkansas.

from some of his hunting excursions. Mother Beatrice Renggli was 29 years old when she was named superior and was eager to fulfill her duties. Although she had a broad education and had obtained a teaching certificate in Switzerland, the State of Missouri had not recognized it. She had to pass the teacher's examination in Missouri, so now she wondered if Arkansas would recognize that license.

Fr. Weibel had achieved his design, and voiced his satisfaction in these words, "With the arrival of the Benedictine Sisters on December 13, 1887, a new era began in the history of Catholicism in northeast Arkansas."[14] The Catholic missions of Pocahontas at that time extended almost a quarter of the State with some 100,000 inhabitants.

To some extent, the challenge of implementing and fulfilling the goals outlined by Fr. Weibel rested on the shoulders of Mother Beatrice. She had the keen ability to evaluate, organize and utilize the capabilities of the other Sisters within her charge. Together they forged ahead to fulfill the four needs:

"1. To open a novitiate
2. To train and admit new members
3. To train Sisters to staff schools in northeast Arkansas
4. To function as an independent, self-supporting unit on a capital that was nonexistent."[15]

Opening of First Schools

On Monday, January 2, 1888, Mother Beatrice opened the school with a total enrollment of 103 pupils. Sr. Walburga McFadden and Sr. Frances Metzler taught the children in the elementary grades. Sr. Walburga taught the primary children in one room and Sr. Frances taught the middle grades in the other room. Sr. Beatrice taught the 43 upper grade students, called the Academy, in the annex to the church, which also served as a sacristy.

Later, Fr. Weibel procured a house nearby and fitted it for a classroom where Sr. Agnes taught 36 children of (in the language of the times) the Colored Race. She transferred her love for the American Indians for the southern Negro at Pocahontas. The white population soon showed resentment to this missionary endeavor of the Sisters. Fr. Weibel received letters of threat that the school for the Negroes

Sr. Agnes Dali and Fr. Eugene Weibel with a group of children at the first black Catholic school opened in the State of Arkansas at Pocahontas 1889.

would be burned to the ground, but he ignored them at first. Because of this antagonism the school was closed the following year.[16]

On January 29, 1888, Bishop Fitzgerald assigned Fr. Gleiszner as pastor of Pocahontas and transferred Fr. Weibel to Jonesboro as pastor. The latter still held the position as spiritual director of the Benedictine Sisters. In this capacity, Fr. Weibel continued to direct the community.

Differences were beginning to surface between Fr. Weibel and the Sisters. In a letter to Abbot Frowin at Conception, June 23, 1888, Mother Beatrice wrote, "Fr. Weibel makes impossible demands on us. He does not allow us to live the way we did at Conception. It is left to your discretion whether or not in the future we remain under his direction."[17] Other letters continued to point out the differences arising between Fr. Weibel and the Sisters. He wanted the Sisters to teach school, not to spend time in Perpetual Adoration.

On June 24, Fr. Weibel invited the Bishop to Pocahontas to bless Convent Maria Stein. He had named the convent after the monastery in Canton Solothurn, Switzerland, where Fr. Weibel had been a Novice until the State secularized it in 1874. The convent stood on the 12 acres on top of "Catholic Hill" that was donated by the Bishop.

Soon Mother Beatrice found reason to consult Bishop Fitzgerald. Mother had ordered Brother Gall to build a rail fence around the property given to the Sisters. The pastor, Fr. Gleiszner, forbade this project. He maintained the field must be left free to provide a road to the Catholic cemetery. Mother Beatrice then suggested that the road be hemmed in on both sides and that the parish provide for the fence on one side, the convent build one on the other side. The indomitable pastor refused. Mother Beatrice then took the case to the Bishop and she soon received an answer.

The Bishop had donated the property to the Sisters, and under no circumstance was it to be divided. The road to the cemetery was to be built around it, not across it. Some opponents said the fence would be burned, but Mother's answer was, "If it burns, we will know who did it." This fence was never burned, but over time it rotted away.[18]

Because Abbot Frowin was the Spiritual Director for the Sisters at Clyde, Mother Beatrice frequently wrote to him for his advice and help. On July 16, 1888, she wrote the following letter,

> "I am sorry to inform your Grace that our dear Sr. M. Walburga has received the last Sacraments. Pneumonia seems to have taken hold of her. If God should take her from me I do not know how I would stand it, she was my best help. It is all the harder to see her so sick, knowing it is caused by too hard labor.
>
> Dear Sr. M. Walburga is resigned to die, only she does not wish to be buried here, the Catholic graveyard being some distance from the convent. She would like to be buried at home. However, I do not know how that would be done, on account of the extreme heat and the expenses that would be connected with such a transfer. I beg your Grace to let me know what I should do in the event of her death."[19]

No letter of reply from Abbot Frowin was found concerning this request, but after Sr. Walburga fully recovered, she returned to Clyde in July 1889. Eight years later, she died on April 28, 1896 and is buried in the cemetery there with the other members of that community. She was the only one of the four original founders of Pocahontas who did not stay in Arkansas.

Again, Mother Beatrice wrote back to Clyde for additional Sisters. During the absence of Mother John, the Subprioress sent Sr. Mechtilde to aid the struggling community. Upon the return of the superior to Clyde, Sr. Mechtilde was recalled because a certified teacher was needed at Conception public school. Later Sr. Rosalia Christen and Sr. Raphaela Kimmet were sent to Pocahontas. They too, were recalled after a short while. On July 17, 1888, Mother Beatrice again wrote to Abbot Frowin to secure his help in obtaining additional Sisters. In this letter she wrote,

> "Our needs are well known to Rev. Mother John as I often asked her, and she also knows well the possibilities and limitations of each one of us. She showed herself rather indifferent and cold—at least toward me. Please let us have at least one experienced, reliable Sister for the kitchen and housework. Sr. Scholastica would be welcome for the kitchen, but she would not be able to manage the housework too as she is unable to work as we must do here. Sr. Genevieve Ketterer is neat and clean and familiar with kitchen and domestic work. Those who can manage these are the right ones for us. We could well use Sr. Scholastica if you can send us more than one."[20]

A number of such pleas were written to Mother John and to Abbot Frown, but there is no record of any additional Sisters being sent to Pocahontas. Sr. Beatrice also wrote to the superior of Ferdinand for help. She wrote the Abbot that she had received an answer from the Superior in Ferdinand and she will send a music teacher who will be accompanied by a sick Sister, in hopes that she may recuperate in the warmer climate.

The enrollment in the school at Pocahontas was beginning to grow and the pupils gave evidence of their achievements at exhibitions and recitals. During the Christmas Season, the pupils presented the operetta "Santa Claus," which proved a great success. Songs and music were under the direction of Sr. Hedwig Mattingly, a music teacher from the Convent of the Immaculate Conception, Ferdinand, Indiana. She and her sister, Sr. Evangelista Mattingly were sent to Arkansas for the benefit of a milder winter. Sr. Evangelista went to Shoal Creek, while Sr. Hedwig remained in Pocahontas. She was highly lauded for her musical ability. At the approach of warmer weather, both returned to their Motherhouse.

Miss Christine Unterberger from Lungern, Canton Unterwalden, Switzerland, who had entered some months previously, had the joy of being invested with the habit of St. Benedict on December 28, 1888. This first investment was a day of celebration for the young community. She received the name of Sister Aloysia when making Religious Profession, and later became the second superior of the community. January 1889 brought a new addition to the community so greatly needed when Miss Maria Wursch came to Pocahontas from Racine, Wisconsin. She had been a Postulant with the Dominican Sisters, who had taught at Pocahontas 1886-1887. Before her departure, she had promised Fr. Weibel to return if he would be successful in obtaining Sisters to found a convent at Pocahontas. When Fr. Weibel had informed her that he had succeeded in obtaining Benedictine Sisters from Clyde, she requested to return to missionary territory. Since she had already been a Postulant, she was invested a few days after her arrival.

During the same winter, a third Postulant arrived, Miss Johanna Sonderegger, who was sent by Fr. Weibel's brother, Roman Weibel of Einsiedeln. To the surprise of Mother Beatrice and the Sisters, Johanna traveled alone across the Atlantic and arrived safely in Pocahontas. She received the religious name of "Frowina" in honor of the Abbot of Conception, who had befriended them. Another Postulant, Miss Catherine Brodell of Pocahontas entered the convent on April 23,1889 and when making Religious Profession received the name of Sr. Eugenia.[21]

First Mission

Since Fr. Weibel was also pastor in Jonesboro, he was anxious to secure Sisters as teachers for the school. During the month of April 1889, Sr. Agnes Dali was sent to Jonesboro to teach in the school. When Sister Maura, OSB, from St. Mary's Convent in Navoo, Illinois arrived, she accompanied Sr. Agnes to Jonesboro. They began classes the first of May of that year; one taught in the church and the other taught in the small sacristy. Two days later a devastating fire swept through Jonesboro. Due to the absence of water and fire fighting equipment, 40 buildings were destroyed. Sr. Agnes gathered the children together and led them in prayer. Shortly after they began to pray, the wind changed and the little church on Cate Street was spared during this conflagration.

The parishioners soon found ways and means to accumulate funds by sponsoring entertainments, suppers and luncheons and thus financed the erection of the school and the sisters' quarters. The structure consisted of two floors with a basement for the heating apparatus and coal bin. The first floor consisted of two classrooms, with a small stage, while the second floor was reserved for the Sisters' quarters. The Finnegan Family donated $400 in cash, and Fr. Weibel gave $500 worth of lumber. The school was opened on May 1, even though it had not been entirely completed. By September 1889 it was in full operation. Sr. Agnes was greatly loved and respected by all the people and the little school flourished.[22]

Mother Beatrice attempted to borrow more Sisters from Clyde and from other communities, but with little success. She realized the small community could not fulfill all the requests she had received for teachers. This growing necessity caused her to request permission from Bishop Fitzgerald to travel to Europe to solicit Postulants. Bishop Fitzgerald willingly endorsed the project and wrote a letter in support of her quest. With the letter of endorsement and blessing of the bishop, Mother Beatrice first went to Clyde to see Mother John, her former superior, and received the prayers and good wishes of the Sisters there. She left the United States in June 1889 on the Red Star Line and traveled to Antwerp.

In Belgium she visited the grave of St. John Berchmans and promised to name one of the Sisters after the saint if she was successful in obtaining a large number of persevering young Sisters. From there she traveled to Germany to make contacts, then she went on to Switzerland, where she made the four-hour climb to her beloved Maria Rickenbach. She set up two stations to contact young ladies, one at Maria Rickenbach and the other at Marie Einsiedeln, where Brother Roman, brother of Fr. Weibel, handled business matters for her. For five months, Mother Beatrice advertised, traveled, visited, lectured, and by the beginning of November 1889, she was ready to return to Arkansas. Rickenbach gave her all possible help as she had obtained one professed Sister, ten young ladies from Switzerland and one from Germany, whom she considered suitable to become good religious.[23]

In her absence, Mother Beatrice had left Sr. Agnes in charge at Convent Maria Stein. Under Sr. Agnes' direction, Brother Gaul had enlarged the Sisters' quarters and she had furnished the two large dormitories with beds and bedding to prepare for the new arrivals. The meager funds of Mother Beatrice were seriously depleted by the trip to Europe. Now, it was a challenge to clothe and feed the growing community.

January 28, 1890 was a day of rejoicing at Convent Maria Stein when the First Profession ceremony was held. Novice Aloysia Unterberger and Novice Anselma Wursch professed their vows according to the formula brought from Convent Maria Rickenbach in Switzerland. The little community was beginning to grow and conditions were improving.

However, this joy was turned to sadness on March 24, 1890, when Convent Maria Stein experienced the first death in the community, as Sr. Frances Metzler succumbed to typhoid fever. A second death followed the same year, when Novice Scholastica Stoeckli, who made her profession on her deathbed, died on November 18, 1890.[24] Both are buried under a row of Cedar trees in St. Paul's Cemetery in Pocahontas, along with 18 other young Sisters who died within those early years.

According to Mother Beatrice's notes, there were other

growing concerns due to the differences arising between the expectations of Fr. Weibel and the goals of the Sisters. Also, the debt incurred by adding the annex to the original dwelling needed to be cancelled. Besides this, she had the obligation of feeding, clothing and inducting the new members into the spirit of religious life. She turned to prayer and entrusted all these concerns to Jesus in the Blessed Sacrament. She held as an ultimate goal for Convent Maria Stein to have enough Sisters to fulfill the teaching obligations in the schools, and have Perpetual Adoration in the Convent.

CHAPTER 4
1891-1897

Divergences Arise

Shortly after Mother Beatrice returned to Pocahontas from a successful recruiting trip to Europe in 1891, to obtain Postulants, tensions began to increase between Fr. Weibel and herself—two strong-willed personalities. However, Mother Beatrice continued to direct the community according to the Constitution and Rules brought from Maria Rickenbach to Clyde and then to Pocahontas. Fr. Weibel often overruled her decisions and gave contrary directions to the young Sisters.

The young superior experienced other difficulties and crosses as well. There were frequent illnesses among the Sisters, as they were not accustomed to the humid climate. Two Sisters died the previous year—Sr. Frances Metzler and Sr. Scholastica Stoeckli. Now other Sisters frequently suffered from a fever. The swamps had not been drained in northeast Arkansas and mosquitoes were breeding in the area. Mother Beatrice herself had contracted tuberculosis, but was later healed. There was so much work to be done, as they had to be in the classrooms, care for the garden, chickens, cows, hogs and kitchen. During many nights Mother Beatrice was up caring for those who were ill.

Convent Maria Stein, Pocahontas — 1890s.

According to Sr. Agnes Voth in Green Olive Branch, Mother Beatrice soon realized that Fr. Weibel did not understand her problems. She could no longer confide in him. Thus serious misunderstandings developed with no arbitrator between them. Fr. Weibel forbade her to write to Abbot Frowin, although he himself frequently informed the Abbot of the situation in accordance with his own interpretations.

Fr. Weibel wrote to Abbot Frowin to recall Mother Beatrice to Clyde and send another superior. He also said that she consulted him, and after he had given her his orders and opinions, she did exactly as she pleased. In the same letter, he maintained that Sr. Agnes was prayerful, obedient, much more capable of making decisions and keeping the order of the day, than was Mother Beatrice. He also wrote that Mother Beatrice purchased food to such an extent, that he forbade her to buy more than $20 worth without consulting him.

However, when arrangements were being made at Clyde to carry out Fr. Weibel's requests, he changed his mind and refused to let Mother Beatrice be removed. He wrote, "She is an excellent teacher and disciplinarian. Under the present circumstances we need her and cannot accept a change."[1]

Contrary to Fr. Weibel's orders, Mother Beatrice wrote to Abbot Frowin, "Fr. Weibel is arrogant and wasteful. He has debts himself and drives us also always deeper into debt. Without telling us he even incurs debts in our name. In everything regarding food, boarding, instructions, the work in the garden and house, he is so pretentious that it is impossible for us to meet his demands. He forces us to give our boarders such food as costs more than they pay. If the cooking is not after his liking or taste, he reproaches the Sister in front of guests and boarders."[2]

Later, Father Weibel did report that great progress had been made in the schools and that the Sisters' pedagogy had improved. The Sisters were now teaching a total number of 250 pupils at Pocahontas, Jonesboro and Paragould. Sr. Agnes had begun the new schools in the two latter places. The Postulants brought from Europe, now Novices, would be a great help, once they made vows and were accustomed to the climate. They also needed appropriate instruction in the Rule, the Constitution and the Benedictine way of life. The young women were eager to learn and generous in spirit, so the future looked bright.

Teachers and pupils in front of Maria Stein Convent/Academy — 1890s.

According to Green Olive Branch, Fr. Weibel reported to Abbot Frowin that Mother Beatrice acknowledged that she was unable to rule the community. He wrote that she requested that an election be held, secretly knowing that she would be elected. Fr. Weibel maintained that the Sisters would elect her out of fear. He found that Abbot Frowin refused to recall Mother Beatrice to Clyde, therefore he made other plans. He requested Abbot Frowin to send another Sister from Clyde, bearing the message of having been appointed superior at Pocahontas, and that Mother Beatrice be moved to the Jonesboro school. Mother Beatrice learned of his plan, and told Fr. Weibel if she were removed, ten Sisters would leave the community. Thereupon, Fr. Weibel decided to enact a different plan, and act quickly, without giving advance notice.

First, he had to take a number of steps to implement his plans. One was the reorganization of the Constitution to legitimatize his designs. Constitution of the Benedictine Sisters at Pocahontas had originally been composed at Maria Rickenbach, Switzerland by Abbot Placidus Tanner, Fr. Claudius of Einsiedeln, who had temporarily been spiritual director, and by Fr. Anselm Villiger (later Abbot Anselm). Copies of the original were taken to Maryville in

1874, then to Clyde, and finally to Pocahontas, Arkansas.

Fr. Weibel obtained a copy of the Constitution and a book from Venice entitled, "Confessarius Monialium." Based upon these contents, Fr. Weibel revised the Original Constitution. He obtained Bishop Fitzgerald's approval for this undertaking and reported to Abbot Frowin the following additions:

1. No one is obliged to reveal his conscience to the superior. *(The decree of Pope Leo XIII forbade superiors to insist upon this revelation of conscience.)*
2. Those with temporary vows also had the right to vote both actively and passively.
3. A new superior was to be elected every three years, and no one could hold office for two consecutive terms.

Fr. Weibel added a number of "Amendments" most of which regarded the operation of schools.[3] Neither Mother Beatrice, nor the other Sisters knew anything about these plans, and by April 14, 1891, Mother Beatrice wrote Abbot Frowin, "Twelve of our 17 Novices are to make their first vows on the 21st of this month. The Most Reverend Bishop himself will accept them."[4]

Fr. Weibel wished to bring about a complete change in the administration of Convent Maria Stein. He wrote to Abbot Frowin, "I shall give the retreat, the Bishop will accept the vows of the Novices according to the new Constitution. Then he will send the Constitutions to Rome for approval. The Bishop also wants to incorporate the community under the laws of the State of Arkansas so that it can operate as a business unit."[5]

School Endeavors

As the community increased in membership, so did the requests for teachers increase from neighboring parishes throughout northeast Arkansas and southeast Missouri. In addition to giving daily instructions in the Rule and Constitutions, Mother Beatrice gave the young Sisters instruction on the current teaching practices, as she had been trained in Switzerland. At this time, there was no available institution to prepare teachers. Whenever she felt they were ready, Mother Beatrice sent the young Sisters out to open the different schools, as requested by the parishes.

Mother Beatrice continued to develop the educational program at Pocahontas and during this era published a small brochure to advertise their school. The front of the publication stated it was printed by "Free Press Printing, Pocahontas, Arkansas."

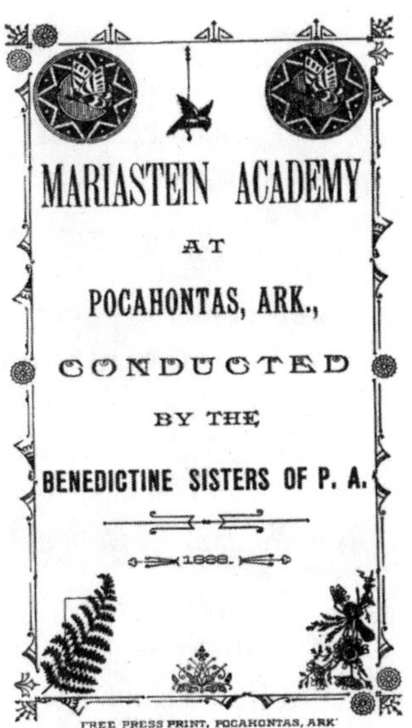
MARIASTEIN ACADEMY
AT
POCAHONTAS, ARK.,
CONDUCTED
BY THE
BENEDICTINE SISTERS OF P. A.
1888.
FREE PRESS PRINT, POCAHONTAS, ARK.

Bulletin announcing curriculum Maria Stein Academy.

Maria Stein Academy

This academy is beautifully situated on shady grounds, on a pleasant hill in the town of Pocahontas, Arkansas. It possesses the advantage of invigorating hill air, with quiet seclusion, which will make it a desirable place for children living in the surrounding bottoms.

The course of instruction embraces all branches, both useful and ornamental. The school opens with the first Monday in September, and closes with the last Wednesday of June.

Terms for Boarders per Month

Board, tuition, laundry, bedding, knitting, plain sewing, crochet, embroidery, German language, bookkeeping $11

For Day Scholars

Inferior Class $1
Higher Department $2

Extra Charges

Tuition for piano per month $3
Use of piano for practice per month $1
Tuition on guitar per month $2

Tuition on oil painting or watercolor	$2
Tuition on plain drawing per month	$1
French	$2
Shorthand	$2
Typing	$1

Wardrobe

Scholars must be provided with towels, napkins, sufficient changes of underwear, also knife, fork, and spoons, combs, and brushes. The use of white aprons and skirts is not allowed on weekdays, and if this rule is not complied with, washing will be charged extra. *Further Information on Request* [6]

According to "In the Beginning," by Sr. Felicitas, summers at Convent Stein were spent in caring for the garden, taking care of the farm animals and studying to prepare for the new school year. By the end of summer, the Sisters were engaged in packing trunks to go to the Missions. Although there was not much to pack, it was an annual ritual engaged in by all the Sisters sent to the mission schools. The usual contents consisted of clothes and the few teaching materials they were able to make and gradually accumulate over the years.

As for travel from Pocahontas in the mid-1890s, only the steamboat was available. The steamboat ran twice a week, and then only as far as Black Rock, which was a slow and inconvenient way of traveling. The Convent possessed two mules, Juno and Johnny, and a large farm wagon, so the Sisters traveled by wagon to one of the three available train stations in the area. They boarded the station at O'Kean, Hoxie or Walnut Ridge to travel to their respective Missions.

Brother Gallus would first load the trunks in the wagon and then the missionary Sisters would climb aboard. They situated themselves as best they could for the ride. After goodbyes and waving of handkerchiefs, the wagon moved swiftly up and down the hills to the riverbank where they would board the ferryboat to cross to the other side. Old Juno was not always willing to take the ride, but after his bucking and balking, Brother Gallus was able to guide the wagon on the ferryboat. After docking on the other side, the mules needed no urging to leave.

Then the wagon continued on the other side to one of the three train stations at O'Kean, Hoxie or Walnut Ridge, where the Sisters would board for their respective destination. The travelers took along lunch which included fresh fruit in season, so they enjoyed their picnic while they traveled through the woods. For those who were to board at Hoxie, it would usually take four or five hours to reach their destination.

Change of Superiors

The year of 1892 began quietly, and members of Convent Maria Stein were operating as usual according to previous schedule. No one expected the sudden change that would shake the community within two weeks. Early in the afternoon of January 14, 1892, Fr. Weibel arrived from Jonesboro, announcing that he wanted the entire community to meet in the lecture room. No one had reason to expect anything other than the customary conference.

All the Sisters assembled in the lecture room, expecting the customary conference. However, before Fr. Weibel began his lecture, he shocked the Sisters by announcing, "Mother Beatrice, has on several occasions, resigned the office of superior of this convent. The Most Reverend Bishop Fitzgerald has accepted the resignation and approved the suggestion that Sr. Aloysia Unterberger be installed as her successor. SEE PROFILE IN APPENDIX. Mother Beatrice was appointed local superior for the mission school in Paragould, in place of Sr. Aloysia. There was no election."[8]

No attempt was made to conceal surprise and consternation of each present. There were tears, as all loved Mother Beatrice and felt that without her, Convent Maria Stein could not exist. The opinion prevailed that the convent was pointed toward disaster without the leadership of Mother Beatrice. There was nothing the community could do, as the Bishop had approved the change. After the lecture, Fr. Weibel made a hasty departure.

The Sisters grouped about Mother Beatrice and begged her not to leave them. However, she tried to console them and began to pack to leave for Paragould the following day. She relinquished leadership of the community forever, and permitted others to lead the institution she loved and courageously began.[9]

In his letter of February 16, 1892, to Abbot Frowin, Fr. Weibel reported that he went to Pocahontas on January 14, and called a Chapter meeting. During the meeting he "accepted" the resignation of Mother Beatrice. (Neither she nor any one else knew anything about the resignation before the meeting.) Mother Beatrice showed herself well-pleased and willing, and proposed Sr. Aloysia Unterberger as the new superior. All the Sisters agreed to this proposal.[10]

On April 21,1892, Bishop Fitzgerald verified the appointment of Mother Aloysia with his seal and letter, and commented on how graciously the community accepted the change. By the Bishop's approbation, Mother Beatrice was given the honor of foundress of Convent Maria Stein with the perpetual title, "Mother Beatrice." She was named local superior of Convent St. Gertrude, Paragould, Arkansas; Mother Agnes was sent to Poplar Bluff, as local superior of that school. She showed no evidence of opposition and gladly went to the assigned school in southeast Missouri.

During her administration, Mother Beatrice had opened nine schools. Besides opening the schools at St. Paul's in Pocahontas, (1888-) and the school for the black children (1888-); she opened St. Roman's, Jonesboro, (Later, Blessed Sacrament 1889-); St. Mary's Paragould (1890-1900); St. John's, Engelberg, (1891-1968); Sacred Heart, Popular Bluff, Missouri (1891-1909); Immaculate Conception, New Madrid, Missouri (1891-1902); St. Edward, Little Rock, Arkansas (1891-1904). St. Boniface, Fort Smith (1891-1903). These latter two schools continue in operation today but under different administration. The Pocahontas community withdrew from them when the Benedictine Sisters from Shoal Creek were able to take over the staffing in the fall of 1903.[11]

Mother Beatrice had fulfilled the assignment entrusted to her from Abbot Frowin and Mother John. She had opened the novitiate, trained and admitted new members, trained teachers to staff the schools, and established a new independent Benedictine house. Personnel had increased five-fold during the five years she had been superior.

The first Novice, Christine Unterberger of Lungern, Canton Unterwalden, Switzerland, who had been received into the community at Convent Maria Stein, had made religious profession as Sister Aloysia on February 28, 1890, was now the superior. She first taught school in Jonesboro, but that same year was appointed superior of the school in Paragould. Now, two years later, she was appointed the second superior of Convent Maria Stein in Pocahontas. SEE PROFILE IN APPENDIX.

According to Green Olive Branch, "Completely on her own, except for obedience to Fr. Weibel, Mother Aloysia governed the community of six older and 18 younger religious for two years." [12] During this time eight new members joined the small monastic community. Sr. Antonia Gehrig, just professed, had died January 9, 1892.

Like Mother Beatrice, Mother Aloysia accepted her difficult role with prayer and patience. Although she was unsure and inexperienced in religious life, she had the duty to lead her companions. Even more challenging was the task of winning the cooperation of the older religious whom she hardly knew. Both she and the community cautiously accepted the challenge, but not without difficulties and misunderstandings.

Olivetan Benedictine Affiliation

Bishop Fitzgerald had approved Convent Maria Stein as a Diocesan Institution, but he wanted a more stable authorization by the Church outside the Diocese of Little Rock. Bishop Fitzgerald pointed out the advisability of obtaining an official declaration of the Apostolic See as to the ecclesiastical standing of the community. Fr. Weibel saw no necessity for this effort, but in a letter dated June 2, 1892, the Bishop wrote that he wished Convent Maria Stein affiliated with an institution outside the Diocese of Little Rock. "I do not share your opinion that Orders, particularly those of women, should be dependent upon Diocesan Bishops alone. The Bishop of today may favor the convent, but possibly a later one would not be so disposed. What will then happen to the organization? It is much better that they become dependent upon a central authority outside the Diocese."[13]

The Bishop authorized Fr. Weibel to go to Europe to secure the appropriate documents to ensure official declaration of the Apostolic See as to the ecclesiastical standing of the community. Fr. Weibel first went to Switzerland to visit his former Abbey Maria Stein that had been re-established, upon returning from France. From there he visited his home in Eschenbach and then on to Einsiedeln, where he conferred with Abbot Basil about the purpose of his trip. The latter had formerly revised the Constitution of the Benedictine Sisters at the convent in Cham, Switzerland. He informed Fr. Weibel that the Abbot General of the Olivetan Benedictines, had the right and the power to accept convents and monasteries into his Congregation.

In October, Fr. Weibel went to Rome to contact Cardinal Parrochi, who established the proper sources, and the process began. Fr. Weibel was introduced to Dom Camillus Maria Seriolo, Abbot General of the Olivetan Benedictines and made preliminary preparation for the affiliation. This undertaking required some changes in the Constitution of Convent Maria Stein. Because the time of his visit was limited and those negotiations took a longer period of time, Fr. Weibel delegated the work to Fr. Thomas of Collegio San Anselmo, (Benedictine House for clerical studies) in Rome.

Abbot Camillus Seriolo gave assurance that everything would be put in order, and all that was now required was a slight revision of the Constitution of Convent Maria Stein, and the formation of the documents. Convent Maria Stein, Pocahontas, Arkansas, would be assured of its status as affiliated with the Congregation of the Montei Oliveto.

While in Europe, Fr. Weibel contacted 32 persons, whom he was to chaperone on the return journey. Most of these were young ladies who planned to enter convent Maria Stein, Pocahontas, St. Scholastica Convent, Logan County, Arkansas, or students who went to various Benedictine seminaries. All met in Einsiedeln and left on

November 27 to meet another group at Basel.

From the group Fr. Weibel chaperoned from Europe, eight of the Postulants came to Pocahontas to enter Convent Maria Stein, one of which was Pauline Hoegger, later Prioress, Mother Walburga. The increased number also increased the need for more room and financing for food and clothing. By the summer of 1893, a second story was added to the frame Convent, which made three large rooms upstairs and three small front rooms. About this same time a new washhouse was built about 50 feet south of the Convent.[14]

Affiliation Document Received

After the close of the 1893 Retreat conducted by Fr. Eustasius, OSB, the Sisters for the first time renewed their vows according to the formula of the Olivetan Benedictines. This form was used until the updated formula after Vatican II arrived. Although the document of Affiliation arrived in Pocahontas much later, it had been dated January 15, 1893, Feast of St. Maurus, a disciple of St. Benedict.[15] The document was written in German and signed by Dom Camillus Maria Seriolo, Abbot General of the Olivetan Benedictine Congregation. The Affiliation document also advised that the community adopt the white habit of the Congregation of Our Lady of Mount Olivet.

That summer the Sisters sewed white habits and donned them for the first time at the Motherhouse in Pocahontas on August 5, 1893, the Feast of St. Mary Major or Our Lady of the Snows, as it is sometimes called. However, the Sisters on the Missions continued to wear the black habit until the following summer, when they had time to make enough white habits for all of them.

Sr. Felicitas Hunkler, Mother Beatric Renggli and Sr. Angelina Boesch in their new white habits — 1893.

In addition to wearing the white habit in honor of Mary's purity, the document of Affiliation also specified that the community imitates Mary's virtues and her love for Jesus. In imitation of Mary's fidelity to Christ throughout His suffering and death, the Sisters were to cultivate a special devotion to honor the Passion of Christ.

Not only did Convent Maria adopt the title, "Olivetan Benedictines," it also adopted the Olivetan formula of profession and the celebration of principal feasts of the Congregation.

The documents also specified that the community would remain under the jurisdiction of the local Ordinary (Bishop), and be affiliated with the Olivetan Benedictine Congregation, headquartered at Monte Oliveto, Chiusure-Siena, Italy. However, it was not clear in the documents if this was actual canonical affiliation or only a spiritual affiliation. In 1907, when Rev. John Baptist Morris, DD, became the Bishop for the Diocese of Little Rock, he wrote to inquire about the status of the Olivetan Benedictine Community in his jurisdiction. He did not receive a definitive answer, as the documents could not be located.

In 1912, Mother Beatrice wrote to Prior Augustine Stocker, OSB, of Subiaco, asking him to inquire about the status of the community. He wrote,

> "The Abbot General states in a recent letter, that you are entirely under the jurisdiction of the diocesan Bishop, though at the same time, contending that your Affiliation is more than spiritual. What is the plus in your Affiliation? I cannot pretend to guess, for if it is not jurisdictional, I am at a loss to find a canonical name for it. I am very sorry that this affair does not let you in peace."[16]

No further information was received concerning this matter. Throughout the years there has been continued discussion on the status of the community. In 1969, Mother Benedicta Boeckmann, OSB, asked Fr. Bernard Sause, OSB, of Atchison, Kansas, who was assisting the community in revising the Constitution, to write once again to Monte Oliveto, to clarify status of the community. Dom Romualdo M. Zilianti, OSB, Abbot General replied,

"About your foundation and your spiritual Affiliation with the Olivetan Benedictine Congregation, at the moment, I have only the writing which I have already mentioned. I am confident however, that we shall find the document, which we are presently looking for and which was lost during the fire. This document, like so many others, was drawn up far from Monte Oliveto, at the time when the Abbot General, after the suppression by the Italian Government, was forced to move from one monastery to another. I am searching for the document in those monasteries in which the Abbot General is presumed to have stayed during that period. I shall see to it that photostatic copies of all documents which I have and shall find are made, and I will send them to you."[17]

However, no other documents were forwarded, but the Abbot General told Fr. Bernard Sause that he understood that the Affiliation was only spiritual.

In 1997, once again, an effort was made to secure clarification on the status of the community. Copies of the letters and documents in Holy Angels Convent Archives were sent to the Abbot Primate Reverend Marcel Rooney, OSB. at San Anselmo, Rome, who in turn contacted Reverend Michelangelo M. Tribilli, OSB, Abbot General of the Olivetan Benedictine Congregation at Montei Oliveto, Chiusure-Siena. The following was his response to Sr. Henrietta Hockle, OSB, Prioress, dated March 11, 1997:

"I spoke with the Abbot General of the Olivetans and it was his idea that your community had only a spiritual association with the Congregation rather than an actual canonical affiliation. However, the documentation which you sent me shows an 1893 letter of actual affiliation. I suggest that you write directly to the Abbot General at Monte Oliveto to ask for a copy of the original document of affiliation. That would tell what type of affiliation it is."[18]

After writing to Reverend Michelangelo M. Tribilli, OSB, Abbot General, the response was the same as the community received in 1969. He wrote that, the way he interpreted the documents, the affiliation was only spiritual.

There were continuous challenges for the young Superior because Fr. Weibel attempted to give contradictory orders to the

Sisters. At last, Mother Aloysia wrote to Bishop Fitzgerald. In a letter dated, October 16, 1893, *she wrote*:

> "I am sorry that I am compelled to write to you concerning the following, but my conscience does not allow me to be silent any longer. Rev. Fr. Director (Fr. Weibel) was here a few days ago and told me in case he would not get a letter from you soon, he would come here and make Pocahontas his dwelling place and visit Jonesboro and Hoxie from here. If he does this, then I may just as well give up all hopes for the future.
>
> The Sisters have already divided themselves into three parts, some hold to Fr. Director, others to Sr. Beatrice and the rest to me, and some Sisters think they only have to obey Fr. Director. You can imagine how Sisterly love – Vows and Holy Rule are observed. I have begged Fr. Director twice to take the heavy burden of Superior from my shoulders, but he never would grant it, and I now beg your Lordship, if you think it good to release one of it.
>
> I am perfectly satisfied to be the last in the community, but to be Superior this way when I have nothing to say to the most important affairs of the convent....
>
> As to the above, I hope you will do whatever you can to restore the true religious spirit among us. I do not think there will be any remedy without a change.
>
> I remain in humble submission to whatever you decide."
>
> Your Lordship's obedient servant,
> Sr. M. Aloysia [19]

There is no record of a response from Bishop Fitzgerald concerning this letter, but there must have been some communication between them, as well as between the Bishop and Fr. Weibel, as a change occurred in the administration the following year.

First Election

By the end of the second year of Mother Aloysia's administration as superior, Fr. Weibel decided to allow the Sisters of Convent Maria Stein to determine the next prioress by vote. The community was called together in the Chapter room and the result of the election was that Sr. Agnes Dali was the first elected superior of the Olivetan Benedictine Sisters in the United States. SEE PROFILE IN APPENDIX.

Mother Agnes was a prayerful person and had expended zeal and energy wherever she was assigned. She was loved and revered by the Sisters and the people on the Missions. Mother Agnes also aided in the completion of the affiliation with the Olivetan Benedictines. She had opened St. Roman's School in Jonesboro and St. Mary's in Paragould, and most recently, she was the local superior at Sacred Heart School in Poplar Bluff. She was ready for any sacrifice and accepted the burden of leadership. She found time to spend hours praying before the Blessed Sacrament. Shortly after her election, Mother Agnes chose Sr. Cecilia Huber as her secretary to assist her in administration.

The problems that faced Mother Agnes were numerous, above all was the poverty in the area. They had no money and neither did the people they tried to serve. The tuition for school was frequently paid by garden and farm produce. Mother Agnes worked tirelessly to help others and willingly gave of her time and energy in this regard.

By 1894, Bishop Fitzgerald appointed Monsignor Weinand H. Aretz as the spiritual director for the Sisters. He worked well with Mother Agnes, and supported her efforts in forming the young Sisters in the Benedictine Rule and Constitutions. This brought a welcome respite of peace to the community. However. Fr. Weibel regained his role, as spiritual director of the Sisters, within a short time. In 1895, Mother Agnes sent a letter to Rome, reporting that 28 Sisters were ready to make their final vows that year, and four were ready to make their first vows. She also reported that Fr. Hugo Fessler, O.P.M. preached the retreat to the Sisters that year. She also noted in her letter, that "For the first time since their affiliation, all the Sisters were wearing the white habit of the Olivetans."[20]

In addition to opening new schools in Arkansas, by 1895, Mother Agnes responded to a request to send Sisters to teach in Muenster, Texas. Fr. Bonaventure Binzegger, OSB, from Einsiedeln, who had become acquainted with the Olivetan Benedictine Sisters, when he was assistant pastor at St. Edward's Church in Little Rock, made the request for teachers. Mother Agnes sent Sr. Anselma Wuersch, Sr. Frances Bossart, Sr. Anna Brunner, Novice Fridoline, Novice Caroline and Oblate Sally Geppert to Muenster.

Mother Agnes wrote to Fr. Weibel in Jonesboro, to inform him of their drastic poverty. She wrote that they could no longer afford to give alms, as they had scarcely enough to buy the needed staples for the community. Also, she wrote they did not have enough money to buy the gold rings for the 28 Sisters who would make Final Vows that year. The Sisters would not have been able to survive without the donations they received from their families in Switzerland. Fr. Weibel sent Mother Agnes small donations from time to time, but money was scarce, so this was only temporary relief. The Sisters of the Missions also experienced the same difficulties, as they also had to make a garden, and can the vegetables they could store for winter. They struggled to survive and they welcomed any alms that would be donated, as well as garden and farm produce.

Jonesboro Fire

During the night of May 15, 1896, while the pastor was away, a heavy storm hit Jonesboro. Lightning struck the tower of the recently enlarged St. Romans' church and fire quickly spread over the roof of the church and adjoining school. Sleeping in the Sisters' quarters were; Sr. M. Anna Brunner, Sr. M. Frances Bossart, Sr. M. Felicitas Hunkler and Sr. M. Angeline Boesch. They were awakened and quickly dressed to escape the flames.

The church bells were rung to summon the people to come to help. They gathered from all directions, but no fire fighting apparatus was available. The hoses were locked behind the doors of the machine house at the train depot, and the caretaker was in Pine Bluff. People dragged furniture out of the church, school and Sisters' home and rectory. All buildings on Cate Street were completely lost when hoses were finally obtained after someone broke into the machine house. Only surrounding homes could be saved.

Within a week, Fr. Weibel purchased another piece of property located two blocks from the Court House in Jonesboro. An old house

Early Catholic settlement on Cate Street in Jonesboro. L to R: St. Roman's rectory, church with combination Sisters' house and school in background. All were destroyed by fire from lightning in May 1896.

was on the property where the Sisters were lodged temporarily. All the furniture that had been rescued was taken to that location. School was resumed within a few days. Mother Agnes recalled Sr. Angelina Boesch and Sr. Frances Bossart to Pocahontas and then sent them to Europe to recruit more Postulants. Sr. Anna completed instruction for the First Communicants, with classes under the trees. Some pupils sat on the rescued benches while others sat on the ground. Sr. Felicitas gave music lessons and they finished the school year before returning to Pocahontas for retreat and summer respite.

Building of the new combination church-school was soon begun. The Jonesboro parishioners held a fair to defray expenses. The Sisters and the people collected articles to be raffled or sold to add to the proceeds. Anthony Weibel, brother of Fr. Weibel, oversaw the construction and by the opening of school in the fall of 1896, the Sisters began classes in the two sacristies and on the balcony of the new structure. Fr. Weibel used part of the balcony as sleeping quarters until the new brick veneer rectory was built. Mrs. Higi, a widow, offered the Sisters the use of her home, until their residence was completed.

Decision to Relocate

Convent Maria Stein experienced a fateful year in 1897. "At one time, 13 Novices, young, promising members, were afflicted with typhoid fever. Novice Gregoria Straub, Novice Boniface Jacobs, and Novice Edeltrudis Limacher fell victim to the dreaded disease. These three Novices were allowed to make their Profession of Vows on their deathbed, even though they had not completed the Novitiate. The other ten Novices recovered and regained their health. Upon close investigation and examination of the drinking water, it was found that the new well which was very deep, had a leak, and matters containing typhoid germs had mixed with the water. The well was closed immediately, and no new cases occurred. This tragedy was one of the reasons that caused the community to relocate the convent from Pocahontas to Jonesboro."[21]

Convent Maria Stein showing garden foreground — 1890s.

Another reason was that by 1897 railroads had come. Jonesboro was supplied with two lines, the St. Louis Southwestern (Cotton Belt), and the Kansas City Southern (Frisco). The Iron Mountain ran through Nettleton, only three miles distant. These advantages in transportation far surpassed those offered by boats on the Black River at Pocahontas, and its one small railroad spur. People in general realized that railroad centers would become dominant trade centers, and spur rapid growth. Jonesboro seemed destined to surpass Pocahontas. Bishop Fitzgerald and Fr. Weibel jointly decided to move the convent and the novitiate of Convent Maria

Stein to Jonesboro.[22]

Mother Agnes also saw great advantages in the change, and took the preliminary steps to have Fr. Weibel supervise the building of the convent and novitiate in Jonesboro. One of the first things he did was to inform the Abbot General of the Olivetans in Sienna of the proposed change. After receiving approval, Fr. Weibel drew up plans, supervised evacuations, and procured materials. Anthony Weibel, his brother, would oversee the erection of the brick veneer building which comprised three stories, plus an attic and a tower for occupation.

The basement housed kitchen, dining room, and laundry. A large cistern was to furnish the water supply, but it was still empty. The second floor was devoted to classrooms, music and art rooms. The third floor, the attic and the tower were planned as sleeping quarters for the Sisters and boarding girls. In 1898, Jonesboro was still a small country town, with no water works nor electric lights. Private cistern and wells supplied water. There were no telephones nor paved streets. There were wooden sidewalks along the main street. Fr. Weibel had a 75 foot well dug, and had a windmill erected on it to draw water.[23]

Shortage of water was not the only problem—there was a shortage of funds. Bishop Fitzgerald sent Fr. Weibel to Philadelphia to solicit funds for the Diocese of Little Rock. He was allowed to keep part of what he was able to obtain for the erection of the building in Jonesboro. In addition, Mother Agnes received permission to send the sisters out on collecting tours. Sr. Raphael Kimmet, Sr. Berchmanns Weber, Sr. Albrica Steffens, Sr. Walburga Hoegger and others helped raise funds. A part of these funds was used to advance the education of teachers and the improvement of schools.

As the result of frequent reports to Fr. Weibel about Mother Agnes, Fr. Weibel removed her from office three months before her tenure was over and appointed Sr. Cecilia, her secretary, as the interim superior, until an election was held. Mother Agnes was sent to Muenster, Texas.

CHAPTER 5
1898-1900

Second Election

As Sr. Agnes Dali packed to leave for Muenster, Texas, where she was now assigned to teach, there was unrest again in the community. The Sisters were concerned about what would happen in the future to their community. Fr. Weibel had removed Mother Agnes Dali from office, three months before the end of her elected term, and appointed the secretary, Sr. Cecilia Huber, as the interim superior.

One incident clearly illustrates the methods employed by Fr. Weibel. The Sisters were all on their missions at Pocahontas, Jonesboro, Paragould, Engelberg, Fort Smith, Wynne, and Forest City, Arkansas; and at Poplar Bluff and New Madrid, Missouri. Mother Agnes had gone with the other Sisters assigned to teach in Muenster and Sr. Cecilia Huber, the assigned interim superior, was at Pocahontas.

On a Saturday morning, Fr. Weibel had returned to Jonesboro from a trip, and came into the residence of the four Sisters stationed at St. Roman's school. Disregarding all formality he announced, "Tomorrow is Election Day." He meant the election of a new Mother Superior. The four Sisters were shocked almost as greatly as they had been when he announced the resignation of Mother Beatrice, January 14, 1892, and the appointment of Mother Aloysia as superior. This time one of the Sisters asked, "How can there be an election with only four Sisters present?"[1]

Fr. Weibel answered that he had the votes of all the absent Sisters in his pocket, except those who were to come to Jonesboro tomorrow. He said that those from New Madrid, Missouri; Pocahontas, Wynne and Paragould would arrive in the morning and they did. The election was held on Sunday between the morning Masses. After Fr. Weibel counted all the votes, (both absentee and of those present, he announced that Sr. Cecilia Huber was the elected superior. According to "In the Beginning," by Sr. Felicitas, "The entire process took less than 30 minutes."[2] SEE PROFILE IN APPENDIX.

Even though the community experienced extreme poverty, Mother Agnes had tried to educate the Sisters by giving them every opportunity to prepare to be teachers. Now, it was Mother Cecilia's responsibility to stretch funds to enable the Sisters to take summer courses being offered at Nashville, Tennessee, St. Louis, Missouri, Chicago, Illinois, and Atchison, Kansas.

Mother Cecilia collaborated with Mother Beatrice to upgrade and improve the schools. Not only were religious subjects stressed, but the curriculum was geared to educate the whole child, both spiritually and academically. In addition, classes in art, music and languages were added to enhance the child's development, both emotionally and socially. The schools staffed by the Sisters became noted for high academic standards and they soon surpassed the public schools at the time.[3]

Because of her educationally inventive mind, Mother Cecilia encouraged the Sisters on all the missions to hold exhibits at the end of the scholastic year. According to Fr. Weibel, "The pupils at St. Paul, Pocahontas, St. Roman, Jonesboro and St. Mary, Paragould presented exhibitions of classroom work, and oral examinations in the presence of a public audience, fit for a college display."[4] The exhibitions grew each year, and some booths displayed drawings, needlework, composition work, and samples of arithmetic and history projects in geography.

Besides improving the educational system in the schools staffed by the Sisters, Mother Cecilia was faced with moving the community from Pocahontas to Jonesboro. After 11 years in Pocahontas, the Sisters had provided Convent Maria Stein with cows to supply milk, butter and meat; chickens to furnish eggs and meat; a garden and orchard that supplied vegetables and fruit. The plan was to move only part of the community to Jonesboro at first, while leaving the Novitiate and some of the Sisters in Pocahontas to maintain the convent and school.

Relocation of Motherhouse

By the end of June, Fr. Weibel notified Mother Cecilia that the new convent building in Jonesboro stood ready for the community. Masons and carpenters had terminated their work, but the interior was still unfinished. Floors were unfinished, windows did not have screens, furniture was practically non-existent. The furniture the four Sisters had at St. Roman's was brought over across the field to the new convent—four beds (cots), four chairs, a table, a small cook stove, and trunks. The Sisters themselves carried these items across the weedy area down to the basement of their new residence. Beds were carried up the narrow staircase to the top floor.

The date of July 4, 1898 was set as moving day for the Sisters in Pocahontas to move to Jonesboro. Since it was a holiday, the farmers took off from their fieldwork, and came with their farm wagons to help. They helped Brother Gallus move the 12 Sisters and 12 Novices, who were to make their first Profession when the Bishop came to bless the new convent.

The men first loaded the wagons with the Sisters' belongings, packed in trunks, plus sheets, pillows and blankets. Then the Sisters and Novices climbed aboard for the trip to Jonesboro. The four Sisters stationed in Jonesboro had a Fourth of July surprise by the unannounced appearance of the Community with only a few personal belongings. According to "In the Beginning," by Sr. Felicitas Hunkler, such surprises were not unusual.

First Holy Angels Convent in Jonesboro (facing west) — 1898.

"After assessing the situation, Mother Cecilia went to the local furniture store to purchase beds and mattresses. Only the latter were available. Beds (army cots) had to be ordered. Fortunately, the newcomers were easily pleased, as mattresses were spread on the floor, and used that way for several weeks until the beds arrived. No one complained about sleeping on the floor nor of the excessive July heat."[5]

It is hard to picture now, but according to newspaper accounts, Jonesboro had no electric lights in 1898. The town was lighted by 62 gaslights furnished by the Sun Vapor Street Lighting Company of Canton, Ohio. City leaders had made plans to secure electric lights. The residential section of the town had plank sidewalks and paving was being planned for the main streets.

Eggs were eight cents a dozen, bacon was nine cents a pound, and the population of Jonesboro was 4,508. There was no sewage disposal system in operation, but talk around town indicated one would soon be installed. The Jonesboro, Lake City and Eastern Railroad (J.L.C.&E.) had stretched its line to Monette, connecting Jonesboro to the outside world. The Southwestern Telephone and Telegraph Company was newly established in Jonesboro and had installed a long-distance line to Harrisburg.[6]

The lack of sufficient water was a growing problem. With so little breeze, the windmill erected over Fr. Weibel's 75-foot-deep well for the convent did not pull up the water from that depth. Unless there was a storm or heavy wind, the Novices had to use the hand pump to draw up the water and this was difficult because of the depth of the well.

Unlike Convent Maria Stein, Jonesboro did not yet possess cows, chickens, garden or orchard. Everything served at table had to be brought from Pocahontas or purchased from peddlers, or from one of the few stores. Furnishings to accommodate four people could not be expanded to furnish convenience for the nearly 30 people. All this required money, and money was a scarce commodity. From the exterior, the convent looked palatial, but the inside lacked the barest necessities. Because of the 30 lumber mills surrounding Jonesboro, lumber was cheap, so Brother Gallus began making chairs, tables, wash stands, and desks. He was engaged in making furniture for the new convent for a long time.

The grounds surrounding the convent were not yet cleared so something had to be done before the Bishop arrived for the dedication. Weeds and dog fennel covered the large space of ground (about 50 feet) between the church and hall and the new convent. Because the Bishop would have to cross this weedy patch when he came to bless the convent, Mother Cecilia sent the Novices out to clear a path through the weeds. After a second day of pulling weeds and bleeding fingers, Mr. Worland, father of Novice Celestine, (the first Jonesboro member of the community), had pity on them and mowed the rest of the path with his scythe and cleared the land for the Bishop.

Holy Angels Convent in Jonesboro (facing east) — 1898.

A New Home, A New Name

A number of names were proposed for the new convent, for it could not be named Maria Stein. That name must remain with the first Motherhouse in Pocahontas, for that name reflected the place on which it was built—on rocks. Some of the Sisters recalled an experience they had had at sea, during one of the crossings, to bring back Postulants. A frightening storm arose and Sr. Remigia Dietsche, who was in charge, urged the group to pray to the Holy Angels for protection. After their arrival on American soil, the soon to be Postulants, attributed their safe crossing to the Holy Angels.

Happily, the name "Holy Angels" overruled all other suggestions and Bishop Fitzgerald, approved this title and dedicated the new convent to the Holy Angels. The Bishop praised the idea and placed the community of Olivetan Benedictine Sisters under the special protection of the Holy Angels.

July 10, 1898, the day for the dedication arrived, with cloudless sky and sweltering heat. However, no one seemed to mind the July sun or the heat. The ceremonies began when Bishop Fitzgerald, accompanied by Fr. Weibel came across the grounds from the church, the Bishop carrying the sprinkler, Fr. Weibel the vessel of Holy Water. First they circled the building, blessing its exterior, then they entered. They found most of the rooms empty. In the dormitories the Bishop saw the mattresses on the floors, in the dining room, a table, four chairs and a few benches. The two cooks had slipped into the pantry and closed the door after them. However, when the Bishop passed by, he opened the door to bless the pantry and also blessed the kneeling Sisters behind the door.

After that, the entire group returned to the church, and the solemn High Mass began. During which, four Postulants were invested as Novices, then, the 12 Novices made profession of First Vows, and lastly four Sisters made profession of Final Vows, or Perpetual Profession. Indeed, this was a memorable occasion in the history of the Olivetan Benedictine Community, now of Jonesboro.

After the lengthy ceremonies in church, the entire assembly returned to the convent for the festive meal. "At the dinner (by mistake), Mother Beatrice served plain hash to His Lordship, the Bishop, while the fine steak which the cook had prepared for the Bishop, and set aside on the pantry shelf for safekeeping, was untouched." [7] Those at head table had the same fare as the community that day.

First group of Sisters to move to Holy Angels Convent, Jonesboro 1898.

In the months following the dedication, attention was focused on convent routine. With heroic efforts, obstacles were overcome and gradually a garden, a grape arbor, and an orchard emerged and supplied the community with fruits and vegetables for the following years.

By February 1899, an epidemic of spinal meningitis raged in the vicinity of Pocahontas. Dr. Esselmann told Mother Cecilia to shield the Sisters from the disease for all who contacted it were certain to die. There was no known remedy so there was very little she could do about it. Sr. Beatrice Renggli and Sr. Mechtilde Schuchert both became very ill, and the latter died that same year.

At the persuasion of Dr. J.C. Esselmann, the Sisters opened a small infirmary in Pocahontas on October 19, 1899. This infirmary, named, "St. Anna's Infirmary," was located near the old Highway 67, at the fork in the road, that leads into the town of Pocahontas. Dr. Esselmann and Dr. J. Hughes used this infirmary to care for the sick. Sr. Aloysia Unterberger, who had nurses' training in Switzerland, was placed in charge. She was assisted part-time by Sr. Eugenia Brodell, and Sr. Fridoline Buck.

According to the record book, the first patient, Miss Mary Peters, age 19, who had typhoid fever, was admitted to St. Anna's Infirmary on October 29, 1899. She was dismissed on November 28, and listed as cured.

At the end of Mother Cecilia Huber's first term as Prioress, (1897-1900), Fr. Weibel conducted a third canonical election in the community. This was the second election held in Jonesboro, which resulted in placing Sr. M. Edward End, one of Mother Beatrice's early Novices, in office as Prioress in 1900. She had come to America with the first contingent of 16 other applicants for membership in the community of Convent Maria Stein. She was well-educated and a skilled teacher, and after profession, she had been assigned to teach in different schools staffed by the community, the last of which was St. John's, Hot Springs. SEE PROFILE IN APPENDIX.

Mother Cecilia, the outgoing Prioress, returned to her favorite occupation of teaching school. She was placed in charge of Immaculate Conception School in Higginsville, Missouri. Mother Edward continued to emphasize education and encouraged the young Sisters to pass the required tests to assume teaching responsibilities. She expanded the ministries of the community by accepting seven new schools, besides staffing the former ones.

Although a few of the Sisters had worked in the small infirmary in Pocahontas, the education of children was emphasized as the primary ministry of the community. Now, however, a new challenge faced the community because of ensuing events. Health care as a ministry of the community would be the beginning of an entirely new endeavor by the Sisters. Mother Edward was faced with guiding the community in making this difficult decision.

Malaria Fever Epidemic

While the doctors were struggling to care for the sick in the Pocahontas area, a malaria fever epidemic was beginning to spread throughout northeast Arkansas. Back in Jonesboro, the doctors were asking for help. Although the Sisters were engaged in their mission of teaching, they were often called upon to help care for the sick, because the nearest health care facilities were in Memphis, Tennessee, Little Rock, Arkansas or St. Louis, Missouri. Mother Alexia, superior of St. Joseph's Hospital in Memphis, was frequently asked to accept charity patients from the northeast Arkansas area. Oftentimes, Fr. Weibel would accompany the poor patients to St. Joseph's and make the request. Patients who had severe cases of fever often died before they could gain admittance.

There was a longstanding need for a hospital in Jonesboro to serve people in the surrounding areas. "Plans had been made in 1896 to provide a small hospital for Jonesboro, but the conflagration had obliterated all plans for this project indefinitely."[8]

Fr. Weibel knew the Sisters were not prepared to take on hospital work, but the fact that several had been doing nursing duties in Pocahontas convinced him that it could be done in Jonesboro. The stroke suffered by Bishop Fitzgerald at Jonesboro, January 21, 1900, confirmed the resolution in Fr. Weibel's mind to found a hospital there. Fr. Weibel concluded that a hospital in northeast Arkansas was a necessity and he resolved to do his utmost to bring it to realization.

Fr. Weibel contacted Bishop Fitzgerald who was ill at St. Joseph's Hospital in Hot Springs, for permission to open a hospital in Jonesboro. "The Bishop reminded him that such undertakings require endowments, and these were not available in Jonesboro. He specified if Fr. Weibel and the Sisters could raise $10,000 as a charity fund, he would acquiesce to the project. However, at the moment, Fr. Weibel could not produce even half that amount, but he promised himself he would do so before long."[9]

When Fr. Weibel presented this project to the Sisters, they were not open to expanding their ministry. Mother Edward and the community reminded him that, according to their history and tradition, they were founded primarily to be adorers of the Blessed Sacrament, not nurses. They engaged in the ministry of teaching as a means of supporting themselves. The Sisters were unwilling to relinquish the traditions they had brought with them from Maria Rickenbach and of Clyde, Missouri.

"Fr. Weibel then began a series of lectures to point out that the very name "hospital" had its origin with the Benedictine Order. According to the Rule of St. Benedict, every monastery and convent should operate a guesthouse, or "hospicium," where strangers could obtain lodging. Even Maria Rickenbach, high in the Swiss Alps, provided accommodations for pilgrims. Guesthouses gradually evolved into hospitals. He reminded the Sisters that St. Bernard, the founder of the Olivetan Benedictines, had given his life to the care of the sick."[10]

He also recalled, that according to the Council of Trent, cloistered Nuns would not be permitted to do this type of work, but they were not cloistered Nuns. He insisted that this community had been founded by him to conduct schools and hospitals. Fr. Weibel continued to instill in them the fact that they were Olivetan Benedictines and St. Bernard, their patron, had given them an example of service to others. He asserted that his aim was to found a convent of laboring Benedictines.

"Mother Edward was deprived of the foresight, aid and guidance that Bishop Fitzgerald would have provided, had he been in the capacity of ruling as the Bishop. While he was recuperating in Hot Springs, he had appointed Fr. Fintan Kramer, OSB of Subiaco, as the Vicar General to rule the diocese."[11] Mother Edward and the Sisters would have to make the decision without the aid of the Bishop. After many lectures by Fr. Weibel, and discussions among the Sisters, the community agreed to operate a hospital.

After he had obtained the consent of the community, Fr. Weibel publicized the need for funds. "He himself made the first donation. The people of Wynne, Arkansas had presented him with a gold watch, as pay for his services, as he refused a fee. He held a raffle for the watch and secured $500 to make the first donation towards a hospital fund. He and Dr. C.M. Lutterloh walked along Main Street, hat in hand, and begged funds to begin the new project."[12]

The Jonesboro civic leaders realized the growing need for a hospital and as the twentieth Century was dawning, the idea was gaining in momentum. The challenge, and one that would be ongoing throughout the century, was to raise the money for the hospital. One local merchant, a Mr. Edward Wheeler, spent days canvassing Jonesboro and surrounding areas to secure subscriptions for the hospital fund. When half of the needed funds of $5,000 had been accumulated, Bishop Edward Fitzgerald approved the founding of a hospital by the Sisters in Jonesboro.

Mr. J.F. Mason, a community leader, who later became the first Advisory Board Chairman, contributed a gift of $100 to the hospital fund. He further helped the sisters by agreeing to let them use his name as security to purchase a building located near the convent. The original hospital was an estate the Sisters purchased from the photographer, Mr. Robinson. The estate, comprising a large two-story house and considerable garden space, bordered the property of the convent and faced Matthews Street.

Hospital on the Frontier

First there was the question of leadership. Mother Edward End was faced with the challenge of appointing not only the Sisters to teach in the schools, but now in addition, Sisters to serve in the hospital. After much deliberation and prayer, she appointed Sr. Aloysia Unterberger, who had been in charge of St. Anna's Infirmary in Pocahontas, to be the first Superintendent of St. Bernards Hospital. Sr. Aloysia moved to Jonesboro to direct the hospital work, leaving Sr. Eugenia and Sr. Fridoline in Pocahontas to care for the patients at St. Anna's Infirmary.

"As soon as Mr. Robinson vacated the building, the Sisters went to work scrubbing, varnishing and transforming it into a hospital. They prepared six rooms, each with a cot, a chair and an orange crate to serve as a table or wash stand. A crocheted doily, made by one of the sisters, covered the orange crate. The "hospicium" of St. Benedict had become a reality in Jonesboro."[13]

On July 5, 1900, the hospital was formally opened. It was named "St. Bernards" in honor of St. Bernard Tolomei, founder of the Olivetan Benedictines. During the Black Plague in Italy during the 1340s, Bernard and 30 of his monks risked their lives to care for those afflicted. Bernard succumbed to the disease and died in 1343.

The first person that was supposed to be admitted to the newly opened St. Bernards Hospital died on the way. According to Craighead County Historian, Harry Lee Williams, the first patient admitted was a D. Parson from Deckerville, who was operated on by

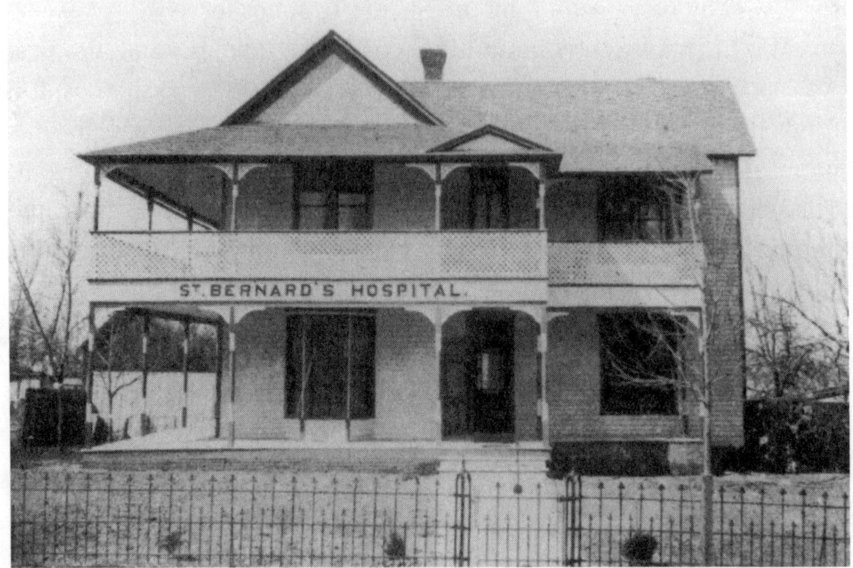

St. Bernards Hospital (facing Matthews Street) — 1900.

Dr. C.M. Lutterloh. Within a week, however, mostly fever patients occupied all six beds.

Food for the sick in St. Bernard's Hospital was prepared in the convent kitchen. Coal oil lamps were used for lighting. Laundry was cared for by the Sisters in the convent laundry equipped with tubs, washboards and homemade soap. The work was hard, but all the Sisters who were able helped.

According to Sr. Hilda Gabler, "Both Dr. Lutterloh and Fr. Weibel had a temper hard to control, but no demand was too great for either of them. If for some reason an order of the doctor could not be carried out, the nurse had better meet the doctor at the door and explain. Dr. Lutterloh would accept a sensible explanation, but without previous interview, there would be a violent explosion supported by Fr. Weibel. Then they would both storm to the superior's office."[14]

Since the Sisters were not trained nurses, there was the issue of developing their skills in caring for the sick. Sisters knew that cleanliness and appropriate food was necessary for the recovery from illness, but that was largely the extent of their medical knowledge. The doctors instructed the Sisters on accepted medical techniques and the Sisters assumed growing responsibilities for the actual care of the patients. This was the growing concern of Mother Edward, as she struggled to educate the Sisters for teaching in the schools, she now had to consider the education of nurses. Sr. Justine Rinke and Sr. Lawrence Jenniman were sent to St. Joseph Hospital in Memphis for further training.

In Jonesboro, the hospital beds continued to remain occupied, because Dr. J.L. Burns and Dr. W.W. Jackson joined Dr. Lutterloh in admitting patients. Dr. J.L. Burns, one of the region's medical pioneers, often brought patients to the hospital in his own buggy. As time progressed, there continued to be a need for additional beds, even though it was difficult to maintain what they already had.[15]

Wood stoves supplied the heat when it was cold, and coal oil lamps furnished light during the night. It was hard to keep these replenished and without water or sewage disposal systems, the efforts of the Sisters to keep the hospital sanitary were heroic.

As the community continued to grow in membership, Mother Edward expanded the missions to which Sisters were sent to teach. During her tenure in office as superior, Mother Edward added seven new schools to the number already established by her predecessors. She stretched the meager funds to educate the Sisters both for the hospital and the schools.

CHAPTER 6
1901-1909

Facing New Challenges

In early January 1901, Fr. Weibel and the doctors persuaded the Sisters to purchase a second house to expand the hospital, as there was a growing need for more beds. A second two-story building was purchased and linked to the first one by a one-story inter-spatial annex. Space had now increased to 20 rooms with better furnishings. "The total number of patients admitted from July 5, 1900 to March 30, 1901 was 180 patients of whom seven had died. Both Catholics and non-Catholics were cared for on equal terms." [1]

The 1901 Yearbook Directory of St. Roman's Church and St. Bernards Hospital has the following entry. "Payment Terms $1 a day. In surgical cases an extra fee, ranging from $2 to $5 is charged for the work in the operating room. Any physician in good standing may be called by the patient; physician's fees are extra." [2]

Advancement in medical care grew from year to year. The Sisters wanted to give good service, the best they could give under the circumstances. In January 1902, Mother Beatrice fell and broke her hip. Although at first, she did not feel strongly about the Sisters taking on hospital work, the help she received after breaking her hip, won her over to this new ministry. From this time on, she became a strong advocate of the health care ministry.

The spirit of service was the goal of the Sisters as they carried out their hospital duties. In speaking to the doctors during a medical staff meeting, Dr. Lutterloh said, " We are all under obligation to the good Sisters for their great devotion and extreme care for the welfare of the patients." [3]

Expansion of Schools

Not only did the hospital flourish, the schools also increased in number and quality. Mother Edward continued the educational efforts stressed by Mother Cecilia and provided opportunities for advanced education for the teachers. With the additional qualifications, increasing number of young Sisters passed the required examinations to assume teaching responsibilities.

Fr. Weibel persuaded Mother Edward to send a Sister out to Engelberg to teach the children in that community. The five-mile distance was too difficult for those children to walk to school in Pocahontas. At first, Mother Edward sent Sr. Hildegard Huerlimann to Engleberg to organize a school. Brother Gallus made a little cart to be pulled by a donkey, for her to ride to Engelberg. She would go out and stay with families during the week and return to the convent in Pocahontas on Saturdays and Sundays.

According to oral history, as told to the author by her grandmother, Mary Weisenbach Thielemier (7/10/1884—8/7/1981), Sr. Hildegard stayed with the Anton Weisenbach family, whose home was near the church. This was the same home where Fr. Weibel had offered the first Mass in that community on December 9, 1885. After a time, Mr. Weisenbach provided a small one-room building on their property for Sr. Hildegard. At first, his oldest daughter, Mary, would stay with Sr. Hildegard during the nights. Then the older girls in the area vied with each other for this privilege.[4]

As pupils increased, additional Sisters were sent to Engelberg and the parishioners erected a school building and a small house as residence for the Sisters. Eventually, the county took over the responsibility for the school and organized it as a public school. The county paid the salaries of the Sisters. They were able to teach religion in the school, as long as the religion classes were held before the beginning of, or after, the official school day. This arrangement continued until 1968, when the school was closed and pupils were transported on the public school buses to Pocahontas for their education.

Mother Edward accepted responsibility for seven new schools in addition to those already accepted by the previous superiors. The following schools were accepted during Mother Edward's term as superior. St. Polycarp School, Carmi, Illinois; Sacred Heart School, New Brunswick, Missouri; St. John Nepomucene School, Dahlgreen, Illinois; St. Joseph School, Cairo, Illinois; St. Patrick School, Cairo, Illinois; St. Joseph School, Pamona or White Church, Missouri; and St. Joseph School, Bon Terre, Missouri.[5]

Branches offered in the schools were religion, English language, literature, history, geography, mathematics, bookkeeping, Latin, German and French. Music consisted of instruction in piano, organ, violin, guitar, mandolin, and accordion. A type of what was later termed "Home Economics," then already introduced, consisted of practical sewing, knitting, and mending. The Sisters emphasized the development of wholesome, amiable, honest, and industrious traits in their pupils. Exhibition of the pupils' work at the end of the scholastic year continued to win wide acclaim from the general public.[6]

Desegregation

Desegregation of the hospital occurred during Mother Edward's term in office. Dr. C.M. Lutterloh was responsible for admitting the first Negroes to the hospital in 1901. There had been a landslide at the local quarry and while some people died, others were saved by amputating their arms and, in some cases, their legs. The operating room of the Sisters' hospital was at that time the only suitable place for care and Dr. Lutterloh asked for use of their facilities.

The Sisters agreed and Negro patients were nursed at St. Bernards until their recovery. The Sisters made every effort to show the Negro patients the same kindness and care they showed to other patients but their actions did stir controversy.

In a remarkable foreshadowing of events that were part of the civil rights struggles over 60 years later, there were letters of threats to burn down the hospital. The threats were serious but the Sisters continued to do all they could to make the Negro patients comfortable.

The prejudice spread to doctors and for a time, Dr. Lutterloh was the only physician who practiced at the hospital, because all other doctors resigned. Gradually doctors who had left returned, and ministered to patients of both races. The controversy had some positive results. The Sisters opened a section of the hospital for Negroes and the hospital continued to grow." [7]

Back in Pocahontas another event occurred which went with little notice by the townspeople. Since the epidemic of Spinal Meningitis had passed, and the people no longer threatened by the disease, the Infirmary had fewer and fewer patients. At that time, most people took care of their sick in their homes as the doctor made house calls. Sr. Eugenia Brodell and Sr. Fridoline Buck, who were caring for the Infirmary, were needed at St. Bernards in Jonesboro as that hospital was growing. According to the Infirmary record book, John Turner, a Pocahontas merchant, the last patient admitted to St. Anna's Infirmary, was dismissed on January 4, 1902. The same record book listed him as cured. St. Anna's Infirmary was then closed and became a part of the history of Pocahontas community. [8]

Sixth Superior Elected

By 1903 another election of superior was due to be held in the community. Fr. Weibel scheduled the election during the summer months, when most of the Sisters were at the Motherhouse in Jonesboro. Sr. Angelina Boesch was elected as the sixth superior of the Olivetan Benedictine Sisters of Jonesboro. SEE PROFILE IN APPENDIX. She was a talented young woman who had become an excellent teacher, esteemed by parents and pupils alike. She had been an eyewitness of the catastrophic fire in Jonesboro in 1896. Ever after, she was a firm friend of Fr. Weibel and tried to anticipate his likes and dislikes. She became superior of 56 Sisters and seven Novices upon her election. She was the first superior that Fr. Weibel permitted to be elected for two consecutive terms. [9]

The community had undergone numerous changes since its establishment in 1887. The original Constitution had been changed by Fr. Weibel, then later revised in 1893 when the community became affiliated with the Olivetan Benedictine Congregation. The remaining personnel in Pocahontas were transferred to Jonesboro, except the housekeeper and the teachers who maintained the school at the original motherhouse. When the community accepted hospital service, it doubled its sphere of service. [10]

Brick Hospital Building Erected

As word spread in surrounding communities about the good hospital in Jonesboro, the need for additional beds became apparent. A brick hospital and chapel connecting the convent with the original building was planned. Fr. Weibel drew up the plans for the new addition while he was recuperating from a nose injury in Memphis. He sent the plans to the Bishop who was recuperating from a lingering illness in Hot Springs.

In approving the erection of the new buildings, Bishop Fitzgerald contributed $1,500 towards the new building fund as a way of encouraging Fr. Weibel and of showing support for the charitable work being done by the Sisters. He included a note, saying, "A little nest egg towards the building fund." Encouraged by the Bishop's gift, Fr. Weibel set to work to raise funds. He had the foundation dug and was able to procure good bricks for $4.50 per thousand, and had them delivered to the place of construction. The wood and material for general purposes came to $4 per thousand feet." [11]

To help finance the operations and the erection of the new buildings, the Sisters raised money by going on solicitation tours, always in the practice of the times, in twos, and never alone. They would ride the trains on payday to logging camps in the area and sell "Hospital Tickets." For $1, a workman could buy a ticket to ensure admission to the hospital and care for one day; in exchange for $9, a workman would receive a hospital ticket that would be good for one year.

No.______ **St. Bernard's Hospital** Ward Certificate $9.00

No. 224 East Matthews Street

Sisters of St. Benedict

Jonesboro, Ark., ________________190___

This ticket entitles M________________________________

upon payment of **$9.00** to admission, medical and surgical treatment, medicine, subsistence and nursing, at the above named Hospital, at any time during one year from date hereof, in consequence of injury or sickness hereafter received or contracted, disabling him from manual labor, subject to the conditions indorsed and signed by him.

The certificate holder agrees to comply with the Rules and Regulations of the Hospital.

Intoxication and drunkenness will not be tolerated in or around the Hospital, and certificate holder breaking this rule will be expelled and certificate cancelled.

Expires________________________

By________________________

NOT TRANSFERABLE

Conditions:

It is understood that insanity, contagious disease, such as consumption, small pox, scarlet fever, diphtheria, erysipelas and all infectious diseases, venereal diseases or injuries existing before the date of this ticket, or arising from the use of intoxicating drink are excluded from the Hospital Benefits under this contract.

*Signature*________________________

Hospital Ticket sold by early Sisters to finance operations and raise funds to build the 1905 40-bed brick hospital building.

These tickets were the first example of hospital insurance, or what developed in the 1990s as managed care. Workmen in effect prepaid the cost of hospital care they thought they might need throughout the coming year.[12]

The Sisters also held raffles for embroidered hand pieces and laces. Some of their families would send fine materials from Switzerland for them to embroidery and offer for sale. Little by little the funds grew as the builders erected the new buildings. In 1904 the annual Christmas collection was made throughout Jonesboro by Mother Angelina. Fr. Weibel sent out "begging letters" to all firms and to many individuals.

The 1905 annex contained private, semi-private and three-bed rooms, as well as a spacious operating room, a sterilizing room, drug and service rooms, an office, parlor and large kitchen and storage rooms. With the new building and the old, which was fully occupied, the bed capacity rose to 50. Electric lights were installed in every room and running water was added to the hospital and the convent.

Forty-bed brick St. Bernards Hospital erected in 1905.

A powerhouse, a laundry and a bakery were also erected to serve both the hospital and the convent. The laundry was equipped with revolving washers, steam-heated drying room, wringer, mangle for ironing sheets, a coal heated ironing stove with 30 flat irons, tubs for board washing and soaking for soiled linens. The machinery for the powerhouse was located in the basement with the hot water heaters.

"Later the Sisters cared, not only for the convent and hospital laundry, but also for that of hotels and barbershops. Thus they earned money to help defray expenses. At that time there was no competition from other steam laundries in Jonesboro. The bakery too, was well equipped. A large mixing trough for making bread dough, mixing bowls for cakes and pies, coal-heated ovens and all other equipment for necessities in baking were available." [13]

Chapel Erected

After the hospital building was completed, the convent chapel was begun immediately. Fr. Weibel had drawn the design in Romanesque style and it was destined also to serve as St. Roman's Parish Church. Up to this time, the Sisters had shared with the parishioners, and used St. Roman's Church Hall. The parish would now rent the chapel on a monthly basis and help defray the costs. The old church hall was converted into an entertainment center.

Altars, statues, stations and pews were moved from the combination church hall into the chapel. The organ was also moved to the Sisters' chapel. "Among the new things in the chapel was the beautiful painting by Paul von Deschwanden. His painting became the center of attraction in the new chapel. [14]

The painting represented the Blessed Virgin Mary seated with the Child Jesus in her arms. She was surrounded by three groups of angels, five in white, five in red, five in gold to represent the 15 mysteries of the rosary. Each angel held a symbol to represent the mystery. Paul von Deschwanden died before the picture was completed. The fifteenth angel, who was to represent the crowning of Mary, was absent. Years later, a Mr. Lehman, an itinerant artist tried to complete the picture by inserting the missing angel at the top. However, it did not seem to fit, so detracted from the original painting.

Deschwanden also painted separate canvases of angels above the side altars. The communion rail was of pine wood and extended from wall to wall. Two base-relief plaques adorn the lower front of each of the two side altars. One represented the Last Supper and the other the figure of Christ in the tomb. The stations were also in base-relief and painted in pleasing pastels.

In 1974, the two plaques encased in side altars, and the stations were transferred to the new convent north of town. The two side altars presently adorn the area in the hallway on the right side of chapel, while the stations, encased in individual structures, similar to European Wayside Shrines, are located outside along the front drive.

The first Mass in the new chapel was celebrated on March 19, 1906. The exterior of the new chapel was made of pressed cement blocks, which were being used extensively at that time for building construction. [15]

Mother Angelina had a plan of her own to honor Mary, the mother of God, by erecting a statue of the Immaculate Conception in a prominent place in the center of the convent courtyard. Financial aid from faithful friends and benefactors came to Mother Angelina for this project. Eventually, this became reality and the Sisters often gathered in the evenings for prayers and singing hymns around this statue. Sidewalks lead to this central area from all four sides and the grape arbor ran along the east side of the yard. When the community relocated in 1974, this revered statue was taken along and again placed in the front courtyard of the new convent. [15]

Holy Angels Convent (inner court) with Chapel built in 1905 on left.

Pocahontas Document

A notice was found during Mother Angelina's term, concerning the perpetual obligation assumed by the community. It reads as follows, and the obligation dates from 1887, but signed by Mother Angelina during her term of office.

"In Perpetual Remembrance"

By the grant of 12 acres of land on which Convent Maria Stein in Pocahontas, Arkansas, His Excellency, Bishop Edward Fitzgerald, has obligated the Convent to take good care of the graves Marvin and Putman which are situated on the grounds close to the Convent.

Moreover, Mr. J. Peters, has donated to the Convent 90 acres of land (northwest of town), in exchange of which the Convent will take care of the grave of his wife Magdalena Peters in the Catholic Cemetery, and will pray for the repose of her soul. The grave is located on the lower enclosure of the Cemetery (on the north side) and is marked with a tombstone and with inscription.

The fulfillment of the above conditions is a duty of justice, which may not be neglected. This document shall be framed, and shall be hung in the refectory or the community room where all the Sisters can read it in order that its stipulations may never be forgotten.

(Signed)
Sister M. Angelina, OSB
Superior Pro Tem[16]

A New Bishop

When it became evident that Bishop Fitzgerald's health was continuing to deteriorate, he requested help. Although Fr. Fintan Kramer, OSB, had been appointed Vicar General, the Bishop felt he needed a coadjutor. On April 18, 1906, Pope Pius X, (now St. Pius X), appointed John Baptist Morris of Nashville, Tennessee as coadjutor to Bishop Fitzgerald with right of succession. The bishop-elect carried out the orders of his superior until the death of the latter.

The young, energetic Bishop John Baptist Morris, DD, performed his first official act when he visited Jonesboro. On April 18, 1906, he dedicated Holy Angels Convent Chapel, and witnessed the vows of seven Sisters. It was the first ceremony of making vows in the new convent chapel in Jonesboro.

Fr. Weibel still functioned as the director of the community and in charge of its affairs. Shortly after the dedication of the chapel, he went with Sr. Aloysia Unterberger and Sr. Meinrada End to Switzerland to recruit additional Postulants. Soon after they returned from this recruiting trip, Bishop Fitzgerald suffered a relapse and died on February 21, 1907. Within a short time, Bishop Morris was installed as the third Bishop of the Diocese of Little Rock.

Shortly after his elevation, Bishop Morris asked the Sisters of Jonesboro to relinquish most of their schools outside the State of Arkansas and to concentrate on those he would designate. In the fall of 1907, the Bishop gave St. Andrew's Cathedral School to the Olivetan Benedictines. To the Sisters of Mercy, who had established the Cathedral school, the Bishop designated a large area in Pulaski Heights as their future home, where they had ample room to grow. The location downtown was too confined for them to conduct both the school and novitiate.

Sr. Antonia Holthouse, Sr. Celestine Worland, Sr. Felicitas Hunkler and Sr. Dominica Weibel were the first Olivetan Benedictines to operate the Cathedral School. The building was small, sandwiched between business structures with very little room for a playground for the pupils. Besides this school, the Bishop permitted Mother Angelina and community to retain schools at Pocahontas, Jonesboro, Paragould, Engelberg, Stuttgart, Brinkley, Hot Springs and Texarkana, Arkansas; at Rhineland and Muenster, Texas; and at Poplar Bluff, Missouri. [17]

Bishop Morris also removed Fr. Weibel as director of the Olivetan Benedictine Community, and at the time, reserved this direction to himself. Fr. Weibel then resigned as pastor of St. Roman's in Jonesboro and decided to return to Europe, giving poor health as main reason. The Bishop refused to accept the excuse of poor health and the need to go to Europe, and said there were health resorts in the United States. He pointed out that Hot Springs was one of the leading Spas in the world. The Bishop recognized Fr. Weibel's administrative ability and persuaded him to go to Hot Springs and to organize a new parish in the southern section of that city. Fr. Weibel agreed to remain in the diocese and carry out the Bishop's request.

He organized a parish and erected St. John's Church on a prominent place in south Hot Springs. Later, Fr. Weibel referred to this building as his masterpiece.

When Mother Angelina was notified of the termination of Fr. Weibel as director of the community, she wrote this in part of Bishop Morris.

> "...We have received the official announcement of the resignation of our founder J.E. Weibel, as director and understand that we are now exclusively under your jurisdiction and direction in spiritual and material concerns. Accept our humble submission to your decrees... As to our connection with Rome, I know that our late Right Reverend Bishop Fitzgerald advised our founder to affiliate to some congregation at Rome saying that not every Bishop was so kind and good to the Sisterhoods as he himself felt inclined to be, and that therefore he must see to it that the Sisters would get a standing and protection... I furthermore know that by our statutes we are subject in everything to the diocesan Bishop. Only in cases where the welfare of the community should be seriously in danger, we have the right to seek protection, and matters will be looked after by the Superior General of the Olivetans in Rome.
>
> I am required to send a yearly report to the General of the Order, giving an account of the principal affairs of the Community... I write this only because you inquired to know as to our standing with Rome..."
>
> *Your obedient children,*
> The Olivetan Sisters, OSB
> *per* Mother Angelina, Prioress [18]

Pictured above (left to right) the 1898 convent building, the 1905 Chapel (slightly back with steeple showing), the new 1905 40 bed brick hospital joined to original frame hospital and connecting hallway to the 1901 frame annex. Picture: courtesy of Craighead County Historical Society.

A New Era

Since Mother Angelina's second three-year term was coming to a close, the year of 1909 brought another canonical election of superior. Mother Aloysia Unterberger was elected as Prioress. She had been appointed by Fr. Weibel in 1892 and served for two years before the first election of a superior was held. Now she was elected superior of the community by majority of vote.

Under Mother Aloysia's direction, the hospital continued to flourish and she soon found it necessary to remove some of the teachers from the schools and appoint them to hospital work. She realized that more Sisters had to be sent off to school to be trained as nurses. Mother Aloysia continued the efforts made by previous superiors to give the Sisters the educational opportunities necessary to prepare for their assigned ministries.

Another pressing need was developing the schools. There were frequent requests from parishes to staff new schools. However, now she must have the Bishop's approval before accepting any new schools. With Bishop Morris' approval, one of the first projects of Mother Aloysia in 1909 was to accept Holy Family School in Nazareth, Texas, through which the community was enriched by four new members from that parish. They were: Sr. Xavier Lange, Sr. Lutgardis Weber, her sister, Sr. Magdalena Weber, and Sr. Michael Lange, all of whom persevered in the community until their death. [19]

"The 1909 medical records of St. Bernards reveal a total of 406 patients treated that year with a grand total of 3,359 patients treated during the ten years since the hospital opened in 1900." [20] As the decade ended, St. Bernards had evolved from an idea to a significant community institution. The Sisters, physicians, community leaders and citizens who had planned, worked, volunteered and contributed to the hospital, had established as foundation that would be further developed in following decades.

CHAPTER 7
1910-1919

Ministry Expanded

Little did the Sisters realize at the time, but as the year 1910 dawned, young Bishop Morris would soon ask the Jonesboro Benedictines to help on a diocesan level. "After purchasing land and establishing an orphanage, the Bishop undertook his next major project, that of establishing a school for boys. With the establishment of St. Mary's Academy, girls already had the advantage of higher education under Catholic auspices. The Bishop felt however, that young men were as much in need of Catholic influence in the higher stages of their education."[1]

As the Ordinary of the Diocese of Little Rock, Bishop Morris inherited the Diocesan assets accumulated by his predecessor, Bishop Fitzgerald, who had been an astute financial manager. Therefore in 1908, Bishop Morris was able to purchase the Arkansas Military Academy on Twenty-Fifth and Gains streets, which was for sale. He opened a school for boys and named it Little Rock College, which was at first operated as a day school.

By 1910, an additional building was added to accommodate boarding students. It was at this time, that Bishop Morris turned to the Olivetan Benedictine Community in northeast Arkansas to request help. Since he had already requested Sisters from the Benedictine Community at Shoal Creek in northwest Arkansas to take charge of the orphanage, he now asked Mother Aloysia for Sisters to take charge of the culinary department at the Little Rock College.

"In September 1910, Mother Aloysia sent Sr. Eugenia Brodell, Sr. Hedwig Peterli and several others to take charge of the kitchen and dining rooms at the Little Rock College."[2] By 1911, the Bishop added a Seminary department and named it St. John's Home

Missions Seminary. On September 19, 1911, the Seminary opened with ten seminarians who had been studying for the diocese in other seminaries. Bishop Morris placed Msgr. W.H. Aretz, the first priest ordained by him, as the head of the Seminary.

As the number of seminarians increased over the years, additional Sisters were sent to the Seminary to serve in the culinary department and to take care of the needs of the priests and seminarians. By 1916, the increase of students at both the Little Rock College and the Seminary, caused both institutions to move to new facilities in Pulaski Heights. New and larger accommodations were provided for the Olivetan Benedictine Sisters who continued to serve in the culinary department.

The Sisters met the daunting challenge to feed the hungry, growing boys, as well as the priest professors, by using ingenious means to stretch the food. Because of the limited budget, a garden was planted on the Seminary grounds and the seminarians helped with the planting and harvesting. The Sisters used various means to make sure no one went away from the refectory hungry. According to oral history, one seminarian, Albert L. Fletcher, (later, the Ordinary of the Diocese), was an active leader in gardening and used a mule to pull the plow for tilling the earth.

Over the years, the Sisters had a great influence with the boys and seminarians and many testified to this influence in later years. Oral history revealed to the author, by different Sisters who had worked at the Seminary, that after ordination, numerous priests wrote back letters of gratitude, for their help and encouragement during their years of study at the Seminary.

One of the earliest fruits of the labors of the Olivetan Benedictine Sisters was the ordination of Fr. Walter J. Tynin of Jonesboro, who was ordained to the holy priesthood in 1911. Since the diocesan Seminary had not opened until 1911, Fr. Tynin attended the Seminary at Subiaco Abbey to prepare for Ordination. Several years after his ordination, he was the driving force in organizing the Alumni Association. A memorial plaque on the door of the Alumni Office, designates it as the Walter Tynin Room.

Fr. Tynin attributed his vocation to the Sisters, who taught him at St. Roman's School. He stated their instruction and example had inspired him to become a priest. Since his mother had died while he was still an infant, and his father was a railroad worker, who had little time for his son, the Sisters played a major role in his formative years. At his First Mass, Fr. Tynin gave a testament of gratitude to the Sisters.

Backside of complex—view from Carson street—L to R: St. Bernards Hospital, Holy Angels Chapel and Convent.

A New Era

In 1912, Bishop Morris appointed Fr. Weinand H. Aretz as the spiritual guide for the Sisters of Jonesboro. He was highly esteemed by the priests, religious and laity in the Diocese. Fr. Aretz was the first priest ordained by Bishop Morris, June 29, 1906. The Olivetan Benedictine Community welcomed their new spiritual guide, who was supportive and encouraging as their membership grew.[3]

Another project of Bishop Morris was a monastery for a new religious order to work in the diocese. He bought property at Armstrong Springs (near Searcy) in 1908. According to oral history, the Bishop asked Fr. Fintan Kraemer, OSB of Subiaco Abbey, his Vicar General at the time, to start an order of brothers, to be called "Brothers of St. Paul." Work began on the project. Some candidates and a priest from France came to help the project. The priest claimed that he had been "assured" that he would be superior. He had also brought some money with him for use of the new "order."

However, when he arrived in Arkansas, he found nothing,

became upset and left, later writing to demand his money back. The new order never got off the ground and the few candidates dispersed. The idea had been a good one but it never developed and there was some embarrassment for the Bishop and especially for Fr. Fintan Kraemer. Bishop Morris was so upset with his Vicar General that the Abbot of Subiaco accommodated by assigning Fr. Fintan to out-of-state missions for many years. As a consequence of this, the Bishop was discouraged, but then turned to the Olivetan Benedictine Sisters in Jonesboro for help.

On July 5, 1911, Mother Aloysia sent Mother Beatrice Renggli, Sr. Meinrada End and Sr. Hildegarde Huerliman to teach in St. Paul's School at Armstrong Springs. After being there a year, Mother Beatrice realized the medicinal benefits of the natural springs and decided to establish St. Paul's Hospice.

However, this endeavor at Armstrong Springs was of short duration, as Mother Aloysia recalled the Sisters to the Motherhouse in 1915. The author was not able to discover the reasons for this decision. By 1921, the Bishop's dream for Armstrong Springs (Searcy) was realized when he secured the Franciscan Brothers of Mount Alverno, Cincinnati, Ohio, to take charge of the buildings and open a boarding school for boys. Bishop Morris dedicated the school on October 4, 1922, and named it Morris School for Boys.[6] By the early 1990s enrollment had declined so it was closed in 1993. The property was later sold and most of the Brothers returned to Mount Alverno, Cincinnati. Brother Richard Sanker worked as counselor at Catholic High School in Little Rock, while several Brothers joined the Benedictine Community at Subiaco.

Opening Vistas

As the Olivetan Benedictine community continued to grow in membership, so did the demands increase in the institutions it served. New needs developed at St. Bernards and Mother Aloysia found it necessary to remove additional teachers from the schools to help in hospital work. St. Bernards had attracted additional physicians, which made it possible to increase services for the people in northeast Arkansas.

"Two of the themes throughout St. Bernards early history were the need to respond to people who needed help and the commitment to provide care regardless of the person's ability to pay. There were accidents at the logging camps and these, as well as accidents from the railroad workers, were frequently treated at St. Bernards. There had been a total of 3,856 patients treated since the hospital opened on July 5, 1900, and nearly a third of these had been charity patients."[4]

"Financial challenges continued throughout the early years. Friends and advisors urged the Sisters to do as other hospitals had begun to do, tell the people they had to pay for services the hospital provided. Although the Sisters listened, they also considered the fact that St. Bernards was the only hospital in northeast Arkansas where poor people could get advanced medical care. In the end, the Sisters continued to care for people regardless of their ability to pay. This policy reflected the Sisters' mission but meant the hospital would continue to deal with financial problems."[5]

Having been organized by the poor especially for the poor, the Sisters decided to give good service to all who needed it, and trust in God that he would help them. And this He did, through the generosity of many good friends. This commitment to serve—and especially to serve those in need—was shared by the people in Jonesboro and the region, who helped the Sisters raise the funds to care for those in need.

The Sisters insisted on high quality care and attracted all kinds of people to help them in their work. Mother Aloysia realized the need for a qualified maintenance supervisor and in 1910, placed an advertisement in a German newspaper. Lawrence Schneider, a German immigrant from the Black Forest area in Bavaria, who was living in Ohio at the time, responded to the ad. After a visit to Jonesboro and a personal interview, Schneider was hired for the position. He served faithfully as maintenance supervisor for both the convent and hospital for the next 48 years.[6]

Schneider was the only person doing the maintenance in the early years. Oral history reveals that he learned the skills of carpentry, plumbing and electrical work from trade manuals and journals and eventually secured a license to handle the needed maintenance. Additional employees were hired as the institution grew.

The floods of 1912 and 1913 brought refugees from the bottomlands in northeast Arkansas, who sought care from the hospital. According to Charles A. Stuck, in The Story of Craighead County, "The Mississippi River levee broke at Wilson, Arkansas in 1912 and again in 1913. These breaks caused flood waters to reach deep into the county. The Frisco Railroad brought nearly 1,500 refugees to the higher ground in Jonesboro, where they were housed in tent camps. Smallpox broke out in the camps and there was great need for medical attention."

To care for the refugees and their patients, the Jonesboro physicians had to divide their time between the hospital and the camps. After the second flood, the citizens of eastern Arkansas appealed to Congress for aid. This effort resulted in the passage of the Flood Control Act in 1917, which was the beginning of the continuing program of flood control on the Mississippi.[7]

The outbreak of World War I overseas in 1914, caused a shortage of medical supplies by hospitals in the United States, and St. Bernards was no exception. On April 6, 1917, the United States joined the allies and declared war on Germany. This caused a shortage of help, as many of the physicians and nurses were called to serve in the military.[8]

Because of the shortage of lay personnel, Sisters were often called on to fill the gaps in staffing. Oral history reveals that many times, Sisters worked double shifts, taking night duty after a full day on the floor. Until the War ended in 1918 and Armistice signed, the staff, the physicians, the Sisters all made sacrifices to maintain the hospital's ability to care for the people who needed help.

School of Nursing

The emphasis on professionalism was reflected on the need to invest in nurses' training. Even though it was costly to send Sisters for training, it was determined to be important for the continued growth of St. Bernards. Mother Aloysia decided that Sr. Hilda Gabler and Sr. Pia Wyss should go to St. Elizabeth Hospital in Lafayette, Indiana to study to become trained nurses. Sr. Hilda took additional courses in hospital administration and Sr. Pia studied to become a certified laboratory technician.[9]

Upon completion of their diplomas in nursing and additional courses, Sr. Hilda was named superintendent of the hospital in 1914 and Sr. Pia was named director of nurses.

The movement toward professional standards in hospitals was now becoming general and the demand for growing professionalism placed new obligations on nurses. It became necessary, for example, for nurses to take State Board Examinations for licensure at the State Capitol. Sr. Hilda and Sr. Pia traveled to Little Rock to take their test, and both passed the examination on October 20, 1919. They were now entitled to use the appendage, R.N. for registered nurse and the registration of the nurses entitled St. Bernards to open it own training school.[10]

"The first class enrolled consisted of ten students, all Sisters. Nine completed the program. These were: Sr. Fredrica Spirig, Sr. Benedicta Stuebi, Sr. Justine Renke, Sr. Lawrence Jenniman, Sr. Lindwina Rhinhard, Sr. Camilla Suter, Sr. Adela Spirig, Sr. Helen Suter and Sr. Magdalena Weber."[11]

In addition to Sr. Hilda Gabler and Sr. Pia Wyss, the faculty of St. Bernards School of Nursing consisted of Reverend J.A. McQuaid, pastor of St. Roman's Church, who taught Ethics, and a number of physicians who taught classes in their respective fields.

According to an early yearbook, the Curriculum for St. Bernards School of Nursing consisted of the following courses:

First Year

Anatomy and Physiology
Bacteriology and Hygiene, Physical Education
Chemistry
History of Nursing Ethics
Pathology and Laboratory Techniques
Principles of Nursing

Second Year

Dietetics
Material Medicines
Medical and Communicable Diseases
Surgical Nursing and Gynecology
Obstetrics and Pediatrics
Psychology and Moral Ethics

Third Year

Eye, Ear, Nose and Throat Nursing
Mental and Nervous Nursing
Emergency Nursing and First Aid
Physiotherapy
Professional and Social Problems [12]

Some of the first lay nurses at St. Bernards.

Expansion of Schools

Just as the hospital continued to grow, so did the requests increase for teachers in the schools in northeast Arkansas. Fr. Fuerst, pastor of the newly founded parish in Blytheville, St. Peter's (later named Immaculate Conception), requested teachers for their school. By September 1915, the school opened on Ash Street, with Sr. Gertrude Poole and Sr. Lucy Staubli as the first teachers. Fr. J.M. Hoflinger, the new pastor in Paragould, also requested, additional teachers, as the school enrollment had increased.

Fr. Joseph Froeitzheim, Pastor and Sr. Rose Muheim with class of first and second grade pupils — 1913-1914.

With the approval of Bishop Morris, Mother Aloysia responded to the request to open St. Elizabeth's School in Eureka Springs, in 1911. Sr. Edward End, Sr. Lutgardis and Magdalene Weber were sent there to teach. However, this endeavor was of short duration. For some unaccountable reason, the school was discontinued in 1912.[13]

Another development opened for the Sisters in Hot Springs. Fr. Weibel, who was actively involved in establishing St. John's Parish in that spa city wished to establish a Catholic Sanatorium for guests coming to Hot Springs for the baths. In his own words, he relates the following:

> "A widow owned two large houses on the property that bordered on that of St. John's Church, Hot Springs. She belonged to the Pentecostal Church to which she willed most of her estate. The two houses were destined to become a hospital or sanatorium for the members of her sect. In 1913, I purchased these two houses and two others for the founding of a Catholic Sanatorium for guests of the middle class who came to Hot Springs for baths... My friends aided me in purchasing these houses."[14]

During the first two years of its operation, Fr. Weibel had hired lay women, but now he turned to the Sisters in Jonesboro for help. At first the Sisters were reluctant, as the outbreak of the First World War in Europe in 1914 affected the Jonesboro Community. These were years of sparse vocations, as the Sisters were no longer able to return to Europe to recruit new members. Bishop Morris had encouraged rather that the Sisters try to recruit postulants from our own country especially in areas where the Sisters ministered. Therefore, Mother Aloysia considered that Hot Springs would possibly be another area from which to attract vocations.

After much prayer and consultation with the Sisters, Mother Aloysia agreed to send Sisters to Hot Springs, to take charge of the Sanatorium, now called St. John's Place. By 1915, Sr. Edward End was sent to Hot Springs to take charge of the institution. Other Sisters were sent to assist in the operation.

Fr. Joseph Froeitzheim, Pastor and Sr. Wilhelmina Galatti with class of third, fourth and fifth grade pupils—1913-1914.

Seventh Superior

During the summer of 1915, Mother Aloysia's second term in office came to a close. Her subprioress, Sr. Walburga Hoegger was elected as the seventh superior of the community. Little did she know at the time, her tenure would extend the longest in the history of the community, as she was elected ten consecutive times and served until 1945. SEE PROFILE IN APPENDIX.

The practice of unlimited successive terms for a major religious superior of women was allowed before Vatican II mandated a limit of two terms.[15]

Mother Walburga inherited the leadership of the community during a crucial period of the community. She taught the Novices by word as well as by example. She helped everywhere: in the kitchen, the bakery, the garden, and above all, the laundry. On Tuesdays, which was the designated wash day, she, along with a few volunteers, arose at 3 a.m., said their prayers and went to the laundry to soak the clothing and ready the articles for the machines. She was first to arrive in the morning and last to leave in the evening.[16]

When Mother Walburga entered office in 1915, the most primitive work methods were being used in the convent. The kitchen stove was stoked with scrap wood obtained from surrounding sawmills. With the aid of small amounts of coal, all food was thus prepared for both the Sisters in the convent and the patients in the hospital. During the summer months, hundred of gallons of fruit and vegetables were canned with the same type of fuel on the same cook stove.

At that time, the Sisters grew most of the food in the convent garden. The produce was used for both, the Sisters at the convent and the patients in the hospital. The Sisters grew Irish and sweet potatoes, beans, peas, tomatoes, corn, okra, carrots, onions, radishes, lettuce, mustard greens, turnips and other seasonal vegetables.

In the low damp area at the foot of the hill and on the slopes along the garden, there were trees of apples, plums, peaches, pears, and figs with rows of blackberries and dewberries that provided seasonal fruits for the table. A long "L" shaped arbor along the sidewalk to the laundry, annually produced from 50 to 100 bushels of a wide variety of grapes, from the Concord to some of the white varieties. Since these ripened at different times, the supply lasted from mid-July until early November.[17]

During her years as superior, Mother Walburga's example of trusting faith in the Providence of God and the power of St. Joseph was evident to all who knew her. When funds were low she prayed and often begged the Sisters to pray. "God will help," was her constant expression, and this He did in numerous instances.

Camp chairs of wood with woven cane seats were in use in the refectory. Five Sisters sat along one side of each long table. These tables formed a large U-shape all around the large room. The Sisters took their meals in silence, while one read from a well-selected book. On Christmas, New Year, Easter, Holy Days of Obligation and legal holidays, conversation was permitted after the superior gave the permission to speak by saying "Benedicite," translated as—Let us bless the Lord.[18]

With great sadness, Mother Walburga prepared for the first funeral while in office, that of Mother Agnes Dali, one of the founders and third superior of the community, June 1915. Mother Walburga had great regard for Mother Agnes, as she felt that she embodied many of the qualities of a model religious. To lose this member of the founding group was doubly hard on her, as she had admired and imitated her.[19]

According to Council Minutes of February 16, 1916.

> In the absence of Sr. Cecilia Huber, Mother Walburga appointed Sr. Beatrice Renggli, Secretary. The minutes continue. She then proceeded to explain that the City of Jonesboro had decided to include East Matthews Avenue in other adjacent streets into an improvement district for the purpose of paving these streets.
>
> For this purpose the city authorities requested the signature of the corporation. Our property extending along Matthews Avenue, the paving will necessarily lay a heavy tax upon our corporation.
>
> The President had tried every avenue to extricate the corporation from this street paving district, but in vain. It was evident the signature could not be withheld without losing the good will of the city authorities and a number of citizens.

Whereupon it was unanimously decided by the members of the corporation that it was better to incur the expense than to lose the good will of the city authorities.

This resolution was then, through the Diocesan Chancery, presented to the Bishop, whose reply was: No objection, if the corporation could bear the expense.

Signed:
Mother M. Walburga Hoegger,
President
Sister M. Beatrice Renggli,
Secretary[20]

Another entry in the Council Minutes, concerning the sale of property owned by the community, occurred on October 29, 1916.

"It was decided to put on sale the 12 acres bought by the community of one Nic Valerius. This property is now cut off from the Convent property by a public street. These decisions being subject to the approval of the Ordinarius, Rt. Rev. J.B. Morris, DD. There being no further business, the meeting adjourned.

Signed:
Mother M. Walburga Hoegger,
President
Sister M. Beatrice Renggli,
Secretary[21]

Educational Opportunities

After close of the First World War, a new hope sprang up in the United States and the Sisters of Holy Angels Convent were caught up in this same renewed spirit of moving forward. New projects were undertaken and new opportunities became available. Mother Walburga experienced her first re-election in 1918 and did her utmost to improve everything within her community. Although the influenza epidemic of 1918 and 1919 caused many to succumb to a premature death, it did not daunt the spirit of those who survived. People were filled with hope of more excellent things to come.

An entry in the Council Minutes concerning the purchase of property occurred on August 6, 1919. After the reading of the minutes of the previous meeting, "The President then suggested the purchase of the two lots between the hospital and Church Street, adjacent to St. Roman's Hall. These two lots have been used for the housing of horses and pigs to the annoyance of the patients at the hospital. The President was unanimously authorized to try to purchase that property if it is obtainable.

The President also acquainted the members that the Visitator had commanded her to have an entrance built into the west side of the hospital to prevent people from running through the chapel when coming to the hospital. The new door necessitated a cement walk and two stairways. New drainage was put in all along the west side of the hospital and the Convent."

Bishop Morris was eager to assist religious communities in providing advanced education for the teaching Sisters in the Diocese. Now, under his direction, the Little Rock College, that had been re-located to Pulaski Heights, would offer the teaching Sisters of the Diocese summer courses beginning in 1919.[22]

Fr. Herbert Heagney, the first President, was assisted by other priest professors for these summer courses for the teaching Sisters. An adequate faculty had preparatory courses in arts, sciences, business administration and music. All these besides the general courses of a liberal arts college were offered. These classes, held exclusively for the teaching Sisters in the Diocese of Little Rock, were well attended by religious from communities throughout Arkansas, and the Jonesboro Benedictines were no exception.

Later however, Mother Walburga wrote a letter to Fr. Gregory Keller to ask for a reduced fee for board and lodging during the summer Normal School. In April of that same year, Fr. Keller at Little Rock College responded in the following manner:

> "Very Rev. and Dear Mother,
>
> Your favor of recent date received. We have considered the matter of board and lodging asking of your teachers during the Normal School and we really cannot see our way clear to making it less.

We agree with you that your rates for extra cooks during the Normal School are very reasonable and expect you will use your judgement in regard to the number of extra cooks that you send.

I wish to ask your assistance again for the priests' retreat that will take place the 12th and the 17th of June at Little Rock College. There will be about 45 priests so we shall need some extra cooks that we ask you to furnish.

Sincerely Yours in Christ,
Gregory H. Keller, Secretary"[23]

Mother Walburga noted the following response to this letter on the bottom of this same page.

"Very Rev. and Dear Father,

I asked $4 per week and railroad fare for each of the extra cooks. I suppose all I can do is to send fewer Sisters to the Normal. We cannot offer to pay $5.50 per week for so many."[24]

As this decade came to a close there was a spirit of enthusiasm and renewed interest in progress in every area of endeavor. Advanced medical practices, along with professional nursing skills were being developed in the hospital, and now school teachers had opportunities to earn credits in advanced education. Indeed, the next decade was filled with promise.

CHAPTER 8
1920-1929

Hopes and Disappointments

The early 1920s were filled with enthusiasm and progress. The War that people believed would make the world a safer place for democracy was over, the boys were home, and there was enough manpower to make a crop and carry on normal business in northeast Arkansas. [1] The economy was strong until the first hint of a break in the inflationary swing early in the summer of 1920. Cotton prices, which had been holding at 35 cents a pound in early spring, began to slip in May and by September had fallen to six cents. There were foreclosures of farms and bankruptcies of businesses in town.

This environment caused business failures, pain for families and eventually concern for St. Bernards. "Shortages of needed supplies and equipment were felt in every area of the hospital. The continuing support of community leaders and the Sisters' willingness to make sacrifices carried the hospital through these difficult years. Financial records during this time show that because of the economy, nearly half of the patients cared for at St. Bernards were charity patients." [2]

Nursing School Accredited

At the same time there were accomplishments. On December 21, 1921, the first class of graduate nurses received their diplomas. By 1922, these graduates took the State Board Examinations and passed successfully. These were: Sr. Fredrica Spirig, Sr. Benedicta Stuebi, Sr. Justine Renke, Sr. Lawrence Jenniman, Sr. Lidwina Rhinhard, Sr. Camilla Suter, Sr. Adela Spirig, Sr. Helen Suter and Sr. Magdalena Weber. [3] This achievement gave St. Bernards School of Nursing added recognition for the quality of care it provided and the quality of its staff.

St. Bernards was chartered by the State Board of Education in June 1921, and accredited that same year. In its second year, the school was opened to lay students and Miss Catherine Murray and Miss Anna Hughes were the first students to enroll. Later, Miss Murray joined the convent and made profession of vows as Sr. Patricia Murray. She transferred her interest to the field of education and became a successful teacher. Miss Hughes then became the sole graduate in her class. The *Jonesboro Sun* carried the following information regarding the nursing school.

"Last night, St. Bernards School of Nursing graduated its first secular nurse in the person of Miss Anna Hughes of Texarkana. Her motto was "Live, Grow, Blossom." She chose the rose as her class flower. Chief speakers for the occasion were Dr. J.T. Altman, chief of surgical staff; Dr. R.H. Willett, chief of medical staff; and Fr. George Strassner, pastor of St. Roman's Parish church..." [4]

The next class consisted of Sr. Stanislaus Niedzwiedz, later supervisor of the operating room, and Miss Anna Weiler.

Nurses proudly holding banner for St. Bernards School of Nursing—1920s.

Educational Opportunities Change

While the Sisters in health care ministry were experiencing success, the Sisters in the field of education experienced a great disappointment. Even though the summer courses offered by the Diocese at Little Rock College were well attended by the Sisters from all the communities, the classes came to an abrupt end in 1921. Although qualified priests were the instructors, there was a disadvantage. The First Class State Teacher's licenses issued at the end of 1921 were invalid. "The certificates had been dutifully face-signed, but the required subjects had not been listed on the reverse side. The Sisters were disillusioned on the discovery of this unfortunate fact."[5]

Later however, the Sisters were relieved to find out that the subjects they had successfully passed carried valid credits, and were honored by the colleges they later attended. This experience convinced the superiors, as well as members of the community, that there was an increasing need for more advanced education for all the teachers. Superiors began to send the Sisters to out-of-state Catholic colleges and to State colleges in Arkansas.

Mother Walburga, who had a deep interest in the mission field, responded to the request for teachers in Weiner. Fr. Strassner had opened a school in Weiner on October 4, 1920, after he became resident pastor. He taught the upper grades in the sacristy, and hired Miss Sophie Ruesewald to teach the children in the primary grades in the church. When Fr. Strassner was appointed pastor in Jonesboro, he prevailed upon Mother Walburga to send Sisters to teach in St. Anthony's School in Weiner, which was now a mission of Jonesboro.

Sr. Cecilia Huber was sent as the first teacher and Sr. Salesia Gerspasch accompanied her as housekeeper. The Sisters made the 20 trip on Sundays on free passes donated by the Cotton-Belt Railroad. They returned on Friday nights. The first eighth grade graduating class took place in June 1922 in the new school built by Fr. Strassner. In future years, two Sisters were appointed to teach in the school until it closed in 1972, due to decline in enrollment.

Sr. Amora Felderhoff and class in St. Paul's Parish, Pocahontas 1920s.

Accreditation of Hospital

The hospital continued to grow and the physicians became interested in receiving approval from the American College of Surgeons (ACS). "Medicine was changing and the ACS decided, following its successful experience of examining the large hospitals, that it should expand its review process to include 50-bed institutions. In 1922, St. Bernards applied for the examinations and received approval." [6] There was great rejoicing in the city and especially in the hospital when the news arrived in the daily paper that St. Bernards Hospital received a class "A" rating.

In making the announcement, The Jonesboro Tribune published the following story,

> "ST. BERNARDS GIVEN PLACE OF HIGH HONOR – National Hospital Council Rewards Local Institution for Services. Thorough investigation is made before Hospital is Awarded Honor. An exclusive telegram to the Tribune this morning brought the first information here that St. Bernards Hospital of this city had been placed on the Honor Recognition Roll of the National Hospital Council. After providing proof of high standards of proficiency in hospital care, St. Bernards was issued the document by the American Medical Association, of which Dr. William S. Thayer of Baltimore, M.D. is president." [7]

The original American College of Surgeons' five-point program included requirements for an organized medical staff with rules and regulations, the maintenance of appropriate medical records, and the availability of X-ray and laboratory services. The medical staff and the staff at St. Bernards met these requirements.

Hospital Sisters—1920s. Front Row, L – R: Sr. Fredrica Spirig, Sr. Caritas Burrgi, Sr. Hilda Gabler, Sr. Martha Bauer. Center Row: Sr. Lawrence Jennemann, Sr. Marcella Huser, Sr. Lutgardis Felderhoff, Sr. Cammile Suter, Sr. Adela Spirig, Sr. Lidwina Reinhard, Sr. Benedicta Stuebi. Back Row: Sr. Justine Rinke, Sr. Helen Suter, Sr. Alexia Suter, Sr. Pia Wyss, Sr. Evangelista Sander, Sr. Stanislaaus Neidzwiedz.

Post-War Activities

Other pressing matters arose during these early post-war years. The convent built in 1898 had become wholly inadequate, as overcrowding became an increasing problem. During the winter months when most of the Sisters were located on the missions, where they taught in parochial schools, conditions were bearable. In the summer however, when most of the members of the community were at the Motherhouse, the Sisters had to sleep crowded in the four dormitories, the attic and in the tower.

Since the air in Arkansas often became motionless during the summer months, rooms became almost unbearable because of the heat. Before the era of fans and air conditioning, it was difficult to sleep on the cots during many of the sweltering nights.

However, because of limited community funds, the Sisters realized that construction of a new convent at this time was not possible.

The hospital was experiencing this same problem of overcrowding and the physicians and local community leaders appealed to the Sisters to build. They expressed their strong desire to expand the hospital and offered to help. The present facilities had reached their capacity and something had to be done if they were to continue to provide quality medical care to the people in northeast Arkansas. Because of this need, and the depletion of vocations, as consequence of the First World War, Mother Walburga called the community together for a meeting during the summer of 1922. The following matters were decided.

1. An effort was to be made to satisfy the need for additional Sisters.
2. Some type of expanded living quarters was to be provided.
3. The most urgent need was a new annex to St. Bernards Hospital.[8]

With the approval of Bishop Morris, Sr. Josepha Waespe and Sr. Ignatia Rohmer were sent to Switzerland to recruit candidates. This effort was to remedy the first situation. The second need was partially solved when the community decided to erect a new Novitiate building in Pocahontas. Plans were drawn for a two-and-one-half story wooden frame building to be used for the new members. "The first floor was to house classrooms, reception room, a kitchenette, and a recreation room. The second and upper stories consisted of dormitories and several private rooms. The second floor was supplied with a number of dormer windows for a plentiful supply of fresh air for sleeping quarters. Mr. Henry Dust, father of two Sisters of the future (Sr. Georgia and Sr. Lenore) was hired to erect the building."[9]

On December 21, 1922, 12 Postulants arrived from Europe. These new arrivals were a promising Christmas gift to Holy Angels Convent. Since the Novitiate building at Pocahontas was not yet completed, the Postulants were housed temporarily in the original log cabin and the annexes added in subsequent years. By April 14, 1923, the new building was ready for occupancy and Bishop Morris blessed the building and canonically moved the Novitiate from Jonesboro back to Pocahontas.[10]

Monsignor W.H. Aretz, Spiritual Director for the Sisters, spoke words of encouragement in German for the benefit of the new arrivals. Sr. Joseph Waespe, one of the solicitors for Postulants, and one of the original class of 1889, was appointed Novice Mistress. Fr. Weibel was present for the dedication, but this was one of his last contacts with the Olivetan Benedictine Sisters, before departing for Europe, when he spent his last years.

Progress was also taking place in other areas of activity. One such place was in Muenster, Texas where Fr. Frowin Koerdt, OSB, erected a large, two-story brick school building for the growing population of Sacred Heart Parish. When the new building was completed in time for the 1924-25 scholastics term, Fr. Frowin requested additional teachers. Mother Walburga responded to Fr. Frowin's request, by sending nine teaching Sisters, plus one Sister for housekeeping.

By the following year, grades nine and ten were added, so the number of teachers increased. The school continued to grow and grades 11 and 12 were added and a separated high school building was erected.

About this same time, the school in St. Paul's Parish, Pocahontas, added grades nine and ten. By 1922, when Fr. Froitzheim had the new parish hall built, the parishioners did not realize at the time that it was to house the complete high school for a number of years. In the first years of the high school, the teachers were Sr. Othmara Luchinger, Sr. Cecilia Huber, Sr. Amora Felderhoff, and later, many others were assigned.

St. Roman's School in Jonesboro now also offered ninth and tenth grades. Sr. Augustine Widmer taught the high school subjects in the north upstairs room of the former rectory, opposite the rooms of grades five and six. Grades seven and eight were taught in the old "Casino," a square wooded structure between the bell tower and the former church, that later served as a parish entertainment center after 1906.

When Fr. Tynin arrived as pastor in Jonesboro on March 30, 1921, he found the arrangements for the school entirely inadequate. He approached Bishop Morris about erecting a school building. After receiving approval to use the $8,000 that his predecessor had collected to build a new church for the Catholics of Jonesboro, Fr. Tynin approached the wardens at St. Roman's. The people in Jonesboro had worshiped in Holy Angels Convent Chapel since 1906, and were looking forward to having their own parish church.

However, these circumstances would have to continue for a while, because Fr. Tynin felt there was a greater need for a school. He also sold the original four lots of Cate Street, where the Catholic buildings had been destroyed by the fire of 1896. With these funds, Fr. Tynin hoped to make complete payment for the new school. Mr. Henry Lesmeister of Pocahontas was hired as the general contractor for the new school, which consisted of four classrooms, plus a combination library-choral-assembly room. The new school was completed and ready for occupancy by January of 1922.[11]

The four teachers who first taught in the new school were: Sr. Alexia Suter taught grades one and two; Sr. Agnes Voth, grades three and four; Sr. Petronilla Hoelnstein, grades five and six; and Sr. Alphonsa Gruenenfelder taught grades seven and eight and served as principal.

Hospital Annex Dedicated 1923

To respond to the third need expressed by community members at their 1922 meeting, Mother Walburga began plans to expand the hospital. Monsignor Aretz had sketched a plan and Architect Henry Kraemer of Memphis, Tennessee, assisted by Architect Brother Christopher Hugenschist, OFM, drew up blueprints for a new fireproof Annex. The Estes-Williams-Ragsdale Construction Co. of Memphis was the successful bidder for the contract for producing the building at a cost of $99,030. Brother Christopher was strict in excluding any defective work or material, but

60-bed hospital built in 1923 (facing Matthews Street).

there were no disagreements in concluding discussions among the architects and the builders. The cornerstone for the new building was laid on October 8, 1922. [12]

The new Annex included maternity and surgical departments, and a total bed capacity of 100. The institution had a loyal, efficient, and devoted staff of doctors, a training school for nurses, and personal supervision of all the floors, departments and rooms by the Sisters. The *Jonesboro Evening Sun* reported: "The new annex of St. Bernard's Hospital was dedicated by the Right Reverend Bishop John B. Morris, DD, and opened to the public on April 15, 1923." [13]

The new building replaced all except one of the old frame buildings and enabled the Sisters and staff to make significant improvements in how the facilities were used. The original 1900 hospital became the nurses' residence. One frame building served as lodging for workmen on the campus. The new Annex also included classroom and dining area for the young ladies in the nurses' training program.

The new hospital was supplied with all modern appliances, elevator, telephone system, etc. This new 1923 addition enabled St. Bernards to care for 1,278 patients that year, a dramatic increase from the 133 it had cared for when it first opened in 1900. Fully one-fourth of these patients were charity patients. [14]

In an article that appeared in a local paper the day after the new Annex was opened, the editor wrote, "Dr. W.H. Newcomb, representative of the American College of Surgeons, delivered an address before the staff of St. Bernards Hospital last night. He

Back side of convent, chapel and hospital 1923 — showing garden and grape arbor in foreground.

reported that he had completed inspection of the hospital Annex and that it had met every requirement of the College and was far better than two-thirds that had been rated as 'Class A' with his institution."[15] In the conclusion of the article, Dr. Newcomb stated that the institution gives noble care to charity patients.

The completion of the new building brought additional debt and there was often limited income since many of the patients the hospital served could not pay their bills. Mother Walburga asked the Sisters to pray that God would help them meet payments on the debt. With the faith and trust in God that had characterized the Sisters' mission since they had come to the United States, the needed money was realized.

In many instances, people often paid their bills using the barter system. For example, Mr. Cash Taylor of Monette paid his son's hand surgery with three loads of hay and corn he delivered for the convent animals. At that time the Sisters kept cows and chickens to supply food and horses to plow garden. There was a chicken house and barn in the area beyond the garden near the corner of present Jackson and Carson Streets, the site the parking deck occupies today.

One Sister recalled another similar financial arrangement. A year after a farmer from Bay, Arkansas, had surgery in the hospital (and could not pay his bill), he returned to the hospital the following summer. He arrived with a truckload of garden produce. He said, "You Sisters were so good to me when I was in the hospital and couldn't pay my bill. I told the Lord if He would help me make a good garden, I would bring a load to you." Since cash was scarce all such gifts were gratefully received.

"Through the 1920s, the Sisters relied on four approaches to financing the hospital. The first was the expectation that some patients would pay their bills. The second was philanthropy and community support. The third was the barter approach and the fourth was the Sisters' continuing work to provide what was needed themselves."[16]

Although the Sisters relied on community leaders, they continued to provide for their own needs as best they could by growing an abundance of produce in the convent garden. Sr. Leona

Steger, who had learned master gardening in Switzerland, was in charge of the garden for many years. Along with helpers, she was successful in providing an abundance of fresh vegetables and fruits for both the convent table and the patients in the hospital.

During the growing seasons, many willing hands helped to prepare the vegetables and fruits for the convent table and hospital patients. Vegetables and fruits not needed for immediate use, were preserved and stored for winter use. The Sisters preserved numerous jars of jellies and jams, used throughout the year.

Not all was work - Community band — 1920s. Back Row, L – R: Sr. Wilhelmina Gallati, Sr. Rosalia Peterli, Sr Petronilla Holestein, Sr. Agatha Haeni, Sr. Modesta Fetsch, Sr. Leonarda Foehn & Sr. Frances Bossart. Sitting, L – R: Sr. Claudia Bichsel, Sr. Columbia Kuster, Sr. Felicitas Hunkler, Sr. Josepha Waespe, Sr. Cecila Huber & Sr. Rose Muheim. Front: Sr. Paula Dietsche, Sr. Teresa Fetsch & Sr. Remigia Dietsche.

Recruitment Efforts

The Sisters soon realized that the 12 young recruits who had come from Switzerland with Sr. Josepha and Sr. Ignatia were too few to fill the vacancies caused by death and the expansion of the hospital. The Community Chapter again decided to send two Sisters to Europe to recruit additional members. Sr. Pia Wyss and Sr. Remigia Dietsche were chosen to go during the summer of 1923.

When they were ready to return with a group of nine eager young ladies, they encountered difficulties in securing visas. The "Quota" for the United States from Switzerland had already been filled and that no more visas would be issued in 1923, and possibly none in 1924.

After repeated fruitless efforts, Sr. Pia was recalled to the

Motherhouse and Sr. Remigia was left with the young ladies in Switzerland. Fr. Weibel, who was also in Switzerland at the time, assisted Sr. Remigia. He found kind people to provide food and temporary housing for the young ladies, and eventually he was able to arrange lodging for them at the Monastery Maria Stein.

Sr. Remigia contacted the United States Embassy in Switzerland as to permits to enter the United States at once and received no encouragement. Mother Walburga also made efforts to obtain the permits, but was not successful. Finally, the community decided to erect a Lourdes Grotto on the grounds of Holy Angels Convent if the young ladies could gain entrance into our country. Soon after this, three young women, who had traveled separately from the group assembled in Switzerland, arrived at the Convent in Jonesboro. These were later known as Sr. Canisia Senn, Sr. Gonzaga Morant, and Sr. Bathildia Keller.

A new plan developed, as the quota of Swiss for Canada was not yet filled for 1924, so the group embarked at Le-Havre for Halifax, Canada. From there they went to the Monastery in Montreal, where they met Brother Andre (later Beatified by Pope John Paul II). Brother Andre assured them of his prayers and encouraged them to have confidence they would be permitted to enter the United States soon.

The Postulants were given lodging at the Monastery in exchange for doing household chores. Some of them were able to secure work in neighboring Catholic homes. During the ensuing month they were learning the English language. In addition, Sr. Remigia led the group in daily prayers and gave beginning instructions in religious life. Their long awaited request was obtained and on November 26, 1924, the group secured the visas to enter the United States.

A grateful Sr. Remigia and the happy group of nine Postulants arrived at Holy Angels Convent, Jonesboro on November 27, 1924. The community rejoiced and thanked God for answering their prayers. The next day when they went to the Novitiate in Pocahontas, the bells were rung in happy jubilation.[17]

The former class from Europe made their Profession of First Vows on July 2, 1924, and after intensive courses in spiritual training and learning the English language, this class made Profession on July 2, 1926. This class included Sr. Frances Hofbauer from Muenster, Texas, plus 11 from Switzerland: Sr. Angela Weber, Sr. Albertine Hutter, Sr. Theresina Grob, Sr. Gonzaga Morant, Sr. Dorothy Sidler, Sr. Bathildia Keller, Sr. Canisia Senn, Sr. Josephine Jud, Sr. Huberta Tochudi, Sr. Theodora Roos and Sr. Raphael Studer.

Incorporation Changes

Although traditions were still highly regarded during this period, the movement toward professionalism in health care affected the organization of the hospital as well as the nurses and physicians. Convent Maria Stein had been incorporated as a benevolent non-profit corporation when it was founded. When St. Bernards Hospital was established in 1900, it became a part of this same institution. However by the early 1920s, the Sisters felt the hospital should also be incorporated as an institution. The decision was made to create an independent institution and on the 20th day of June 1923, the community took official action and the Clerk of the Circuit Court of Craighead County, Arkansas, recorded the following document.

The legal document concerning incorporation of the hospital, dated September 30, 1928, begins as follows,

> "WHEREAS, Mother Walburga Hoegger, President, Sister Aloysia Unterberger, Vice-President; and Sister Beatrice Renggli, Secretary, have filed in the office of the Clerk of the Circuit Court for the Western District of Craighead County, their Constitution or Articles of Association and Incorporation in compliance with the provisions of the law with reference to incorporating benevolent, educational and other non-profit corporations, together with their petitions for incorporation under the name and style of Convent Maria Stein and St. Bernards Hospital, which petition has been duly presented to the Circuit Court within and for the Western District of Craighead County, Arkansas, on September 3, 1928, being a regular day of the September 1928 term of said court and which petition has been duly granted by said court and order and judgment incorporating said corporation duly entered record. They are

therefore, hereby declared a body politic incorporate by the name and style aforesaid with all powers, privileges, and immunities granted in the law thereunto appertaining." [18]

Gordon Keller, Clerk of Circuit Court, Craighead County, Arkansas, signed this document.

Prevailing Customs

Customs brought from Kloster Maria Rickenbach and practiced in monastic communities throughout Europe continued to be observed at Holy Angels until the late 1940s and early 1950s. The Superior conducted the weekly Culpa Chapters and gave encouragement and exhortations to the Sisters. Two other customs were practiced: (1) asking the Superior's blessing when leaving for a mission trip, and again when returning to the premises; and (2) asking pardon when breaking or ruining something belonging to the Convent.

All permissions were still obtained exclusively from the Superior. She distributed small articles from toothpaste to medicines. She signed lists for needed clothing and handed them to the mistress of the sewing room. At recreation, candy was passed out on special feastdays or holidays. Christmas gifts were limited to a few holy cards and medals.

"Mail that arrived during Advent were tied into a neat bundle, together with an apple, an orange and a handful of nuts, and a similar measure of candy were on a paper plate at each Sister's place at the Christmas breakfast table." [19] During the Christmas Season, "Stille Nacht" was sung each evening before supper by the light of little candles on the tree. Later small electric lights replaced the candles, and the ceiling lights were turned on only after the Sisters had finished the song.

Lent also had special observances. In keeping with the Rule of St. Benedict, the Sisters obtained permission before undertaking any special practices. On the Saturday before Lent, the Sisters wrote down the acts of mortification they wish to practice during the Holy Season. These were presented to the Mother Prioress before the

First Sunday of Lent. Then each Sister appeared in person before her to receive her blessing and the corrected "Lenten practices," signed by the Prioress.

According to oral history, on Wednesdays and Fridays the Sisters also performed some act of penance in the presence of the community. On Fridays, the entire community kept complete silence, saying only what was necessary and speaking in low tones. Before supper, the Sisters recited five Our Fathers with outstretched arms in the refectory.

Observance of Holy Week, followed traditions brought from Maria Rickenbach. The Mass on Holy Thursday was celebrated with great solemnity, followed by the procession to the repository. "The menu at table for Holy Thursday was as follows: Breakfast - hot water, coffee, bread, and butter. Noon - fried eggs, mashed potatoes, greens, chow-chow, Swiss crackers and coffee. Good Friday rising time was 5 a.m. Prime, Terce, Sext, and None were said after morning prayer at 5:20. At 5:45 meditation followed along traditional manner. Then followed breakfast as on the previous day.

At 8 a.m. the Mass of the Pre-sanctified was celebrated without Holy Communion for the Nuns. Dinner was at 11:30 a.m. followed by the 'Tre Ore' or three-hour adoration service in the chapel for both the convent personnel and the members of the parish. At 2 p.m. Fr. Kordsmeier, Pastor of the parish, had sermon followed at 2:30 by the Stations of the Cross by Fr. Evans, the Chaplain at the Convent."[20]

At 3 p.m., the "Good Friday Chapter" was held during which each Sister, on bended knees, asked pardon of all the rest before the crucifix. After the ceremony, the superior gave each Sister an individual penance to be recited with outstretched arms in honor of some part of the Savior's Passion.

The schedule for Holy Saturday was modified, similar to that on Good Friday. However, after morning prayers and breakfast on Holy Saturday, the Sisters dyed over 300 eggs. Patients in the hospital received a colored egg along with some candy. On Easter morning, each Sister received two colored eggs on a paper plate with candies. The schedule on Easter followed the usual Sunday schedule.

The daily "horarium" or order followed the customs practiced at Maria Rickenbach and in many European convents at that time. The Sister arose at 4:30 a.m. and recited in Latin the Hours of Prime, Terce, Sext, and None of the Little Office of the Blessed Virgin Mary in Latin. Meditation followed, with the Prioress or her representative reading out the points for consideration. On ordinary days when the community had a chaplain, Mass followed at 6 a.m. When the parish priest substituted, he only distributed Holy Communion to the members of the Community except on Good Friday.

After breakfast each Sister began her assigned work. Nurses went directly to the hospital, teachers went to school after making up their beds and tidying their cell or place in the dormitory. At 2 p.m. the bell summoned all to spiritual reading in the community room. One Sister read while the others listened and sewed or did some kind of handwork. This was followed by Vespers chanted in the Chapel, after which the Sisters recited the rosary in common. A period for assigned work followed until supper at 6 p.m.

The evening meal consisted of corn mush or cooked rice. To this was added a vegetable and hash, made of chopped meat, potatoes and a few onions in a heavy gravy. Only water was served at the evening meal for the drink. Recreation followed after supper until 7:30 p.m. when Matins and Lauds were recited together in Chapel. This was followed by night prayer before retiring in silence for the night. Only necessary speech was permitted during this night silence, which lasted until after breakfast the following day.

Other Happenings of the 1920s

Patriotism of the Sisters was evident as they were encouraged to vote. On November 24, 1926, Sr. Pia Wyss, Sr. Stanislaus Niedzwiez, and Sr. Regina Willett were the first from Holy Angels Convent to vote in the polls.

Fr. Weibel received word from Bishop Morris that he had recommended him to be made a Monsignor. He chose Pocahontas as the place of his investment by the Bishop on August 31, 1926. As an expression of gratitude from the community, Holy Angels Convent furnished the red vestments. Monsignor Weibel then visited Holy Angels Convent, his parish in Engelberg, and all his former missions in northeast Arkansas before returning to Switzerland.

The spring of 1927 brought disastrous floods to areas around Jonesboro. Some were caused by heavy rains, others by a break in the levee of the Mississippi River at New Madrid, Missouri. On Tuesday, April 19, 1927, water covered miles in northeast Arkansas. In many areas people had to evacuate their homes and flee to higher elevations. Since Jonesboro is located on Crowley Ridge, many came to Jonesboro. For nearly two weeks, St. Bernards was overcrowded with people in rooms, wards and hallways. For more than a week, travel from Pocahontas was prohibitive.

Additional trouble developed at the hospital because of a failure to remove a sponge from a woman's abdomen during an operation. On January 14, 1929, Mr. Staudemeir from Manila came to the hospital to collect $500 for this neglect. The hospital and doctor were able to settle this matter out of court.

New Convent

By late 1927, the community decided it was time to build the needed addition to the Convent. To save costs the new Annex was to be added to the 1898 building. Msgr. Aretz, who was now professor at the Seminary in Little Rock, returned to Jonesboro to draw up plans to join the original Convent on the north. The new building would serve both as a Convent and as the future Holy Angels

New Holy Angels Convent — 1929 (facing Jackson Street)

Academy. Mr. Henry Kraemer of Memphis was hired as the general architect. The total cost of the building was $132,300.[21]

Msgr. McQuaid and Mother Walburga broke ground for the construction of the new convent on August 28, 1928. According to community records, the cornerstone was laid on October 30, 1928. Contents enclosed were: a list of the living and of the 42 deceased members of the community, pictures of Bishop Morris, Msgr. Aretz, Msgr. Froitzheim, Msgr. Weibel, Mother Walburga as Prioress, Mother Beatrice as Foundress and Lawrence Schneider, maintenance supervisor of hospital and convent, who oversaw the construction. Also enclosed were copies of *The Guardian*, the *Jonesboro Sun*, and other publications.

The companies of Stehle, Fischer, Misktish of Jonesboro, and Thompson of Memphis, Tennessee were contractors for the general construction, heating, plumbing, and electricity in that order. "The final design of the building provided an entity of the four stories as a counterpart to the 1923 addition to the hospital. Both were constructed of dark red brick, fire-proof with unique facades."[22]

The statue above the convent entrance was one of the Blessed Virgin Mary by Kaletta. The two upper stories were to serve the Sisters, while the two lower ones were designated for the boarding and day students of Holy Angels Academy. Hot and cold water, central heating, electric lighting were provided throughout the building. Cleaning, moving and arranging the new convent quarters came about gradually.

The first time a radio was permitted to be used publicly in Holy Angels Convent was on May 4, 1929, when the Sisters were allowed to listen to the inaugural address of President Herbert Hoover. This was shortly before the dedication of the new Annex on April 16, 1929, by Bishop John B. Morris, DD. According to the *Jonesboro Tribune*,

> "Backed by centuries of the Roman Catholic Church with a display of pomp and ceremony which has been unrivaled in Jonesboro for years, attended by the highest church dignitaries in the State, Holy Angels Convent was appropriately dedicated today."[23]

Relocation of the Novitiate

With the completion of the new Convent building, the community decided to move the Novitiate back from Pocahontas to Jonesboro. With the additional space in the new building, the Senior Sisters moved into new quarters and the Novitiate members could occupy the original 1905 building. This move would benefit the Postulants and young Sisters who had not completed high school. They could join in the classes taught to the secular students. The Postulants and Novices would also become better acquainted with community customs.

Monsignor Fletcher, Spiritual Director of the Community, concurred with this decision and Bishop Morris approved this move. Therefore, Sr. Josepha Waespe, Novice Mistress, plus the Novices and Postulants moved to Jonesboro. According to the Diamond Jubilee Brochure, "The Novitiate was moved on April 17, 1929." [24]

Sr. Joseph Waespe with group of Postulants (Future Sisters) Pocahontas 1928. Back Row, L – R: Sr. Aloysia Kleiss, Sr. Frowina Hacker, Sr. Thomasina Walterscheid, Sr. Theodora Roos and Sr. Georgia Dust. Front Row: (did not stay) Sr. Michael Lange, Sr. Imelda Pels and Sr. Philippa Wavrick

As the 1920s drew to a close, outside events well beyond the control of the Sisters and community leaders began to affect St. Bernards just as they had a decade earlier. On October 24, 1929, the Stock Market took a plunge. That day has been referred to as "Black Friday," and it seriously affected the economy for the next decade. Although this did not immediately affect the citizens of Jonesboro, it would have devastating effects in years to come.

During the summer months crops looked good and everyone felt 1929 would be a good year. No one realized that the rain received on May 29 would be the last rain in the county for 76 days. The American Trust Company in Jonesboro closed its doors on November 1, and the Jonesboro Roller Mill, one of Jonesboro's oldest business institutions burned on November 6.

At the close of 1929, people could not afford to pay for medical treatment in the hospital, so many people went without the help they needed. School tuitions were left unpaid, as many fathers of families had lost their jobs and were without work. By the end of 1929, the citizens of Jonesboro had fallen on hard times. St. Bernards Hospital and Holy Angels Convent were not exceptions.

CHAPTER 9
1930-1939

Uncertain Times

"January 1930, was unusually cold. At times, the temperature fell to nine below. People suffered much, and beggars in groups from 25 to 40 per day arrived at the convent-hospital kitchen requesting food." [1] Although the Depression continued into the early 1930s, several significant events occurred at the beginning of this decade that had far-reaching effects on the community in years to come.

The first was the appointment by Bishop Morris of Monsignor Albert L. Fletcher as Spiritual Director of the Olivetan Benedictine Sisters, April 6, 1930. He succeeded the late Msgr. Weinand H. Aretz, who died Oct. 1, 1929. This was a consequential appointment, as Msgr. Fletcher later became the Ordinary of the Diocese of Little Rock, and continued to have a great influence on the community for the next 42 years until he retired in 1972.

The second significant event in the community at the beginning of this decade, was the completion of the outdoor Lourdes Grotto. This was the fulfillment of a promise Mother Walburga had made in thanksgiving for the entrance of the European Postulants into the United States. On April 30, 1930, Fr. William Kordsmeier blessed the Grotto and offered Benediction. The Sisters sang hymns at this outdoor service, which was the first of many to be held in following years. [2]

Grotto of our Lady of Lourdes — built by Lawrence Schneider in early 1930s. (Temporary Corpus Christi altar erected for the feast).

An event of lesser significance for the community, was the Ordination Fr. George Carns, the second local son to the holy priesthood. Bishop Morris had ordained Fr. Walter Tynin, the first native son of Jonesboro, in 1911. On Sunday, May 4, 1930, Fr. Carns offered his First Mass in Holy Angels Convent Chapel, which still served as parish church for St. Roman's congregation. He was the son of Mrs. Cecilia Carns and the late Frank Carns, and also brother of Sr. Gerarda. Fr. Carns received his early training by the Olivetan Benedictines at St. Roman's School. In addition to the pastor, Fr. William Kordsmeir, a number of visiting clergy attended the celebration.

In spite of unrelenting financial pressures, the Sisters continued to care for those who came to St. Bernards for help. "Although there was occasionally good news—such as the opening of the rice mill in Jonesboro in December 1930—the Depression was far from over. Food that had been used by some patients to pay their hospital bills was now scarce. In January 1931, the American Red Cross estimated over 15,000 people suffering from hunger in northeast Arkansas." [3]

As the Depression continued to worsen, the Sisters' responsibilities continued to expand, while the financial resources available to meet them continued to contract. There was little income from the hospital and neither from the schools. The schools could not forward money home to the Motherhouse, since they had none to send. Families had no income, since fathers had no work. In lieu of paying tuition, the people tried to provide food for the teaching Sisters on the missions.

Mission Sisters at Sacred Heart School, Muenster, Texas—1930s. First Row, L – R: Sr. Mechtildis Schuechert, Sr. Angelina Boesch, Sr. Lucia Staubli. Second Row: Sr. Matilda Sparber, Sr. Michael Lange, Sr. Anastasia Ruegg, Sr. Agnes Voth, Sr. Gebharda Truniger. Third Row: Sr. Bertha Frei, Sr. Ignatius Rohmer, Sr. Leonarda Foehn, Sr. Eymard Lemmer.

At first Mother Walburga held fast to her trust in God that there would be the money needed to make the interest payments on the hospital Annex and the new Convent. Soon these obligations turned unto a "nightmare" which caused sleepless nights. Again friends and advisors urged the Sisters to tell people they must pay if they wanted hospital services.

In spite of mounting financial pressures, the Sisters held fast to their mission of providing Christ-like care to all who needed it. No child was turned away from the schools because their parents could not pay tuition. Frequent and fervent prayers were offered for Divine guidance during these difficult years. From time to time, unexpected benefactors would come forward, which enabled the Sisters to meet their obligations—sometimes at the last minute.

During this time, most businesses understood how important the hospital was to the Jonesboro community and northeast Arkansas, and as a result were patient in expecting payment for supplies. One business however, insisted on being paid in full, in advance of filling the hospital's order.

"Mother Walburga was not easily intimidated, responded that the whole account would be paid but there would be no future orders. Mother Walburga dealt with financial pressures by being faithful to her promises and sent small checks on accounts due as often as she could. As conditions improved, the Sisters returned to their usual practice of paying all bills promptly." [4]

Holy Angels Academy

One of the encouraging signs of the 1930s was the fulfillment of a dream—long held by the Sisters—that of having an Academy for girls. In spite of uncertain financial times, Mother Walburga was intent on opening the Academy on the first two floors. The newly completed Convent building was completed and provided ample space for the Academy.

"Mother Walburga appointed Sr. Cecilia Huber, who had obtained her M.A. degree at Loyola University in Chicago in 1926 as the principal. Sr. Cecilia served in this capacity until her death in

1943. Sr. Ambrose Bruggemann, who had attained her B.A. degree from Mary Wood College, Scranton, Pennsylvania in 1926, was appointed teacher and disciplinarian. Other Sisters were appointed to assist in the Academy.[5]

Holy Angels Academy — (lower two floors of Convent) — opened 1930.

There was a fully equipped art studio with a competent instructor, Sr. Bernardine Grueninger, who had obtained her training and credentials in Switzerland. She offered pencil sketching, charcoal, water and oil painting. She also taught crafts, ceramics, and wood carving.

The music studio offered courses in organ, violin, theory, harmony, history of music, and counterpoint. Wind and string instruments were also listed as selections."[6] Some of the first music teachers included: Sr. Felicitas Hunkeler, Sr. Josepha Waespe, and Sr. Modesta Fetsch.

Sr. Claudia Bischsel, who had training in library science, was appointed librarian. The library numbered 2,500 books classified according to the Dewey Decimal System. Sr. Claudia also kept study hall in the library. Holy Angels Academy opened on August 8, 1930.

According to records, all standard high school subjects were offered. English in all its forms, both spoken and written, various branches of mathematics, the social sciences, general science, chemistry, biology, plus the foreign languages of Latin, French, and

German were initially offered.

"In the fall of 1931, Holy Angels Academy was fully accredited as a Class "A" four-year high school by the Arkansas Department of Education. During the first years of its operation only the first two grades of secondary education were offered. In September 1932, grades 11 and 12 were added."[7]

The first graduating class in 1934 consisted of the following: Mary Cecilia Gatz, Mary M. Heimberg, Maxine Holmes, Josephine Staudt, Loretta Stewart, Mary Rose Frankenberger (later Sr. Louise), Sr. Geraldine Homer, and Sr. Florentine Tempel. The citizens of Jonesboro recognized the results of the educational endeavors of the Academy and commended the Sisters for their initiatives. Academy students were noted not just for their uniforms, but for their outstanding politeness and achievements.

Deprivations and Depression

"Shortly after the opening of the Academy, repercussions of the 1929 Stock Market crash were beginning to be felt by the Sisters at Holy Angels and by those working at St. Bernards. Farmers lost their lands, many employees lost their jobs and with them their income and sustenance. People lost money, banks failed, and even Mother Walburga became fearful to deposit small amounts that dribbled in from the hospital and from the scant salaries paid teachers of some of the schools."[8]

The Sisters maintained both the hospital and the schools, in hope of more favorable times to come. However, for a while, the situation became worse instead of better. Throughout these troubling times, a number of people who felt indebted to the Sisters, stepped forward to assist during this time of need.

According to Sr. Agnes in Green Olive Branch, one such instance of gratitude came from a Marie Orf of Oklahoma. During her early years, she attended St. Roman's School and took violin lessons from Sr. Modesta Fetsch. Her parents were too poor to defray the cost of her education or music lessons. Because of her unusual musical talent, Sr. Modesta continued the lessons.

Now, Miss Orf, a successful musician, returned to Holy Angels, and requested all the bills she owed to the school and music conservatory. Marie said the benefits she had received from the Sisters were priceless, as they helped her family through the Depression. She then wrote a sizeable check, plus a bonus in gratitude for the kindness of the Sisters. [9] It was incidents like this that helped the Sisters through these challenging times.

Sr. Rose Mulheim and band at St. Paul's School, Pocahontas—1930s.

"Times were so difficult that people could not afford to go to the hospital because there was no way to pay the bill and by February 1933, the census had dropped—there were only 34 patients in the entire hospital." [10]

The Depression also affected the Sisters in other ways. Citizens used to loan the Sisters their cars, but during the Depression, according to Sr. Agnes Voth, "People also hesitated to lend their cars for the use of the Sisters when they wished to undertake longer trips. They could afford neither the wear and tear on cars nor meet gas expenses to run them. Hence, Mother Walburga purchased the first car for the Convent in 1933." [11] Convent maintenance men continued to chauffeur the Sisters, since at that time, Sisters were not allowed to drive.

Fr. Wm. J. Kordsmeier, pastor, and Sr. Fridoline Buck, teacher with first and second grades pupils in front of newly dedicated Blessed Sacrament Church, Jonesboro — 1933.

New Parish Church

October 17, 1933, was a memorable day for Jonesboro, both for the parish and also for the Sisters. Bishop Morris dedicated the new parish church in Jonesboro and changed the name to "Blessed Sacrament," in accordance with the emphasis Pope Pius X had placed on the Real Presence of Jesus in the Blessed Sacrament. Now services in the Convent Chapel were conducted only for Sisters but visitors were always welcome. Families with loved ones in the hospital, frequently joined the Sisters at their Mass.

While the impact of the Depression was severe, there continued to be busy years for the School of Nursing. "There was great rejoicing when Sr. Mildred Felderhoff and Sr. Thomasine Walterscheid received a scholarship to St. Louis University, especially when they returned with Bachelor of Science degrees in addition to their registered nurse (R.N.) licensure from the State. Sr. Mildred and Sr. Thomasine were named assistants in their respective fields." [12]

Overcoming Prejudice

Although the Sisters and the citizens of Jonesboro had established bonds of friendship and trust from the beginning of their mission, there was a period in the 1930s that saw outbreaks of prejudice toward Catholics both in Jonesboro and around the country. One example was reported in Green Olive Branch.

"A certain Mr. Jeffers, an itinerant preacher, infringed upon the rights of some of the citizens. He vowed destruction of everything Catholic, in particular of all that was connected with the convent and the hospital. He took possession of one of the Baptist churches and tried to drive out the original minister. Next, he set up a tent two blocks from the hospital. Uninformed people flocked to hear him and brought him farm produce that he sold. He vowed never to set foot in a Catholic hospital. He simulated ceremonies of the Catholic Church, and on the day before he planned to ridicule the Mass, tragedy struck.

The young man he trained to be his 'altar boy' was seriously injured in a car accident. The child was brought to the hospital and diagnosed with a brain concussion. Jeffers stormed to the hospital and in an outburst, cried out, 'Where is my boy?' Sister Adela Spirig, who was in charge on first floor, explained the serious condition of the child and that the hospital, its staff and physicians were doing all they could for the boy. Sister told him, he was free to go in at any time. Jeffers stormed into the room saying, 'Then I'll perform a miracle; I need that boy tonight for services.'

Within minutes, the child died. At 1 a.m. on October 26, 1931, Jeffers' tent was destroyed by fire. He later erected a meeting house, called a 'Tabernacle,' one block from the hospital on Matthews Street. Eventually the violence and disorder instigated by Jeffers and some of his followers caused civil authorities of Jonesboro to ban him from the city forever and prejudice against the Sisters and hospital subsided." [13]

By contrast, an encouraging recognition was cited on November 4, 1931. Monsignor John J. Healy, Diocesan Superintendent of schools and hospitals visited Jonesboro and brought peace and hope to the community. He inspected the Academy and St. Roman's School and commended the work of the Sisters. He also visited St. Bernards and commended the Sisters on the amount of charity performed by this institution.

Another encouraging recognition came on October 29, 1932, when Sr. Felicitas Hunkler was informed that she was named District Examiner of Arkansas State Music Association in northeast Arkansas. This honor gave statewide recognition to Holy Angels Academy Music Conservatory and to the Community.

News from Switzerland brought the announcement of the death of Msgr. John Weibel on March 3, 1934. He was buried near the Cistercian Convent in Eschenbach, his native city, where he spent his last days. The Community mourned his death, especially Mother Beatrice Renggli, Sr. Angelia Boesch, Sr. Edward End and Sr. Cecilia Huber, who had served as superiors while he was the Spiritual Director of the Sisters.

Election Again

Since Mother Walburga's term of office was to expire in 1933, an election was scheduled that summer. After the usual 6 a.m. Mass and breakfast, Msgr. Fletcher officiated, for the first time, at the election of the new superior, which was conducted in the library. As was the custom, two priests acted as tellers to assist him. Complete silence was observed by the Sisters until after the election and Msgr. Fletcher announced that Mother Walburga was re-elected superior for the seventh time on July 3, 1933.

Following this, all assembled in the chapel for Benediction and the singing of the "Te Deum." Then, as was the custom of the time, each Sister approached Mother Walburga and acknowledged her as the Prioress by kissing her ring. Following this a festive meal was then served in the refectory. [14] According to oral history, Mother Beatrice influenced the entire community for nine times to re-elect Mother Walburga as prioress of Holy Angels Convent. By letter she obtained permission from Bishop Morris to allow the community to re-elect Mother Walburga again and again for a span that reached 30 years. His letter was read to the assembled Sisters before election. Not all the Sisters agreed with Mother Beatrice, but these were the minority and were easily out-voted.

Hospital Advisory Board

In the mid-1930s, Rev. John J. Healy, recommended that St. Bernards begin a drive for funds in order to defray burdening expenses, and still allow continued charity to those who urgently required it. "In June 1935, the Hospital Advisory Board was organized with these founding members: Rev. William Kordsmeir, pastor of Blessed Sacrament Church, (formerly St. Roman's), M.P. Welch, A.G. Patteson, Gordon Crenshaw, Eugene Barton, H.L. Weil, and A.M. Heringer. The Advisory Board's mandate was to develop a permanent relief fund for the hospital and their efforts the first year realized the sum of $3,025 collected through the hospital drive." [15]

No one can exactly say when, but the Depression eased and financial conditions gradually improved. There were continuing small signs that things were slowly getting better throughout the mid-1930s. With some, it was the father of a family getting steady work. With others, the Depression eased when the farmer's bills were paid and he sold a crop for enough money to live comfortably into next crop time.

Disaster Strikes

While the economy continued to get stronger, disaster of another kind struck in January and early February of 1937. The St. Francis River again overflowed its banks and flood victims were brought to Jonesboro. Mother Walburga wrote in her diary,

"One thousand more people came to Jonesboro last night. Heaviest flood results were experience in Black Oak, Trumann, Marked Tree, Lake City and Caraway, all of which were almost entirely under water. People live in tents without heat, light, bedding or sufficient protection. All public buildings of the city are filled to capacity. The hospital is much overcrowded. Pregnant mothers suffer the most. St. Louis sent $100, so did Pocahontas. Next day, Pocahontas sent additional $107 for the refugees. Illness and suffering are indescribable." [16]

Five thousand people were temporarily added to the population of Jonesboro and the residents reached out to help the unfortunate refugees; some even shared their guestrooms. According to oral tradition, strain on the hospital caused strain on the laundry and the kitchen. Beds doubled and tripled in rooms, corridors, everywhere where space was available. A number of Sisters helped to give comfort to the additional patients and their families. Academy girls also volunteered to help in caring for the sick.

Sr. Florentine Temple related one incident that occurred while she was on duty helping people affected by the flood. "We set up four beds on the enclosed porch to use as a temporary maternity ward, which was filled immediately. Dr. E.J. Stroud went to check on patients, and since there were no chairs, sat on the edge of the bed to talk to a lady. After he finished his rounds, and came to the desk, Sr. Florentine noticed bed bugs crawling all over the doctor's coat.

The poor lady was covered with bed bugs, as she had been living in such unsanitary conditions. The patients were all given immediate attention in an antiseptic bath. The bed sheets, mattresses and all were sent to the sterilizing room to control the pests before they would spread throughout the hospital." [17]

People of Jonesboro were most generous in sharing what they had to relieve the suffering of those who had lost everything in the flood.

With the passage of time, people were able to rebuild their lives. Since the economy was improving, more people were now able to pay for medical services. Farmers were faring better since they started rotating their cotton crops with rice and soybeans. As business conditions improved, hospital conditions improved.

Chapel Expansion

In anticipation of the Golden Jubilee of the founding of the

Olivetan Benedictine Sisters, the community voted to renovate the chapel. A.J. Kraemer, an architect from Memphis was hired to inaugurate plans for the work. He let the contract to a Mr. Buffalo, who began renovation at once. During February and March the refectory was remodeled. An addition to the refectory was also built. "Excavation for the Novitiate refectory had to be made under the new addition of the chapel. The area was to be the same width, as the old refectory and reach up to the hall of the old Convent. Total expense of excavation was $43.34. This covered cost at $5.00 per day of labor with a team of horses and shovels of two of Mr. John Hockle's boys." [18]

New drainage pipes were also installed that ran down to Jackson Street with greater decline than the flat expanse toward Matthews Street. This was supposed to eliminate the below ground-level Novitiate dining room from flooding. However, this did not eliminate the problem, as many times later, the Novitiate members were involved in mopping water after a heavy rain.

During the renovation of the chapel, services were held in the refectory. The retreat lectures and confession were also heard in the room that formerly served as a library in 1898. Bishop Morris requested that the dedication of the chapel and the celebration of the Golden Jubilee be postponed until October 1938.

During the renovation an incident occurred that showed the spirit of faith and confidence of Mother Walburga. The four Batesville granite pillars for the new chapel entrance had arrived, but the builder told Mother Walburga that he would have to have an electric crane to install them. However, she prayed and asked the Sisters to pray that the workmen could install the pillars without the expense of an electric crane. "On April 29, 1938, the pillars were easily set in place without a crane." [19] The renovation of the chapel was completed without injury to any of the workers.

Golden Jubilee

Preparation for the celebration of the first 50 years since the establishment of the Community involved nearly every Sister, plus a number of volunteers from the parish. First, the newly renovated chapel had to be thoroughly cleaned from top to bottom. The tile floor had to be cleaned with gasoline. Sr. Wilhelmina Gallati painted the statues and the Stations of the Cross.

Sisters in procession entering the renovated chapel on Golden Jubilee, October 1938. Sr. Hilda Gabler first in line and in center Mother Walburga (left side of pole with two visiting Sisters from Fort Smith). Others: Community members unidentified.

New clear windowpane was again installed in the side windows in lieu of stained glass. The plan was to replace them with stained glass whenever finances allowed the expense. According to Mother Walburga's Diary, Fr. Kordsmeier donated the tabernacle in memory of his parents. The Brady family donated the beautiful Crucifix to hang above the main altar. (Later, when the Convent was re-located in 1974, this same crucifix was brought along and now, mounted on a large cross, hangs above the present Eucharistic altar.) The priests of northeast Arkansas donated the high altar. A Wick pipe organ from a firm in St. Louis was installed and the Ralph Budde Company of Jackson, Tennessee, installed new oak pews. (These same pews were transported to the new chapel when the Convent relocated north of town in 1974.)

Sr. Bernardine Grueninger marbleized the altars and the communion rail. It was noted in the Day Book, that the Protestant people in Jonesboro sent flowers to decorate the chapel for the event. Every Sister helped in one way or another to prepare for the Jubilee celebration, which extended over October 3rd and 4th, 1938.[20]

On October 3, Bishop Morris officiated at a Pontifical High Mass, blessed the renovated convent chapel and reviewed the history of the community during his sermon. Fr. William A. Kordsmeier, pastor of Blessed Sacrament Parish, and a number of other visiting clergy assisted the Bishop. The Jubilee was also a celebration to commemorate the Silver Jubilee of Mother Walburga, as Prioress of the Community and the 73rd anniversary of the religious profession of Mother Beatrice Renggli (foundress), who had made profession at Maria Rickenbach in Switzerland. In addition, the celebration also commemorated the Golden Jubilee of profession of Sr. Eugenia Brodel, and the Silver Jubilee of profession of Sr. Paula Deutsche, Sr. Lioba Suter, and Sr. Amora Felderhoff.

Community in choir in renovated chapel. — Golden Jubilee Celebration 1938.

The banquet for clergy and Community, which followed the Mass on October third, was held in the nurses' dining hall and their classrooms in the new hospital Annex. According to Sr. Agnes, "For the first time in the history of the Community, a five course banquet was served to the Sisters with place cards, decoration, and all adjuncts, all of which had been planned by Sr. Georgia Dust." [21] There were 151 professed Sisters living at that time. Fifty-three others who had professed vows in the Olivetan Benedictine Community had died by 1938.

The second day of the Jubilee celebration was opened to the townspeople, as they had been supportive of the Sisters, since relocating to Jonesboro in 1898. The public officials and parishioners, as well as relatives and friends were invited to an afternoon reception and open house. "The largest money gifts of the

Jubilee were: proceeds from Sr. Magdalene Weber's crocheted table cloth which brought $112.50, and other donations which amounted to $318.50."[22]

According to oral history, to honor all deceased Sisters on the occasion of the Golden Jubilee of the Community, Sr. Regina Willett and Sr. Frederica Spirig made artificial floral arrangements for the graves of each of the 53 Sisters who had died by 1938. Twenty of these had been buried in St. Paul's Parish Cemetery in Pocahontas, under a row of cedar trees, while the remaining 33 Sisters were buried in Holy Cross Cemetery in Jonesboro. These floral arrangements were put out on the graves for the first time on All Souls Day and used for a number of succeeding years.

Closing Days of Decade

As the decade of the 1930s drew to close, Jonesboro and St. Bernards had recovered from the Depression and the flood of 1937. A number of improvements were made in the hospital. No longer would the Convent kitchen prepare meals for patients. A separate kitchen was established in the hospital to prepare the meals for the patients. "The hospital Diet Kitchen was opened formerly on October 20, 1938, and special salads and desserts were added to the daily menu for the patients. Sr. Georgia Dust was in charge of this new department and directed the operations."[23]

By 1938 however, a harassing situation arose in Jonesboro when a site for the new jail was selected in the vicinity of the hospital. All nearby property owners signed a protest to this location. The city employees had already delivered lumber and supplies to the selected site. Mr. M.P. Welch and his coworkers continued efforts to stop the erection of the jail on lots 10 and 11 in the proximate vicinity of the hospital.

"The City Council met on December 29, 1938 to discuss the possibility of another location. Finally, to the relief of the Sisters and the neighboring residents, the City Council voted on the last day of the year to relocate the jail to a site on the other side of town. The hospital purchased the two lots for $500 and the supplies for $150"[24]

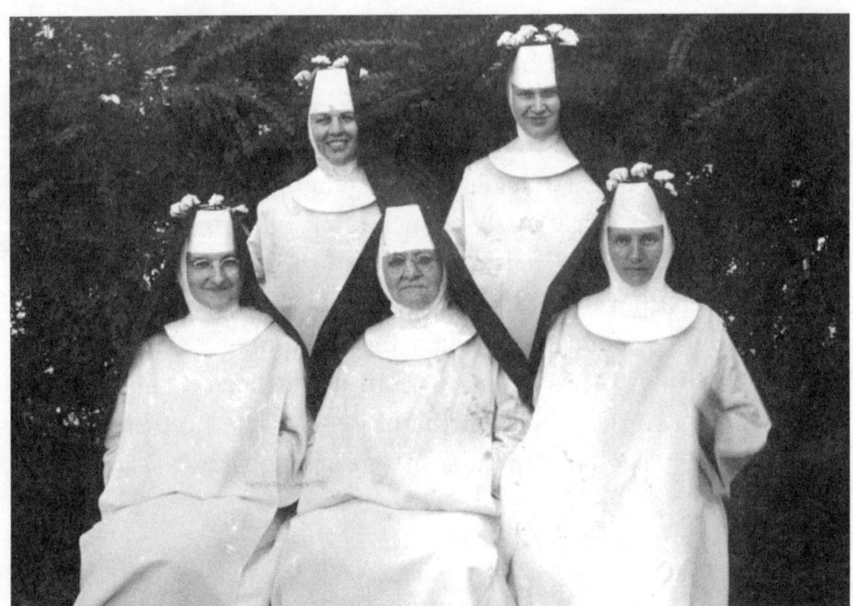

Profession Class with Mother Walburger — 1939. Seated, L – R: Sr. Louise Frankenberger, Mother Walburger Hoegger, Sr. Bernadette Kaufman. Standing: Sr. Helen Swirczynski and Sr. Eymard Lemmer.

By 1939, war broke out in Europe and tensions began to build in America. Adolph Hitler ordered invasion of Poland. Benito Mussolini invaded Albania. Britain and France objected and President Roosevelt asked both dictators for pledges of nonaggression for a period of ten years. On September 3, 1939, however, Britain and France declared war on Germany and Italy. At first, the United States stayed out of the war and only assisted the allies with shipments of supplies. The U.S. would eventually become involved in the Second World War and its involvement would affect the Sisters and how they would be able to serve patients at St. Bernards. As the decade closed, uncertainties prevailed and tensions continued to build across the Nation, which affected Jonesboro and the Benedictine Community.

CHAPTER 10
1940-1949

The War Years

In 1940, war was raging in Europe, but at least during the early phases citizens of northeast Arkansas were not significantly affected. Jonesboro and St. Bernards Hospital were both experiencing growths. The Sisters, physicians and townsfolk were working together to build a better future. The continuing increase in numbers of Sisters throughout the 1930s had strengthened the nursing staff, as well as the teaching staff for the schools.

The year 1940 brought another national honor to St. Bernards. "It was on the occasion of the Silver Jubilee of the Catholic Hospital Association, which had been organized in 1915. The association recognized Catholic hospitals that had been in existence for 25 years or more. Mother Beatrice, foundress of the Olivetan Benedictine Sisters in Arkansas, accepted the award for St. Bernards. She was presented the 'Distinguished Service Cross,' in recognition for her work and the work of the Sisters and community leaders."[1]

Due to his age and growing health problems, Bishop Morris requested a coadjutor to assist in administering the diocese. Instead, Pope Pius XII gave him an Auxiliary in the person of Monsignor Albert L. Fletcher. The Olivetan Benedictine Sisters rejoiced when they heard the news that their spiritual director would now be named a Bishop. On April 25, 1940, Monsignor Fletcher was consecrated Bishop of Samos and Auxiliary Bishop of Little Rock. A delegation of five Sisters attended the ceremony in Little Rock, while the other Community members listened to the radio broadcast of the festivities.[2]

Aid came to the Sisters in various ways. On May 7, 1940, the police brought a number of wild ducks to be used in the hospital. The fowl had been taken from lawbreaking hunters who shot them out of season. Duck was served to patients who considered this a special treat.[3]

"During the summer of 1940, 18 Sisters took courses at Arkansas State College. Sr. Cecilia Huber registered them all for fees at a total of $333, for the six-weeks courses of all."[4] Schools continued to thrive during this period. Sr. Gerarda Carns was sent to St. Louis University in October to earn a M.A. degree with a major in mathematics. During this same month, according to Mother Walburga's Diary, 14 of the latest arrivals of Swiss Sisters obtained their citizenship papers and prepared for a teaching career.

Sr. Jerome Locken with third and fourth grades class in Pocahontas. (Note convent in background and church on left) — 1940.

St. Bernards continued to experience growth and the hospital's limited bed capacity led once again to discussions about expanding the hospital. According to the *Lamp*, the Yearbook for Nurses, "Patients are constantly being put on a waiting list. Citizens of Jonesboro, who have always been patrons and generous benefactors of the hospital, are advocating the enlargement of the now existing institution."[5] The Advisory Board held discussions concerning another addition to St. Bernards Hospital as well as the need for a new nurses' residence. However, before any plan developed, the impact of World War II reached northeast Arkansas.

On October 29, 1940, the United States instituted compulsory military service. More than 16 million young men registered with their local boards. Two such boards were set up in Craighead County. In March of 1941, Congress passed the "Lend-Lease" bill, which offered military resources on a lend and lease basis. It was the largest gesture of aid that the United States had made and it furnished the allies with materials critical to their ability to defend themselves.

In April 1941, five Academy girls participated in the Journalism Contest at Arkansas State College. The *Echoes* staff received a cup to recognize their outstanding work. This same staff inaugurated the *Angelus,* an annual for entrance into the Quill and Scroll Society.[6]

Due to failing health of Mother Beatrice Renggli, who had been serving as Secretary since 1915, Sr. Cecilia Huber was named Secretary of the Corporation Convent Maria Stein and St. Bernards Hospital. M.M. Robinson, Notary Public signed a Certificate of verification, dated November 22, 1922, to document change.[7]

On December 7, Japan bombed the United States naval base at Pearl Harbor. The next day, President Franklin Roosevelt declared the United States to be at war for the second time within a generation. The United States was now engaged in World War II against Japan, Germany and Italy.

People in northeast Arkansas who had not previously been affected by the war now began to feel it effects. "Rationing of materials and supplies was initiated for everything from sugar for the household to gasoline for the cars. Everyone received a ration book for limited supplies of specific goods for a month at a time. Although rationing continued throughout the war, there was no ration of care at St. Bernards. The Sisters continued the service they had always tried to give. If a shortage occurred the Sisters did without so patients could have what they needed."[8]

In early 1942, the already overcrowded conditions at St. Bernards expanded, when the instructor of 12,000 Army recruits, in training for the Air Corps at Arkansas State College, asked the Sisters to help care for soldiers who developed pneumonia because of inadequate living quarters. A large number of young men were treated by Army doctors and local physicians until the Army was able to provide facilities for the care of the sick at the camp.

Throughout the war, St. Bernards faced the challenge of finding people to care for patients as doctors and nurses became involved in the war effort. The School of Nurses became a Cadet Corps and many graduate nurses served with the Veterans Administration in Army Hospitals at home and abroad.[9]

Sr. Hilda Gabler and Sr. Mildred Felderhoff (left) and Sr. Pia Wyss and Sr. Thomasine Walterscheid (right) with St. Bernards Cadet Corps of Nurses.

On July 10, 1942, the annual Corporation meeting of Convent Maria Stein and St. Bernards Hospital brought about some changes in personnel. According to the minutes,

> "The President (Mother Walburga) then reappointed Sr. Perpetua Reinart, Vice-President. Due to a serious protracted illness, Sr. Cecilia resigned her office as Secretary in the spring. Sr. Antonia Holthouse was appointed Secretary. This appointment met with unanimous approval. The following Council members were then appointed: Sr. Eugenia Brodel, Sr. Josepha Waespe, Sr. Rose

Muheim, Sr. Felicitas Hunkeler, Sr. Cecilia Huber, Sr. Celestine Worland, Sr. Pia Wyss, Sr. Justine Rinke, and Sr. Hilda Gabler."[10]

At this same time, personnel shortages were surfacing at the hospital. Some of the employees acted on their desire to contribute to the war effort and found jobs in ammunition and defense plants. As a result, St. Bernards began to experience a shortage of trained personnel. The relationship between the Sisters and the community served the hospital well, and many Jonesboro women came to the rescue as Red Cross aids. "These women were important for two reasons, first because of the actual help they gave, and second because their spirit of service, was a boost for overworked employees."[11]

Soon after celebrating her Diamond Jubilee (75 years), Mother Beatrice Renggli's health rapidly began to decline. The last five years of her life were, for the most part, spent in a wheelchair. She still managed to keep the convent financial account and to help with the accounts of the hospital. Sr. Agatha Knauf was assigned to be her attendant both for day and night.

"At the age of 94, the burden of keeping her mind alert in conversations with people became more labored. Dr. P.M. Lutterloh, her personal physician, kept a close watch on her. On September 6, 1942, Fr. William Kordsmeir was called to administer the last rites. He came again on September 7th at 11:30 p.m. to give her his blessing.

At 6 p.m. Sr. Felicitas Hunkeler came into her room to sing, "Maria zu Lieben..." for the last time for her. Immediately after, Sr. Agatha noticed a functional change and called the hospital Chaplain, Fr. Joseph Milan who came with the visiting priest, Fr. Frowin Koerdt, OSB. Both gave her absolution and blessing for her departing soul. Mother Beatrice breathed her last about 6:30 p.m. on September 7, 1942. Her body lies buried at the head of the third row in Holy Cross Cemetery in Jonesboro, along with 109 other Olivetan Benedictine Sisters."[12]

In 1943 Sr. Bernardine Grueninger, art instructor in the Academy began to paint entire crib sets on canvas, stretched on boards and supported by easels. In December of that same year, she displayed one set on the west porch of the 1923 annex of the hospital. This display of the Christmas story, in a background of appropriate scenery, included stable, shepherds, kings, beasts and birds. Patients, visitors and townspeople came to view her masterpiece and marveled at her ability. She also made some sets suitable for outdoor display, which she sold for $50 each. [13]

Christmas Crib display painted by Sr. Bernardine Grueninger.

The Sister of Holy Angels Convent experienced sadness when they heard news on the radio, that on February 16, 1944 the United States bombed the oldest Benedictine monastery (built in 529 A.D.), the Monastery of Monte Cassino, Italy. The Germans had captured the strategically located monastery and converted it into a fortress, from which they fought. The historic structure was destroyed, but the Nazi eventually surrendered.

Minutes of the July 3, 1944 meeting of Corporation Convent Maria Stein and St. Bernards Hospital, revealed another change in personnel. "Owing to the death of Sr. Cecilia (September 13, 1943) a member of the Board of Consultors, the President, (Mother Walburga), proposed Sr. Modesta Fetsch, as a member. This met with the approval of all the members." [14]

In Craighead County, as everywhere else throughout the U.S., people carefully followed the news about the war. There was great rejoicing when the Germans surrendered to the Allies on May 7, 1945. Following Germany's surrender the United States concentrated on the Pacific front. On August 6, 1945, the U.S. Air Force dropped an atomic bomb on Hiroshima and three days later dropped another on Nagasaki, with the same devastating results. Three days after the second bomb was dropped, Japan surrendered and the war was over.

The period following World War II was a period of dramatic growth and change. Throughout northeast Arkansas, young men, husbands and father were coming home to their families. It was a time of rejoicing and reuniting with loved ones. The post-war period was an economic boom time in northeast Arkansas and across the country.

First American Prioress

During 1945, a change was also in the air at Holy Angels. After 30 years, Mother Walburga's tenth term as Prioress expired during the summer of 1945. A canonical election was scheduled during July when most of the Sisters were at the motherhouse. This 1945 election resulted in a change in leadership of the Community. On July 2, 1945, Sr. Perpetua Reinart was elected the eighth Prioress of the Olivetan Benedictine Community of Jonesboro. She was the first American born Sister to be elected Prioress of the Jonesboro Community.

Mother Perpetua had been born in Roselle, Carroll County, Iowa on November 12, 1888, but the family had moved to Lindsay, Texas in 1900. She entered the Community and made her first vows in 1911. Since she had served as Subprioress under Mother Walburga, she was already familiar with the administration of the Corporation. SEE PROFILE IN APPENDIX.

Following the election, the customary annual Corporation Meeting was held to elect a president. The minutes of the July 2, 1945 meeting reveal the following:

"Of the 121 actual members of the Corporation, 91 answered the

Roll Call. The absent 30 were represented by their proxies.

Since the three-year term of our President, Mother Walburga had expired, the first duty of the assembly was to elect a President. Sr. Eugenia Brodel proposed that a chairman be appointed for this meeting. Sr. Celestine Worland made the motion that Sr. Felicitas Hunkeler act as chairman pro-tem. The motion was seconded by Sr. Edwarda End and approved by all the members.

"The chairman proceeded to the election of a President, nominating Reverend Mother M. Perpetua Reinart for this office. All members arose in assent, after the motion had been seconded by Sr. Josepha Waespe. The chairman's duty being completed, she retired as such.

The President then appointed Mother Walburga Hoegger as Vice-President, Sr. Antonia Holthouse as Secretary. These appointments met with unanimous approval. The following Council members were then appointed: Sr. Eugenia Brodel, Sr. Joseph Waespe, Sr. Felicitas Hunkeler, Sr. Celestine Worland, Sr. Pia Wyss, Sr. Justin Rinke, Sr. Hilda Gabler and Sr. Modesta Fetsch.

The minutes of the last general and special meetings were then read. A detailed account of the finances stating receipts and disbursements for the fiscal year, January 1, 1944 to January 1, 1945 was read to the Corporation members. A copy of the same is attached to these minutes. A copy of the financial report will be sent to their excellencies, Most. Rev. Bishop John B. Morris and the Most. Rev. Bishop Albert L. Fletcher.

The date selected for the 1946 Corporation Meeting was set for July 3, 1946, subject to change."[15]

These minutes were signed by the Prioress, Mother Perpetua Reinart, and Secretary, Sr. Antonia Holthouse.

Mother Perpetua continued the same schedules as Mother Walburga. The Little Office of the Blessed Virgin Mary was prayed in Latin and the Rosary was recited by the Community each afternoon. Rising was at 4:30 a.m. and the daily "horarium" continued as it had been observed, since its earliest days with few modifications. Mother Perpetua was conscientious about observing the daily "horarium" and set the example by always being present for community prayers.

According to oral history, her place was seldom empty in choir, unless she was away attending the annual retreat for superiors or when she visited the missions.

"One of the first major changes Mother Perpetua made was to open a Juniorate. It was housed in a dwelling on Jackson Street with Sr. Stella Kaiser in charge."[16] According to the records, Rev. Conleth Overman, the retreat Master that summer, had recommended it. Young girls could attend the Academy, while receiving some modified experiences and training to discern a religious vocation. Three girls from Muenster, Texas were the first applicants.

Shortly after this change in leadership, Mother Perpetua was faced with an unexpected challenge. The Pastor at St. Paul's Parish in Pocahontas, Fr. Edward Yaeger, approached Mother Perpetua about purchasing part of the land owned by Convent Maria Stein in Pocahontas. He wanted to build a rectory and new school. According to records in the archives, Mother Perpetua called a Council meeting to discuss the request. The Council members decided first to confer with Bishop Morris before giving any answer to Fr. Yaeger. On July 16, 1945, a Council meeting was called at which all members were present. Excerpts from the minutes of this meeting are as follows:

"This meeting was held to inform the Council members of Fr. Yaeger's plan of building. His plans are the tearing down of our Convent Maria Stein and using the better part of our property along Convent Street for the Parish Plant. A new Convent is to be built further north.

"The Council was unanimous in its opposition of the proposal, the cradle of our Community should be kept as a memorial for future edification. The humble beginning of our flourishing Institute should ever be kept before the members of this Community as visible example of the heroic sacrifices of the first members."[17]

Mother Perpetua communicated this decision to Fr. Yaeger and nothing more was heard of this until the following year.

After 22 years as pastor and builder of Blessed Sacrament Church and parish hall, Fr. Kordsmeier was transferred from Jonesboro. Fr. Kordsmeier had also served on the Hospital Advisory Board and assisted the Sisters in many ways during his tenure in

Jonesboro. On November 12, 1945, Fr. William Kordsmeier came to bid the Sisters good-by. The Sisters were saddened to see him leave, for during the early years he had often substituted as chaplain for both hospital and Convent, in addition to serving as pastor to the parish. His memory was held in esteem by all who knew him.

For the second time in the Twentieth Century, the Sisters at Holy Angels, along with the Catholics of the Diocese of Little Rock, mourned the death of their Ordinary. Bishop John B. Morris, DD, died on November 22, 1946. Bishop Morris had been the Ordinary from June 11, 1906 until his death, a span of 40 years Throughout this time, he had been a faithful guide and protector of the Olivetan Benedictine Community.

The funeral services for Bishop Morris were held at St. Andrew's Cathedral in Little Rock, with Samuel Cardinal Stritch, DD, his cousin, as the principal celebrant at the solemn requiem. According to records, a large number of Archbishops, Abbots and over 150 clergy attended the funeral. A delegation of Sisters from Holy Angels, along with religious from throughout the diocese, attended these services in Little Rock. Interment of Bishop Morris was in the Crypt below the Cathedral, along with his two predecessors, Bishop Andrew Byrne, DD and Bishop Edward Fitzgerald, DD.

A New Ordinary

Shortly after the death of Bishop Morris, Pope Pius XII named Auxiliary Bishop Albert L. Fletcher as the fourth Ordinary for the Diocese of Little Rock. Installation was set for March 10, 1947. Mother Perpetua, Sr. Philomena Willimann and Sr. Hedwig Peterli traveled to Little Rock to attend the installation of Bishop Albert L. Fletcher, DD, as the fourth Ordinary for the diocese. A number of the Sisters from various missions in Arkansas also attended the celebration.[18]

In February, 1947, the new pastor of St. Paul's in Pocahontas contacted Mother Perpetua again about the land his predecessor had tried to obtain. He had received a previous briefing from Bishop Fletcher about the property belonging to the Sisters, so he made another approach to Mother Perpetua. She therefore called a Council meeting on February 21, 1947. She presented the matter at hand: "Rev. Father Hinkley had our property and the Parish property surveyed. He gave us a copy of the blueprint. After being told that the decision of the Sisters was, No, that is they do not want to give up the North end of our property, Rev. Fr. Hinkley informed us that he was asked by the Most Rev. Bishop Albert L. Fletcher, in case the property was not obtainable, to give the Sisters the first chance to buy the lots adjoining our property from the Parish. The Parish had originally paid $1,500 for the land. The Sisters agreed to pay $1,500 for the above mentioned lots. After receiving the Warranty Deed, a check of $1,500 was given to Rev. Father Hinkley." [19] These minutes were signed by Mother Perpetua and Sr. Antonia.

Candidates from Texas 1947: L – R: Future Sr. Cabrini Arami, Sr. Joan Hess and Sr. Mary John Seyler.

Plans Accelerate

Meanwhile, with the war over, plans for the new hospital building, originally discussed years earlier were resurrected and by 1947 discussions began in earnest. However, following the war, building codes became more stringent and the old building, constructed in 1905, no longer met government regulations. It would have to be torn down, or at least no longer used for hospital purposes. The installation of a sprinkler system also would be required.

This would mean the hospital would lose 50 beds, just as many as they had planned to add. An architect carefully examined the building and decided that with appropriate changes it could be used for at least 15 more years.

Since the Community owned and administered the hospital, the Prioress and the Sisters made the decisions concerning St. Bernards. Mother Perpetua, with the Community vote, decided to delay erecting any new building and instead update the existing one as far as possible and install a sprinkler system.

Another persistent problem needed to be addressed for the operating rooms. According to the doctors, it is almost impossible to do without fans in the operating rooms. Mother Perpetual called a Council meeting to discuss the problem. In the minutes of the Council meeting of June 6, 1948, she stated, "They (doctors) are now using gases which are highly explosive and it is dangerous to use fans while they are administered. Therefore, we have to air-condition our operating rooms in order to make them safe for the use of such anesthetics as ethylene and cyclopropane, which are greatly in demand now. There are other reasons which really oblige us to air-condition the operating department."[20] The Council approved this expenditure to purchase the needed air-condition units.

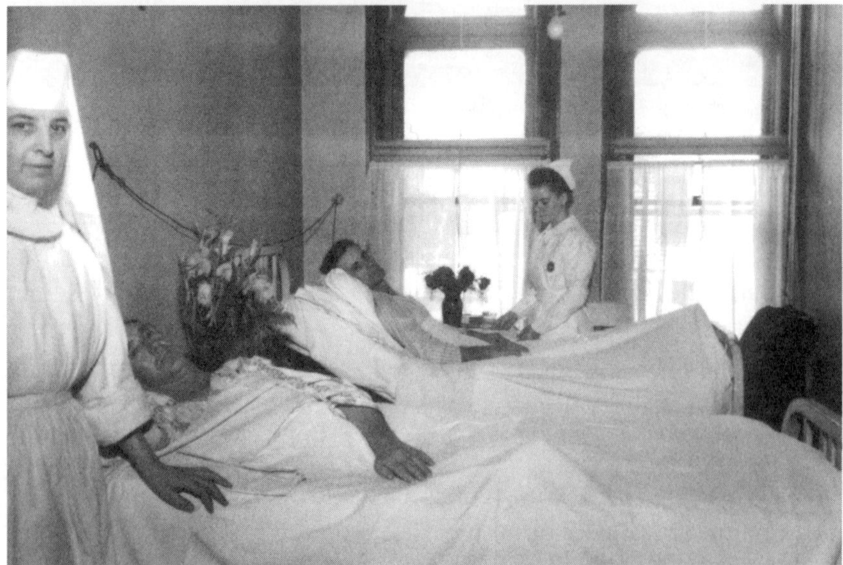

Sr. Mildred Felderhoff with patients in hospital semi-private room.

Improvements and Renovations

According to the Book of Ecclesiastes (3: 1-8), "There is a time for everything under the heavens," and at Holy Angels, it was now time for fixing up the Convent. Early during Mother Perpetua's tenure, she installed new machinery in the laundry. The old equipment needed to be replaced, so a new steel washer, additional dryers, and presses were added. A new and larger-size mangle was installed. Because of the increase in linens needed for the hospital and that of the growing community, lay people were hired to assist the Sisters and Academy girls who worked part-time to help pay off their tuition. For the first time, African Americans (called colored people at the time) were among the employees hired to assist in the laundry.

The Convent was completely refinished with paints and varnishes. According to records in the archives, the kitchen was also improved with the installation of stainless steel table tops, dish washers and food warmers. A new water heater, stainless steel sinks, and galvanized shelves were also installed. New equipment that was purchased included an electric mixer, a grinding machine and a slicing machine. Other significant improvements included the installation of a new walk-in refrigerator and spacious walk-in freezer.

Mother Perpetua again renovated the chapel. The altars were redesigned from the Romanesque to Liturgical. New sandblasted windows were installed. These Sr. Bernardine Grueninger painted in Campana Crystal colors to filter sufficient light into the chapel on ordinary days of sunshine. The process of outlining the symbols and pictures with heavy black lines gave the effect of stained glass windows.

Renovated Holy Angels Chapel — 1940s

Designs on the side windows depicted Jesus Christ in the Holy Eucharist and Mary, Mother of God, with titles from the Litany of Loretto. Other symbolic designs included the twelve degrees of humility and Benedictine Saints from the early centuries. The small back windows depicted the Eight Beatitudes. The windows in the choir loft represented the twelve Apostles and the Archangels. The rose window above the choir loft symbolized the Blessed Trinity. During the summer months, a number of young Sisters were called upon to assist in this project. The apprentice "artists" worked under the direction of Sr. Bernardine to fill in the outlines drawn by Sr. Bernardine.

Expansion Again

The needs of the hospital continued to persist. Often people had to wait an hour or more in the ambulance before a room could be made available. Something had to be done immediately to expand the facilities to accommodate the growing number of patients needing care. After prayerful consideration and discussion with the community, Mother Perpetua decided to act.

"On April 12, 1948, Msgr. John Healy, Msgr. Edwin Hemmen, Pastor of Blessed Sacrament Church, Dr. P.W. Lutterloh, Mr. Alan Patteson, Mr. Eugene Barton, Mother Perpetua, and Sr. Hilda Gabler assembled to reorganize the Advisory Board and to begin the formulation of plans for the new annex. They were resolved to relieve the growing inadequacy of hospital rooms and conveniences. This group decided on preliminary accumulation of funds preparatory to actual sketching of plans for construction." [21]

The plan for the new residence for nurses, which was originally considered, had to be abandoned because of costs and priority was given to building the hospital annex. Construction costs to meet the medical requirements for hospitals had now doubled since the construction of the 1923 building. "A fundraising drive began and again, the citizens of Jonesboro and surrounding areas pledged generous support to the building fund for a second Annex to St. Bernards Hospital." [22] The Sisters again helped to raise money for the building fund by holding bazaars and raffles.

Reaching Out

As they had for over 50 years, the Sisters at Holy Angels continued to reach out and support people in need. In May 1948, the United States Immigration Office solicited sponsors for displaced persons from Poland who had been captured and imprisoned by the German Army. The Sisters at Holy Angels and St. Bernards Hospital sponsored four of these displaced persons from Poland and provided them room and board while they worked in the hospital. Their living quarters were in one of the old wooden frame buildings on the grounds, no longer used for the hospital.

"One in particular, Alexander Kopiecki, worked as an orderly, since he had some previous medical training. Alex was a diligent worker and went on to complete college at Arkansas State College and serve in the U.S. Air Force. He moved to St. Louis, found good employment in the medical field, and married. Still, he continued to keep in contact with Sr. Helen Swirczynski, who had been in charge of the workmen's dining room when he was in Jonesboro. In 1998, Alex sent Sr. Helen an autographed copy of a book he published about his life. In this book, he pays great tribute to the Sisters in Jonesboro." [23]

Education Enhanced

Mother Perpetua placed great emphasis on education. Records reveal that on June 8, 1948, Mother Perpetua was re-elected for a second term. One of the first decisions she made during her new term was to send Sr. Celine Truebenbach, Sr. M. Michael Lange and Sr. Eymard Lemmer to Atchison for advanced studies at summer school. Sr. Theresina Grob, Sr. Geraldine Homer and Sr. Jerome Locken were sent to St. Louis University.

Sr. Leonarda Foehn and Sr. Modesta Fetsch received a Bachelor Degree in Music from Fontbonne College, St. Louis. They also received the designation as Catholic Choirmasters.

Postulants 1949 L – R: Future Sr. Romana Rohmer, Sr. Dennis Dougherty, Sr. Monica Swirczynski, Sr. Mary Anne Nuce, Sr. Dominica Wise and (center-postulant left community)

During this same summer, 15 Sisters attended the course in Gregorian chant given by Miss Pierick at the Cathedral of St. Andrew Parish Hall in Little Rock. They received six credit hours from the Teacher's College in Conway. Although crowded, they doubled up and stayed at the Sisters living quarters at St. Andrew's School.

The "mission Sisters" joined in with the "home Sisters" during the summer months to help with the canning of garden produce. According to Sr. Agnes in Green Olive Branch, "On August 4, 1948, they canned 200 bushels of peaches. In addition, 100 gallons of jelly were made and 140 gallons of tomatoes were harvested and canned from the convent gardens. Besides all this, there were the usual supply of beans, corn and other vegetables to be preserved."[24]

When summer school was over, and most of the Sisters were at the motherhouse, it was not "all work and no play." Fourth of July programs were frequently held in the auditorium. These included skits and talent acts with elaborate costumes. The Sisters "raided" the Academy costume closet for their riggings. A community orchestra also performed, with Sr. Leonarda Foehn as the lead violinist. According to Sr. Agnes in Green Olive Branch, "The first Lawn Supper was held at Holy Angels Convent on August 1, 1948. Three tables were arranged, and to avoid confusion, these were named, Fides, Spes, and Caritas. Each was designated by a different color, and matching cards were distributed to expedite serving. The same food was available at each table. After the meal there was a brisk entertainment which all the Sisters greatly enjoyed."[25]

On August 15, 1949, the largest class up to that time in the history of the Community of all American-born Sisters made profession of Perpetual Vows. This Class consisted of: Sr. Camille McNeil, Sr. Rose Lynch, Sr. Henrietta Hockle, Sr. Julia Pruss, Sr. Pauline Morath, and Sr. Barbara Ritter. In succeeding years, larger classes made Profession of Vows in the Community. During those years, Jubilee celebrations were also held on the same day. Plays and skits were frequently held in conjunction with these celebrations.

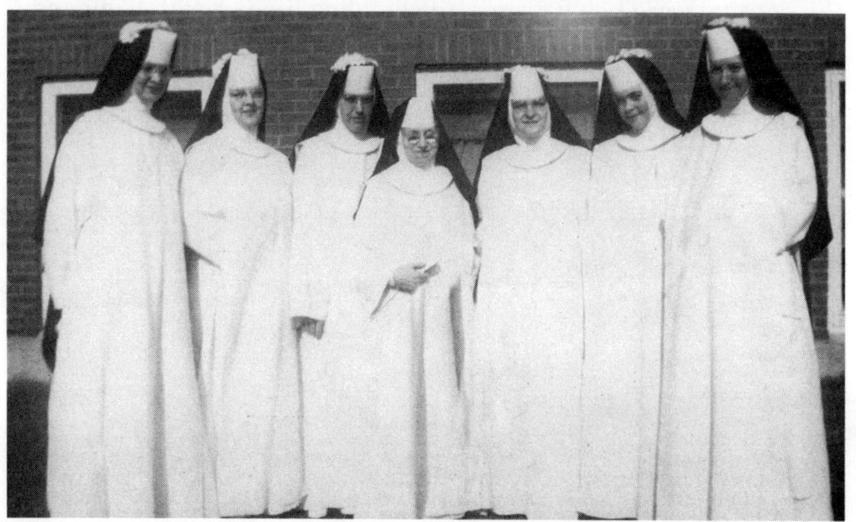

Sr. Alexia with Perpetual Vows Profession Class L – R: Sr. Barbara Ritter, Sr. Pauline Morath, Sr. Julia Pruss, Sr. Alexia Suter, Sr. Henrietta Hockle, Sr. Rose Lynch and Sr. Camille McNeil.

The Community continued to respond to requests for teachers in Parish schools throughout Arkansas. In 1949, at the request of the new pastor, Fr. John Boyce, Sr. Claudia Bichsel and Sr. Gabriel Koechner were sent to reopen St. Peter's School in Wynne after a closure of 39 years. This school closed again in 1973, due to a decline in enrollment.[26]

As new members continued to join the community, additional space was needed. Mother Perpetua had the second, third, and fourth floor porches on the west side of the 1929 Convent building enclosed with glass and linoleum placed on the floors. With added heating units, this made expanded work and study space on the second and third floors and additional sleeping quarters for Sisters on the fourth floor. There was a positive spirit among the young Sisters, as they were eager to make sacrifices and willing to accept the inconveniences of the time.

The hospital also experienced growth, as census records for 1949 showed that St. Bernards treated 6,486 patients for a grand total of 87,292 patients since the hospital opened in 1900. The Advisory Board and the hospital management set a goal of $600,000 to cover a 60-bed addition. As the decade came to a close, plans for the hospital were being drawn, the building fund was growing and a new annex was on its way.[27]

CHAPTER 11
1950-1959

Golden Jubilee of Hospital

As the decade of the 1950s dawned, the community began preparation to celebrate the Golden Jubilee of serving patients for 50 years in St. Bernards and the drive was begun to raise funds for the new addition. The hospital was growing along with the population of Craighead County, which had now reached 260,500.

For the first time since St. Bernards was founded, the Sisters decided to reach out to make a general area-wide public campaign for funds. Leadership of the Jonesboro community and of northeast Arkansas supported the drive for construction of the new wing, which was estimated to cost $600,000.

Mother Perpetua Reinart announced that, "Included in the $100,000 contribution made by the Benedictine Order was $10,000 left to the fund by M.P. Welch, the late business and civic leader of Jonesboro." As Mother Perpetua presented the initial contribution, she said, "There is no greater need or worthier cause than the enlargement of the hospital facilities here at St. Bernards. This pledge was made possible by united efforts and careful savings." [1]

This expansion reflected the Sisters' commitment to serve everyone who needed help. According to the June 22, 1950 edition of the *Jonesboro Sun*, W.L. Gatz of Paragould, Chairman of the Hospital Advisory Board, announced that 16 of the 60 beds to be added this year to St. Bernards Hospital would be reserved for Negroes. According to Mr. Gatz, "The decision to reserve slightly more than 25 percent of the additional beds was made Wednesday at a meeting of the Advisory Board and three representatives of the Negro Interdenominational Ministerial Alliance." [2]

The highlight of the Golden Jubilee of the hospital celebration was the groundbreaking ceremony for the new addition. In the absence Bishop of Fletcher, Monsignor John J. Healy, Director of Catholic Hospitals for the Diocese of Little Rock, was scheduled to officiate at the ceremony.

According to the July 4, 1950 edition of the *Jonesboro Sun,* "Reverend Healy will address those gathered to help celebrate the Golden Jubilee and will bless the ground on which the 60-bed annex will be constructed. Mayor Herbert Bosler will speak representing the City of Jonesboro. Charles Frierson, who helped direct the public subscription campaign, which raised approximately $340,000 toward the building cost, is also to make an address. The special ceremonies will begin at 3 p.m. on the east side of the hospital grounds. Conducted tours of the present hospital facilities will be offered for those interested. Hospital officials invite the public to attend."[3]

On July 5, 1950—the actual Jubilee Day—there was a pouring rain, but even that failed to disperse or daunt the crowd gathered for the groundbreaking ceremonies. Monsignor Healy turned the first spade of earth. During Mr. Frierson's address, he pointed out that Mother Perpetua announced that the Sisters had decided to forgo the possibility of applying for federal aid. For the remaining $260,000 needed to build the 60-bed annex, the Sisters decided to borrow the money and pay it back from earnings. He concluded his remarks by saying, "The hospital has always belonged to the people of this territory, and it still will."[4]

Community Loss

While the community was celebrating the Golden Jubilee of the hospital and all the activities of the groundbreaking ceremony, Mother Walburga became seriously ill. She was moved to a hospital room next to the chapel, where she died on July 12, 1950. As she lay dying around 7 p.m., most of the Sisters gathered near her room to pray and sing her favorite hymn, "Salve Regina." Mother Walburga's death marked the end of an era, as she had led the community and the hospital for 30 years as Prioress.

Mother Walburga had frequently prayed for rain and cooler

weather for all-important functions of the community, and this prayer was answered on her funeral day. A refreshing shower the day before had cooled the air for the many guests who attended the service. Since Bishop Fletcher was in Rome, Monsignor Healy, Vicar General of the Diocese of Little Rock, celebrated the solemn Requiem Mass.

The Rt. Reverend Paul Nahlen, OSB, Abbot of Subiaco Abbey, and also a number of Monsignors and Priests attended the funeral Mass. In addition, City officials and townspeople from Jonesboro and the surrounding area swelled the overflow crowd in chapel. Interment was in Holy Cross Cemetery in Jonesboro. Mother Walburga's body lies buried in the third row, next to that of Mother Beatrice, with the 109 other Sisters buried in the parish cemetery.[5]

Balancing the Enterprise

During the time the Community was placing emphasis on hospital ministry, the schools were not neglected. Because of the continued growth in enrollments throughout the diocese, Mother Perpetua responded to requests to send additional Sisters to teach in the parish schools. During the 1950s, summer school was an accepted way of life for most of the young Sisters. Retreat schedules were always adjusted to accommodate college schedules. New schools were being built and additional classrooms were added to accommodate the growing enrollments. According to Bishop Francis P. Keough, DD, President of the National Catholic Education Association in 1951, "Teachers were to prepare the children and youth for life as Citizens of Two Worlds." Religious instruction in schools kept pace with the steady acquisition of secular knowledge.

To parallel the emphasis being placed on religious education in schools, Mother Perpetua placed renewed emphasis on Community prayer and religious formation of the Sisters. She had a Community prayerbook compiled, containing all the prayers said in common, prayers to be said while dressing, morning and night prayers, De Profundis, Visit to the Blessed Sacrament, Novena prayers for special feasts, the Hour Prayer and others for private use. All the former prayers said in German were now translated into English. This Community prayer book was published by the Abbey Press, St. Meinrad, Indiana, December 2, 1950.[6]

Class of Novices Entering Chapel to make First Vows—1950 L – R: Future Sr. Monica Swirczynski, Sr. Dominica Wise, Sr. Romana Rohmer, Sr. Dennis Dougherty and Sr. Hildegarde (Mary Anne) Nuce.

Sr. Mary Anne presenting candle to Bishop Fletcher during Profession ceremony.

Since the Community handled the hospital affairs, the Council was frequently involved in making decisions for the direct operation of St. Bernards. According to Council Minutes of April 26, 1951, Monsignor Healy reported to the Sisters,

> "It does not appear necessary at present to borrow as much money as we had anticipated. 150,000 to 175,000 dollars should be sufficient, and it should not be necessary to borrow the money this year. This will be another savings provided the bankers will let us make this change without changing the rate of interest. Mr. Bill Gatz will meet with the bankers in a few days.
>
> Monsignor Healy also discussed the new appraisal of our buildings. The installation of the automatic sprinkler system has not only increased the value of the non-fire resistant buildings, but it has greatly reduced the insurance rate.
>
> Whereas, all our buildings and equipment at cost minus the depreciation were valued at $281,507.46. They are now valued at over a million dollars, therefore it will not be necessary to mortgage all our property. The hospital buildings alone are considered sufficient collateral for the loan. The buildings are now insured adequately without having to pay a great deal more for premiums."[7]

Changes Made

The Council was called on November 8, 1951 to discuss two items: first, the adoption of habits made of a new material, a cotton gabardine, which seems not to wrinkle so badly, but is more expensive than the cotton flannel; and second, a change in schedule for rising in the morning. All seemed in favor of both propositions so they were presented to the Community for a vote. Minutes of the Chapter meeting held on November 11, 1951, reveal the following.

"Members of the Community were made acquainted with the item of the proposed material for the new habit at a meeting on November 11, 1951, presided over by Reverend Mother Perpetua. Mother pointed out that these habits were to be worn by all on Sundays and those who had to appear in public. Two habits were on exhibit and the Sisters could look at them and see what they thought about them. The secret vote was held and it was a unanimous yes.

The condition—if the goods held up under several washings—was laid down. This will be tried out.

"A change in the schedule for rising was proposed. The Sisters were to get up at 4:55 a.m. instead of 4:30 a.m., morning prayers at 5:25 a.m., followed by Holy Office (Prime and Tierce), and then the points of meditation to follow, these to be read in succession without colloquies. Sext and None would follow the Mass after saying the Indulgence Prayer to Jesus Crucified. A vote was cast on this and it, too, was almost unanimous."[8]

Dedication of Hospital Addition

By July 11, 1952, the new hospital addition became a reality, when Bishop Fletcher, DD, officiated at the dedication. Beside Church dignitaries, state and local dignitaries also participated in the ceremonies. With this new addition the hospital now had a 150-bed capacity. The Sisters were able to continue their commitment to serve and maintain traditions begun earlier in the history of the Church. During the ceremony, Mother Perpetua stated, "There are many small and large gifts from friends, and of course whatever a Sister receives in the line of duty goes into the Community fund. Her needs are taken care of that she may devote herself to the service of Christ in the person of the sick and needy who will come in greater number with a greater St. Bernards."[9]

The 1952 hospital East Wing addition.

Constitution Revised

While placing emphasis on community life, Mother Perpetua also had the Constitution revised. This Constitution was a major revision to the one brought from Maria Rickenbach and used with minor revisions and adaptations throughout the first 65-year history of the community. This revision was in order, since now the new members entering the community were exclusively from the United States. In addition to the Council, the entire Community was invited to give suggestions. After a number of meetings, the revisions were completed and agreed upon by community vote.

This revised Constitution, entitled, "*Constitutions of the Olivetan Benedictine Sisters, Holy Angels Convent,*" was published in 1952. On the first page inside the front cover, Monsignor John B. Scheper, Diocesan Censor Librorum, is listed as giving his "Nihil Obstat,"on December 5, 1952, and Bishop Albert L. Fletcher, DD, as giving his "Imprimatur" on December 6, 1952.[10]

Mother Perpetua also commissioned a "*Book of Ceremonies,*" to be compiled in English for Investment of Novices, Profession of Temporary and Perpetual Vows, and the Renewal of Vows on the Twenty-Fifth and Fiftieth Anniversaries of Profession. This ceremonial book was published in Jonesboro in 1953. On the first page inside the front cover, Monsignor M.F. Donavan, (Censor Delegatus) is listed as giving the "Nihil Obstat," and Bishop Albert L. Fletcher, DD, as giving his "Imprimatur," both on August 4, 1953. This book was used for the first time for Investment Ceremonies on August 24, 1953. According to Sr. Agnes in Green Olive Branch, "Mother Perpetua also added the *Missa Recitata* and the Conventual High Mass with all the Sisters singing."[11]

A New Era

"In accordance with the Constitution of the Olivetan Benedictine Sisters, an election of Mother Prioress is to be held every three years. This necessity was fulfilled in 1954 both according to the original and the revised Constitutions."[12] By the summer of 1954,

Laundry day during the 1950s. Sisters standing, L – R: Barbara Ritter, Romana Rohmer, Leonarda Foehn and Richard Hess. Lay help: Mrs. Ed (Marie Novak), R.N.

Mother Perpetua's third term drew to a close, so she announced that July 2, 1954, as the date set for the election of the Prioress. This date was selected, as most of the Chapter members could be at the Motherhouse. At the close of the annual retreat, on the eve of July 2, Bishop Fletcher arrived in Jonesboro to conduct the election. He brought with him two priests from the Seminary to serve as tellers.

After the 6 a.m. High Mass in honor of the Holy Spirit, the Sisters gathered in the community room on third floor of the Convent for the election. After the opening preliminaries about the procedure and reading of the Rule, the Bishop and the two tellers retired to the library to await the vote of the Sisters.

Each Sister then filled out her ballot, sealed it, and proceeded into the library to drop the ballot into the chalice in front of the Bishop. The Sisters then filed back in silence to the Community room to await the results of the election.

After the ballots were counted and a majority was reached, Bishop Fletcher summoned the Sisters back to the library to hear the results of the election. He announced that Sr. Philippa Wavrick, a noted musician, was elected as the ninth Prioress of the Olivetan Benedictine Community. Mother Philippa was born in Burke, Idaho. She was baptized Cecilia Ruth in St. Alphonsus Church in Wallace, Idaho. Shortly after, the Wavrick family moved from Idaho to Arkansas where they settled on a 680 acre farm near Hardy. SEE PROFILE IN APPENDIX.

After the election process was completed, the Sisters processed to Chapel where the Bishop held Benediction of the Blessed Sacrament, followed by the Community singing the "Te Deum." As was the custom at the time, each Sister then filed to the front of Chapel in order of seniority, to promise obedience to the new Prioress by kissing the ring on her finger. This closing ceremony was followed by a festive meal in the dining room.

According to custom, the Community assembled again on the afternoon of July 2, 1954, to select a president for the legal Corporation of Convent Maria Stein and St. Bernards Hospital. Excerpts from the Minutes of that meeting reflect the following:

Of the 131 eligible Chapter members, 106 were present to answer the roll call."The first duty was to elect a new President. Sr. Leonarda Foehn proposed that a chairman be appointed for this meeting. Sr. Teresa Fetsch made the motion that Sr. Lucia act as chairman pro tem. The motion was seconded by Sr. Perpetua.

"The chairman proceeded to the election of a President, nominating Reverend Mother Philippa Wavrick for this office. All the members arose in assent after this motion had been seconded by Sr. Josepha. The chairman's duty being completed, she retired as such."

"The President then appointed Sr. Amora Felderhoff, Vice-President, Sr. Antonia Holthouse, Secretary and Sr. Thecla Lothenbach, Procuratrix."

"The following Sisters were nominated by the President for the office of Councilors and elected individually and separately by the majority through secret ballot of the Chapter. Sr. Fridoline Buck, Sr. Josepha Waespe, Sr. Stanislaus Niedzwiedz, Sr. Gerarda Carns, and Sr. Florentine Temple. In addition to these the President appointed the following four: Sr. Imelda Pels, Sr. Ida Egli, Sr. Maura Jorski, and Sr. Thomasine Walterscheid."[13]

According to Community custom, the Vice-President of the legal Corporation, also served as Subprioress of the Community. Therefore, Sr. Amora served in this capacity throughout Mother Philippa's tenure in office.

Shortly after Mother Philippa was elected Prioress, Fr. Edward

McCormick came to Jonesboro to request Olivetan Benedictine Sisters for St. Michael's School in West Memphis. Fr. McCormick wanted to reopen the school, which had been previously staffed by the Dominican Sisters of St. Catherine, Kentucky, and the same Community that staffed Siena College in Memphis, Tennessee. Since the Dominicans had ceased to teach in small schools, St. Michael's was one of the ones they left.

Mother Philippa sent Sr. Frances Hofbauer and Sr. Jane Frances Dallmer as the first Olivetans to teach in West Memphis. Fr. McCormick came to Jonesboro to take them to West Memphis on August 24, 1954.[14]

Customs Change

Sr. Philippa Wavrick's election as Prioress in 1954 began the prologue of renewal in the Community. She was a kindred soul of Pope John XXIII. The windows were opened, doors were unlocked, and a new breeze filled the air. Although Mother Perpetua Reinart (1945-1954) had been the first American Prioress of the Community, it was Mother Philippa, whose vision led the Community across the threshold to the Twentieth Century in customs and practices.

Up until her election, Sisters did not drive cars. If public transportation was not available, Sisters always had a chauffeur (one of the maintenance employees) to take them wherever they needed to go. First, Ed Novak, later James Novak, Ed's nephew, drove the Sisters for years. Permission to drive was a "break-through" for many of the Sisters. Mother Philippa gave permission for the Sisters to drive and soon additional cars were purchased as travel needs increased.

Next change was the option to swim. The Wavrick family had donated frontage property on the Spring River in Hardy to the Community. One day, Mother Philippa surprised the Sisters when she announced all were invited to go there for an outing. Soon swimming and enjoyable trips to Spring River in Hardy became a favorite Community outing. Later, the Community built a cabin on the property to afford more opportunities for the Sisters. After weeks of walking the floors at St. Bernards or teaching in the classroom, overnight stays at the cabin on Spring River became a coveted relaxation.

Another change occurred right in the back yard of the Convent. To provide relaxation for the Sisters, a swimming pool was built behind the Convent between the grape arbor and the building. This pool was enclosed with an eight-foot high board fence to provide privacy for the Sisters. At first, some of the doctors and hospital personnel were curious about what was going on behind that enclosure. However, when told about it, they were happy the Sisters had this new healthy opportunity for relaxation.

Summer School at St. Scholastica College Duluth, MN — 1956. Sr. Henrietta Hockle, Sr. Charlotte Jones, Sr. Carmelita Myers, Sr. Barbara Ritter and Sr. Georgia Felderhoff.

Mother Philippa continued to place great emphasis on education. She encouraged all the Sisters to become certified in their fields of teaching or nursing. In addition to attending Siena College in Memphis, a number of Sisters attended Benedictine Colleges in Atchison and Duluth, as well as, DePaul University, Chicago and Creighton University, Omaha. Those destined to work in the hospital attended St. Mary-Corwin Nursing School in Pueblo, Colorado, Sacred Heart School of Nursing, Yankton, South Dakota, and other noted education centers.

Due to the growing increase in membership in the community, there was a shortage of sleeping spaces for new members. Even though the Novitiate attic was utilized for sleeping quarters, they still needed room. The Council decided to discontinue accepting boarders for the Academy, beginning for the 1954-55 school term. The dormitory and private rooms on the second floor, formerly used by the Academy boarders was now utilized by the young Sisters.

Because of the hot, humid summers in northeast Arkansas, discussion arose on air-conditioning the Chapel. After conferring with air-conditioning consultants and with Lawrence Schneider, chief maintenance engineer, about the cost of air-conditioning the Chapel, Mother Philippa presented the matter to the Council. This decision was met with overwhelming approval. Therefore, the Chapel was air-conditioned and used for the first time during the summer of 1955. This addition brought welcome relief to both the Sisters and the visitors who attended the ceremonies of Investment and Profession of Vows on August 14 and 15, 1955.

In the Chapter meeting held on July 10, 1955, the Sisters addressed four significant topics that would affect the Community in future years. The first (1), closing St. Norbert's School in Marked Tree due to small enrollment; second (2), accepting a mission in Lake Arthur, Louisiana; third (3), recitation of the Divine Office; and fourth (4), discontinue wearing the mantles for Holy Communion.

According to the Minutes of this meeting, in order to accept the mission in Lake Arthur, it would be necessary for the community to close St. Norbert's School in Marked Tree. During the discussion, it was proposed that, if the Community voted to close Marked Tree, two Sisters would go there every Sunday to teach religion.

Mother Philippa stated that Fr. Pelous, Pastor in Lake Arthur, was eager to have at least two Sisters at first to teach Catechism and to visit in the homes. Later, they would establish a school and then need additional Sisters. She further stated, "I will ask for volunteers who feel they are capable of doing that kind of work."[15]

According to the Minutes, the Community voted by secret ballot in favor of closing St. Norbert's School in Marked Tree and accepting the mission in Lake Arthur, Louisiana.

The third and fourth topics were addressed as follows:

3. Divine Office – "The recitation of the Divine Office was favorably received. It was suggested that Compline be said in the evening instead of following Vespers, then Compline would become our official night prayer and Prime our morning prayer. Matins would drop out entirely." (Majority votes favored adopting the Divine Office as proposed.)
4. Mantles – "There was more opposition to doing away with the mantles. Some maintained that it was part of our garb and therefore we should wear it for Holy Communion. Also the mantle is a good coverage for those who are not so careful about their appearance. The idea of it being a part of our garb was easily refuted by stating the Holy Father's desire that Sisters simplify their garbs to conform with change of time.

Question posed – Should we wear the mantle for Holy Communion from May 1 to October 1" [16] (Results showed that majority favored not to wear the mantle from May 1 to October 1).

On August 25, 1955, Sr. Frances Hofbauer (Superior), Sr. Martina Bolds and Sr. Madonna Gahr left for their new Mission in Lake Arthur. The Olivetan Benedictine Monks had settled in Lake Arthur sometime earlier and built Regina Coeli Monastery. When they relocated later, they left the Monastery to the Parish to be used by the Sisters.

Throughout the succeeding 25 years, a number of other Sisters served in Maria Goretti Grade and High School in Lake Arthur. Happy memories are shared by the Sisters who experienced the "Cajun" warmth and hospitality during their years in the Bayou State. Due to the decline of Vocations by 1980, the Community voted to withdraw from Lake Arthur and concentrate on prior commitments in Arkansas and Texas.

In addition to Sisters going off to study, a special series on the Liturgy and Benedictine Spirituality was inaugurated in 1955 at the

Motherhouse. Fr. Wilfred Tunik, OSB, from St. Pius X Monastery, Pevely, Missouri, traveled to Jonesboro to give monthly lectures. It was Fr. Wilfred, who instructed the Sisters in the rubrics in praying the Divine Office in English using the Monastic Diurnal. The first hour recited was Compline, which was the beginning of a new era at Holy Angels. "This is the day that the Lord hath made. Let us be glad and rejoice in it." Thus spoke Fr. Wilfred as he inaugurated instructions on the Divine Office on the eighteenth of October, the Feast of St. Luke, the Evangelist.

Father further stated, "I do not believe there is to be a day of greater importance in the history of your Community than this day. And I do not think any event in the history of your Community will ever equal in importance, in dignity and in effect the event that will transpire today; namely, the introduction of the English Office into your Religious Life. I think that, because we cannot live well unless we pray well, and we do not pray well unless we understand what we pray.

"I hope the English Office will be the occasion of the flourishing of all the virtues for you, especially that of love for one another, that of devotion to your Community, that of zeal for the service of God."

"Beginning today, you are going forward to pray with the Church as she proceeds through the year from day to day. As your proceed with her, as she draws you along day by day, your soul will be fed, you will be lifted up into the arms of your Heavenly Father."

That day will indeed remain forever in our memories, although the Sisters spent many practices on the Hour of Compline, after two periods of intense instruction and practice with Fr. Wilfred, the Community sang their first Hour of the Divine Office in English.[17]

During the summer of 1956, the Community again voted on a change in the material for the habits. Mother Philippa displayed samples of factory-made dacron habits (full length) with scapulars. Each Sister was measured so the habits would fit properly. Mother Philippa announced that two new habits would be ordered for each Sister, and worn for Sundays or out in public. The old ones would be used for everyday and around the Convent.

Original Convent Building Replaced

Although the official motherhouse was relocated to Jonesboro in 1898, Sisters continued to live in the original Convent building in Pocahontas. Some taught in St. Paul's Parish School, while several others did support work in housekeeping and gardening. A significant development occurred in February of 1956, when it became apparent that the Sisters in Pocahontas needed new living quarters. According to Pocahontas contractors, the old convent buildings were beyond repair. Since the Community owned the property and buildings in Pocahontas, this responsibility rested with the Community.

On February 12, 1956, the Council members voted in favor of replacing the buildings. "It was decided that Mr. Wm. Barthel be contacted to draw up a plan and estimate expenditures for the erection of an entirely new Convent. We hope the work can start in April. Detailed plans will be made after general plan and estimates are given."[18]

On June 10, 1957, the new facility was dedicated by Bishop Albert L. Fletcher, DD and named, Immaculate Heart of Mary Convent. The Sisters stationed in Pocahontas were happy to be able to move into their new quarters. Especially the younger members, who had been sharing the dormitory in the old two-story Novitiate building. The Monks of Pius X Monastery in Pevely, Missouri, were engaged to make furniture for the new Convent in Pocahontas, including beds, desks and even the beautiful Chapel furnishings.

Immaculate Heart of Mary Convent, Pocahontas — 1958

On June 10, 1957, Mother Philippa was elected to a second three-year term. The Community continued to grow and the ministries in hospital work and in Catholic schools continued to flourish. In the spring of 1958, another custom changed in the Community. Mother Philippa announced that a small glass of fruit juice would be served for breakfast in addition to the usual menu of coffee, cereal and toast. She stated that doctors had recommended this addition for health reasons. For the first time on Mothers' Day that year, the Sisters enjoyed the special treat. This custom of having fruit juice for breakfast has continued to present time.

Policy Change

Up to this time, it was customary for the Convent to provide transportation for the Sisters to go to and from the Missions. Several of the Missions at a greater distance were allowed to use the car during the school year and then return home in it at the end of the school year. On November 26, 1957, a Council Meeting was called to discuss a particular problem concerning one of the cars.

"The first point of discussion was the Sisters' car at Holy Souls. The car the Sisters are now using is in such bad shape, that repair is very expensive, and driving it any distance is unsafe. The question was: Should the Convent buy the car and have the Sisters at Holy Souls pay the Convent installments, or should Holy Souls Parish furnish the car for the Sisters?

"After due deliberation, the Council decided that the Convent should buy a station wagon for greater accommodation and have it for use at home during the summer months and in going to and from the Mission."[19]

Later this policy was changed as a diocesan policy was inaugurated that mandated parishes should furnish the cars for the Sisters on a Mission.

New Openings

Although Our Lady of Fatima Parish in Benton, had been established earlier, the parishioners built a school in 1957. However, it did not open because Fr. Charles McGinnis, the Pastor, could not find Sisters to teach there. The building stood empty until 1959, when he petitioned Mother Philippa for Sisters to teach in the school. The Council approved to send two Sisters to Benton to teach the first four grades. The plan was to add a grade each year until all eight grades would be represented.

According to Sr. Agnes in Green Olive Branch, Sr. Alberta Krebs and Sr. Laura Schneider were sent to Benton on September 9, 1959. "The Sisters were assigned to live in the rectory while the pastor confined himself to the small room in the school, later designated 'the office.'" The school was first called Notre Dame, but later changed to that of the Parish, Our Lady of Fatima. The Sisters' Convent was completed the following year, and as additional grades were added, additional Sisters were assigned to teach in Benton.[20]

Although the school continues to flourish today in the hands of competent lay teachers, 1998 marked the last year, Sisters would be stationed there. The loss of Community members and the decline in vocations caused this change.

Sr. Jane Frances Dallmer's third and fourth grade class at Holy Souls School, Little Rock, Typical Classroom—1950s.

In April 1959, Fr. Joseph Lauro pastor of St. Elizabeth Church in Eureka Springs, northwest Arkansas, begged the Sisters to staff a hospital there. After discussing with the Council, Mother Philippa published the fact that the Olivetan Benedictines agreed to staff Carroll County Hospital in Eureka Springs.

"When Mayor C.C. King was informed of their willingness to assume responsibility, he and the city officials immediately arranged to build the hospital as a 26 bed institution."[21] According to records, Mother Philippa sent Sr. Stanislaus Niedewitz, RN, as superior and administrator of the new hospital with Sr. Hilda Gabler as Record Librarian and adviser. Sr. Mathilda Sparber accompanied the two Sisters and served as housekeeper.

Another opening in the Bayou State occurred for the Olivetan Benedictine Sisters in the Spring of 1959, when Bishop Schexnader requested Sisters to teach Religious Education in a Catechetical Center in Erath, Louisiana. Mother Philippa accepted this invitation and sent Sr. Lucia Staubli and Sr. Aloysia Kleis to begin the new adventure. They were accompanied by Sr. Anselma Haverkamp as housekeeper and cook.[22] Other Sisters staffed this center for the next few years, but the Community withdrew in 1962 due to decline in vocations.

While all this activity was going on at the Missions away from the Motherhouse, the hospital also continued to expand its range of services. In 1959 St. Bernards requested and received a license from the Arkansas Pharmacy Board to open a pharmacy. Before this time, some medicines were kept on hand in the Central Supply, others were delivered from the local drugstore when physicians prescribed them. Sr. Rita Sparber, Hospital Administrator, advertised for a pharmacist and John Turner, who had graduated that same Spring from the Pharmacy School at the University of Tennessee, responded to the ad. After Mr. Turner came for an interview with Sr. Rita, she said, "You are an answer to prayer," and he accepted the position.

As the first pharmacist at St. Bernards, Mr. Turner started in a small room, but over the next 25 years, he saw the pharmacy grow from a small room to a full-size department where now more than 23 full and part-time employees work.

New Organ

Since the original organ in the Convent Chapel had been used since 1905, it was now out of order for quite some time. Mother Philippa could not find anyone to repair it. She called a council meeting on November 28, 1959, to discuss the possibility of purchasing a replacement. According to the Minutes of this meeting, the cost of a new organ would be $6,000. It was suggested that the organ could be paid for with the income from making Hosts for the different parishes, and from gift money the Sisters receive.

The Council voted to approve this purchase and expressed hope that the new organ could be installed by Christmas.[23] According to oral history, Mother Philippa, an accomplished musician and composer, was the first to play on the new organ. Since the Chapel adjoined the hospital on the south side, she would sometimes surprise the patients by filling the hallways with beautiful renditions of familiar hymns.

New entrance to chapel.

As the decade of the 1950s drew to a close, the spirit of Mother Beatrice continued to live on in the elected leadership of the Community. Vocations were on the rise and membership in the Community continued to grow. Catholic Schools were flourishing and new hospitals were on the rise. The Olivetan Benedictines of Jonesboro continued to respond to these needs as far as personnel allowed.

During this time, the Juniorate also attracted young ladies right after graduating from the eighth grade. They could enter the Juniorate and attend classes at the Academy, while discerning their vocation. Although vocations came from Jonesboro and various other places, a significant number of young ladies came from Sacred Heart School, Muenster, Texas. Housing needs for the new members soon became a growing concern at Holy Angels.

This influx of vocations at Holy Angels parallels that of other Religious Communities throughout the country. This time was considered by some historians, as the "Golden Age" for Vocations in the United States. However, during the rapid growth and development after the close of World War II, there was a restlessness in society that spilled over to religious communities in the United States.

CHAPTER 12

1960-1969

Era of Changes

As the decade of the 1960s unfolded, changes implemented during the 1950s were only the beginning of what was to follow. Although Mother Philippa had implemented a number of changes since taking office in 1954, she was only the bridge between the tightly-structured old ways and the burgeoning life-style soon to come as a result of the Second Vatican Council of 1962-1965.

Pope John XXIII astounded the world on January 25, 1959, by announcing his intention to convoke the 21st Ecumenical Council, the first since Vatican Council I (1869-1870). On Christmas Day, December 1961, he officially convoked the Second Vatican Council for some time in 1962.

After almost four years of preparation, the Second Vatican Council opened on October 11, 1962, closing three years later, December 8. Although John XXIII died on June 3, 1963, his successor, Pope Paul VI vigorously pursued the agenda set out by his predecessor. He intended to complete and implement the Council convened in 1961 by John XXIII.

Of the sixteen documents produced by the Bishops at Vatican II the one most pertinent to religious communities was the Decree on the Appropriate Renewal of Religious Life, promulgated on October 28, 1965.

The appropriate renewal of religious life involved two simultaneous processes:

"1) A continuous return to the original sources of all Christian life and to the original inspiration behind a given community and
2) an adjustment of the community to the changed

> conditions of the times... constitutions, directories, custom books, books of prayers and ceremonies... are to be suitably revised and brought into harmony with the documents of the Sacred Synod.

This task will require the suppression of outmoded regulations." [1]

Academy Closes

Due to the growing increase in membership in the Community, there was a growing concern for bed space for new members. The decision made in 1954 to discontinue accepting boarders for the Academy had an adverse effect on the enrollment. Girls who had formerly attended from Weiner, Blytheville and as far away as Little Rock and southern Missouri were no longer able to attend. Too few local girls registered to warrant the teachers holding a class.

By the summer of 1962, the Community Council decided that the Academy, which had been opened by Mother Walburga in 1930, was to be closed. The girls already enrolled in grades 10, 11 and 12 had to transfer to the Jonesboro Public School to complete their high school studies.

Sr. Bernardine Grueninger in art room with fine arts class — 1960s.

Unrest

The unrest that had begun to infiltrate religious communities in the 1950s escalated in the 1960s and the Jonesboro Community was no exception. The national media and various publications were reporting changes taking place in religious communities throughout the country, and this caused a number of the Olivetan Benedictines to reconsider their vocation and some asked for a dispensation from their Vows.

Mother Philippa made efforts to respond to this unrest by providing varied options for recreation, such as listening to classical music, swimming and outings at the cabin at Hardy. However, this did not stop the trend. This was only the beginning of the exodus that would follow in succeeding years. By the year 1962-63, Mother Philippa separated the Junior Professed Sisters from the Novitiate and placed Sr. Georgia Felderhoff in charge, while Sr. Louise Frankenberger continued with the Novitiate. The following year, Sr. Georgia was also placed in charge of the Novitiate.

Nursing School Closed

Sr. Pia Wiss bidding farewell to nurses at the close of the School of Nursing — 1962.

By 1962, St. Bernards School of Nursing, which had been chartered in 1921, had to be closed. The American Hospital Association enacted new regulations that required Nursing Schools to be affiliated with a College or University. A program for a Registered Nurse would now entail a four-year degree program, instead of the three-year program offered by St. Bernards.

This regulation effected a great hardship on young people in the area who were interested in pursuing a career in nursing. Arkansas State (College) University was not prepared to offer a degree in nursing at that time. However, in collaboration with St. Bernards, ASU administration began plans to open such a program by 1968.

Honorarium Increased

On June 18, 1962, Bishop Fletcher sent a letter to Superiors of all religious Communities in the diocese, stating the increase in "honoraria" for the teaching Sisters.

"The honorarium for each Sister teaching in the parochial schools in the Diocese of Little Rock having a total enrollment, including kindergarten, elementary and secondary pupils of 75 pupils or less, shall be $65 each month for 12 months beginning September 1st of each year. For Sisters teaching in schools having an enrollment of 76 pupils or more, the honorarium shall be $75 per month for 12 months.

The parish is to provide, free to the Sisters, the convent with proper furnishings, light, water, heat and telephone. In the event the parish does not provide the above, each Sister teaching in the parochial school is to receive an additional $120 per year." [2]

Up to this time, the parishes had paid $50 a month per each teaching Sister. However some of the parishes were not able to provide even this amount, but the Sisters continued to teach regardless of what they paid. The parishioners were eager to help as much as possible by providing fresh vegetables from their gardens and those who lived on a farm contributed fresh meat on occasion.

Most parishes held a "Pantry Shower" for the Sisters upon their return from the Motherhouse in late August. The parishioners were generous in contributing some of their canned goods to help during the winter months. Although the Sisters received contributions of food and were provided housing and utilities, other expenses would arise.

The local Superior would use the monthly salaries to pay for other mission expenses and send the remainder to the Motherhouse.

In some instances, there was very little cash left to send back to the Motherhouse. During the annual Community Chapter each summer, a report was read telling the amount each mission sent to the Motherhouse. This information sometimes created a competitive feeling among the local Superiors, as some were reluctant to spend money for the needs of the local community, just to be able to send more money home. This practice of reporting this information was later discontinued.

New Iberia

After the dedication of the New Iberia Parish Hospital, on September 11, 1960, Sr. Mildred Felderhoff, the first Administrator received wide acclaim from the civic community for her expertise in operation. Bishop Maurice Schexnader, DD, Diocese of Lafayette, Louisiana, also took notice and spearheaded a drive to build a home for the aged next to the hospital. The Diocese purchased land adjacent to the hospital and erected the building. "It was built to accommodate 75 aged residents, regardless of sex, religious affiliations, race or nationality."[3]

After completion of the building in 1961, Bishop Schexnader turned to the Olivetan Benedictines to operate the facility, named "Consolata Home." Mother Philippa responded to his request by appointing Sr. Benedicta Boeckmann, as the first Administrator of Consolata Home. Sr. Benedicta held a Certificate of Administration of Nursing Homes from the Catholic Hospital Association Training Program. She organized and administered the diocesan sponsored retirement home with distinction, regardless of race, color or creed.

Residents in this facility had the advantage of having their doctor close by since it was on the same grounds as New Iberia Parish Hospital, which was also operated by the Olivetan Benedictine Sisters of Jonesboro. A resident Catholic priest was available whenever needed by the residents. The home grew in popularity and soon there was a waiting list for admissions. The Bishop, himself, frequently visited the home, as he felt it was his special project for the people in that area.

Day Care

Due to a shift in the residential area in Little Rock, the downtown St. Andrew's Cathedral School, staffed by the Jonesboro Benedictines since 1907, was closed in 1961. The pupils then transferred to St. Edwards School just a few blocks away. A new ministry, a "Day Nursery," was begun in September of that same year at the former St. Andrew's Cathedral School. Sr. Modesta Fetch was named superior and taught music. Sr. Regina Willett, Sr. Christopher Flowers and Sr. Dominica Wise were assigned to the Day Nursery. The following year, Sr. Dominica directed the Day Care Program and Sr. Modesta continued as superior and music teacher.

Sr. Dominica continued her studies and later received a degree in Early Childhood Education. She has continued in administering the Day Care Program to the present time. The Day Care was relocated in 1969 when the St. Andrew's Cathedral property was sold. The Day Care was renamed "Little Angels Day Care" and relocated to St. Theresa's Parish in south Little Rock. [4]

Lay Administrator at St. Bernards

The decade of the 1960s also brought about further changes to St. Bernards. "After having directly administered St. Bernards for the first 61 years, the Sisters decided it was time to hire a lay administrator. Government regulations, legal requirements, the proliferation of specialties and rising standards required leadership with expertise in these fields.

In consultation with the Advisory Board, Mother Philippa Wavrick and the Sisters' Council hired John W. Foley of Flint, Michigan on July 18, 1961 as the first lay administrator. He had been assistant administrator at St. Joseph's Hospital, a 408-bed hospital in Flint. He and his family moved to Jonesboro in August 1961." [5]

To ensure a smooth transition and a continuation of the Sisters' mission and tradition of service at St. Bernards, Sr. Thomasine Walterscheid, who was certified in hospital administration, was named Associate Administrator. The Sisters continued as heads of a number of hospital departments and many worked on the floors.

Hospital Corporation Separated

St. Bernards had been incorporated with Convent Maria Stein as a benevolent non-profit institution since 1928. However, in response to continuing changes in both health care and Church regulations, the Sisters felt it was now time to establish two separate corporations. Mother Philippa Wavrick and the entire Chapter of Sisters voted to separate the Corporation Convent Maria Stein and St. Bernards Hospital into two distinct corporations, namely Olivetan Benedictine Sisters, Inc. and St. Bernards Hospital, Inc. All Sisters (permanent members) are "ipso facto" members of both corporations. The first meeting of St. Bernards Hospital was held on July 2, 1962.

The Resolution signed on June 15, 1962, by Sr. Antonia Holthouse, Secretary of Convent Maria Stein and St. Bernards Hospital states, "The affairs of said corporation, operating under the name and style of St. Bernards Hospital, Inc. shall be operated exclusively for charitable, scientific and educational purposes as stated in the Articles of Association of St. Bernards Hospital, Inc."[6]

At this time the Sisters named a Governing Board for St. Bernards. The Governing Board structure formalized the strong bonds between the Sisters and the Jonesboro community leaders. "Membership shall consist of 11 voting members, five of whom shall be members of the Olivetan Benedictine Sisters, including the Prioress of Holy Angels Convent, and the other six shall be lay citizens of Jonesboro or the northeast Arkansas community."[7] In 1967, when a business manager was engaged for Olivetan Benedictine Sisters, he was designated as one of the lay board members to represent the Community. In addition to the Governing Board, the bylaws called for an Advisory Board with members to be appointed by the chairperson of the Governing Board. Certificates separating the corporation to the Olivetan Benedictine Sisters, Inc. and St. Bernards Hospital, Inc. were signed by the Clerk, Searcy Taylor, and filed for the record in the office of the Circuit Court for the Jonesboro District of Craighead

County, Arkansas on June 16, 1962.[8]

Both the governance and the structure of the hospital continued to evolve in response to health needs. "By June 10, 1962, Sid Frier, the Jonesboro architect who had carefully checked the construction progress of the north wing of the hospital, declared it was ready for occupancy and could be opened for use. On July 8, 1962, Mr. Foley announced that the new annex had been built and the older sections modernized without any public solicitation of funds and that memorial gifts to purchase equipment for the new $1 million annex were being accepted.

Mr. Foley stated, "A Federal grant under the Hill-Burton Act paid nearly $600,000 but the remainder is being paid from hospital funds, memorial gifts and donations. Twelve doctors on the staff at St. Bernards made memorial gifts to the hospital that will furnish an entire floor of the annex. To furnish a room, a memorial of $750 is required." [9]

The total number of beds was raised to 207, with new X-ray, pathology and pharmacy departments, new emergency rooms and laboratories. A tunnel connected the hospital with the newly constructed laundry, enlarged and modernized to care for both hospital and Convent laundry.

Diamond Jubilee

On August 15, 16, and 17, 1962, the Olivetan Benedictine Sisters celebrated their Diamond Jubilee of founding. The Community commemorated their 75th year of service to northeast Arkansas. The special Diamond Jubilee bulletin published for this occasion stated, "To begin a three-day Diamond Jubilee celebration, the Olivetan Benedictine Sisters of Jonesboro, Arkansas, chose the Feast of Our Lady's Assumption."

The first day, August 15, was appropriately designated as Community Day for the Sisters and their Relatives. Contributing a major role in the celebrations and ceremonies of this first day, 11 Sisters pronounced their Perpetual Vows. Following the Pontifical Mass by Bishop Albert L. Fletcher, DD, a festive meal was enjoyed by all in the Convent Refectory.

August 16, Clergy Day, was attended by many of the priests, especially from parishes where the Sisters served. The day opened with a Pontifical Mass celebrated by Bishop Fletcher and assisted by the visiting priests. This second day reached its climax with the consecration of the new Jubilee Bell, "Walburga," which was destined for the new motherhouse whenever it would be built. Following the Ceremony of the Bell, the Bishop dedicated the new wing of St. Bernard's Hospital, which was completed in August.

Jubilee Bell, christened "Walburga" by Bishop Albert L. Fletcher, DD on October 16, 1962

The final day of the Jubilee celebration was devoted to friends and benefactors. A silver tea was held in their honor. A large crowd visited the Convent that afternoon and enjoyed a tour of the facilities, both, the public areas of the Convent and the new hospital wing. The tour was followed by refreshments and visiting with the Sisters in the auditorium.

Health Care Expanded

Health care needs continued to change and in April of 1963, St. Bernards opened a 25-bed section for chronically ill convalescent patients. Mr. Foley announced, "After an extensive remodeling program, the section formerly known as H-2 (1905 brick building), has been converted into a cheerful, modern unit. Because the amount of nursing care needed is less, rates are considerably lower than those in the general hospital." [10] The unit was named "Justine Hall," in memory of Sr. Justine Rinke, one of the first nursing Sisters at St. Bernards.

Also in 1963, the Sisters of Mercy, contacted Mother Philippa about assuming responsibility of operating Mercy-Gazzola Memorial

Hospital in Brinkley. Due to a shortage of personnel, the Sisters of Mercy wanted another Community to administer the hospital. They asked to transfer both property and administration to the Olivetan Benedictine Sisters. Mother Philippa and Community acceded to the proposal and accepted the administration on December 28, 1963.

The official transfer of the property took place at midnight on December 31, 1964. Sister Thomasine Walterscheid was appointed the new administrator. Sr. Eileen Schneider was assigned to the business office, while Sr. Elaine Willett, R.N and Sr. Benita Drew, R.N. were assigned nursing duties. The people of Brinkley were agreeable to the change and supported the efforts of the Jonesboro Benedictines. A nursing home was later added to provide care for the senior citizens in that area. [11]

Mother Philippa undertook a second million-dollar enlargement of St. Bernards in 1963. According to the Jonesboro Sun, June 8, 1963, "Ground breaking ceremonies would be held for a 200 bed addition to St. Bernards at 2 p.m. today. This is the second phase of a three-part expansion program. The new wing is being built with money from a Federal Hill-Burton Grant and a bond issue, which will be paid from hospital revenues.

"The ceremonies will take place immediately east of the present hospital building at the corner of Matthews and Carson. Church, hospital and civic officials will participate in the ceremonies. Bishop Albert L. Fletcher, DD, of the Diocese of Little Rock will officiate." [12]

The Jonesboro Benedictines accepted a fifth institution of healing when the Muenster Memorial Hospital was built. Sr. Mildred Felderhoff, a native of Muenster, was appointed the first administrator of the Muenster Memorial Hospital, which was opened on January 19, 1964. Fr. Alcuin Kubis, OSB, the local pastor of Sacred Heart Church blessed the new hospital building.[13]

Hardy Property

According to records in the Archives, the Community purchased 170 acres for $25,000 in Fulton County, near Hardy in 1964. The property known as the "Hightower Place" bordered the south side of Spring River and adjoined that of Godfrey Wavrick. Mother Philippa signed the purchase agreement, dated March 11, 1964. The Warranty Deed read as follows: "KNOW ALL MEN BY THESE PRESENTS: *That we, Frank L. Souter and Allean Souter, his wife for and in consideration of the sum of Twenty Five Thousand and no/100 to us paid by Olivetan Benedictine Sisters, Inc. do hereby Grant, Bargain, Sell and Convey unto said Olivetan Benedictine Sisters and unto their heirs and assign forever, the following lands, lying in the County of Fulton and State of Arkansas, to wit:* S 1/2 NW, NE of SW, Pt. NE NW 30 acres, Pt. NW NEW 10 acres, Pt. West 1/2 NE lying on South West side of South Fork of Spring River, and containing in the aggregate 170 acres more or less, all lying in Sec. 12 Township 19 N. Range 6 West, of the 5th Principal Meridian in Arkansas." [14]

This Warranty Deed was signed by William D. Graybill, the Notary Public, on the 11th day of March, 1964 and filed for the record in the County Clerk's office by L.W. Love, Clerk.

Mother Philippa envisioned that the future Motherhouse would someday be built on this property. However, there were different opinions among the Sisters. Some felt favorable to the idea, while others thought it was too far away from the Medical Center and the College in Jonesboro. Consequently, no immediate plans were made at that time. Bishop Fletcher, the Ordinary, had not yet approved the location for the new Motherhouse, as he wanted more time to study the proposal. He requested that copies of all papers and documents pertaining to the property be sent to him.

Changes Continue

By 1964, another change was implemented in the Jonesboro Community. Up to this time, only the nurses were allowed to wear wrist-watches. They needed a watch with second hand when taking blood pressure in the hospital. All other Sisters wore pocket watches, which were usually worn on a pull chain under the scapular.

Because of changing customs and the increased cost of repairing pocket watches, Mother Philippa announced that all the Sisters would now be allowed to wear a wrist-watch. On December 12, 1964, the Community purchased from Capital Jewelers in Little Rock, for a sum of $1,231.96, wrist-watches for all those who requested one. A footnote was penned on the bottom of the statement, "Most of this amount was refunded." [15]

Jubilee Celebration 1965 — Seated, L – R: Mother Walburga Hoegger (65) and Sr. Eugenia Brodell (75). Standing, L – R: Sr. Paula Dietsche, Sr. Lioba Suter and Sr. Amora Felderhoff (50).

In the spirit of ecumenism and in compliance with the wishes of Pope Pius XII to simplify the religious garb, the Olivetan Benedictines made a major change in 1965. Mother Philippa proposed that a soft collar be used instead of the traditional pleated "collarium" or coif historically worn by Benedictines. Because of the time consumed in pleating the "collariums," (and machine breaking down frequently), the Sisters voted overwhelmingly for this change.

The sewing department, under the direction of Sr. Conrad Frankenberger, began sewing in earnest and the Sisters worked "over time" to make the new collars and headbands to meet the desired deadline. According to records in the archives, "On June 15, 1965, the Feast of the Sacred Heart, the Sisters donned for the first time, the circular, soft collar. A white band on the veil was used to go over the headband and tie behind the head. However, the long habit and scapular were retained."[16]

Another first for the Community occurred in December 1965. According to the *Jonesboro Sun*, December 29, 1965:

"Open House was held for the first time Sunday (December 27) and Monday nights at Holy Angels Convent for the purpose of informing the public of the way of life at the Convent.

"Sisters took the visitors on tours of areas, which had never been opened before to non-Catholics. They saw the beautiful paintings in the art department and visited the recreation room, chapel, TV lounge, Novitiate, music library, sewing department, dormitory—even the print shop. It's going to be an annual affair, so plan to attend next year."[17]

As Mother Philippa continued to respond to changing times, she was open to new opportunities. A local banker, Herbert McAdams, who handled some of the Convent's accounts, offered to provide flying lessons to Mother Philippa. He felt this would save her time in visiting the distant missions and when attending meetings.

Mother Philippa accepted his offer and took her first flying lesson on October 1, 1965. Truman, her instructor, commented that she was a quick learner. She clocked enough flying hours to secure a pilot's license, but by the time she left office in 1966, she had not yet clocked enough flying hours to be able to take up passengers.

Because of the need to educate the young Sisters so they could obtain certification for their respective ministries, the Council voted to purchase a House of Studies in St. Louis near St. Louis University. On January 4, 1966, Mother Philippa signed a purchase agreement for $28,430 for a residence at 4335 Maryland Avenue.[18] Priests of the Holy Family Community had a House of Studies across the Street. They willingly offered Mass for the Sisters in residence there. A number of young Sisters in residence there attended classes at Marillac College, operated by the Daughters of Charity, and some attended St. Louis University. The house was later sold when the need diminished.

During the 1960s, Mother Philippa initiated the study to revise the Constitutions of the Olivetan Benedictine Sisters by appointing all the Sisters to work in groups on revision committees. She assigned a presiding Sister for each group to write down and submit suggestions proposed by the Sisters.

After completing the proposed document in 1965, Mother Philippa submitted it to Bishop Fletcher, the Ordinary, in hopes to have it approved before the end of her fourth term. However the document was never approved. Bishop Fletcher wrote that he had not had time to study the proposed document, since he had been spending so much time in Rome attending the Sessions of the Vatican II.

As summer 1966 drew near, Mother Philippa completed her fourth term in office. She had served as Superior for 12 consecutive years and had led the community through changing times. Changes would only escalate in future years for her successor. Mother Philippa announced the date set of the election, July 2, 1966, and readied the office for her successor. On the day before the election took place, she assigned Sr. Amora, the Subprioress, to be in charge of the Community, and quietly left the Motherhouse for an extended vacation. After she returned from her vacation, she was assigned to the music studio located at the former St. Andrew's School in Little Rock, where the Day Nursery was now conducted.

The promulgation of the Documents of Vatican II (1962-65) were only the beginning of the changes that would impact religious communities in the future. The next Superior of the Olivetan Benedictines in Jonesboro would face not only great challenges, but also great sorrows. Changes being made in religious communities throughout the country also had an impact on the Jonesboro Benedictines.

Tenth Superior

Due to a conflict in his schedule, Bishop Fletcher was not able to conduct the 1966 election. He appointed Msgr. Joseph Murphy to officiate as presider and Msgr. M.F. Donavan and Fr. Joseph King as tellers. The Sisters elected Sr. Imelda Pels and Sr. Patricia Murray as witnesses. [19] On July 2, 1966, the Sisters chose by secret ballot

Sr. Benedicta Boeckmann as the tenth Superior of the Olivetan Benedictine Community. Mother Benedicta, baptized, Christine, was born at St. Elizabeth, Missouri. Six years later the family moved to Knobel, Arkansas, where she grew up. Christine entered the Olivetan Benedictine Community in Jonesboro on September 31,1931, and made First Profession as Sr. Benedicta on August 15, 1933. SEE PROFILE IN APPENDIX.

Mother Benedicta had served as Administrator of St. John's Place in Hot Springs from 1948 to 1955. For the next five years she was in charge of the Juniorate at Holy Angels. Since 1960, she had been assigned as Administrator of Consolata Home for Senior Citizens, in New Iberia, Louisiana until she was elected Superior.

On the afternoon of election on July 2, as was the custom, the Sisters gathered in the Community room to elect a President of the Corporation. In the absence of Mother Philippa, the outgoing Prioress, Mother Benedicta requested Sr. Amora to act as temporary chairperson, to ask for nominations for a new President of the Corporation. Sr. Perpetua nominated Mother Benedicta and Sr. Agnes seconded this nomination. The Sisters unanimously voted by hand to accept Mother Benedicta as the new President of the Corporation of the Olivetan Benedictine Sisters, Inc.

During the course of this meeting, Mother Benedicta announced that Sr. Geraldine Homer was appointed as Subprioress. Other appointed Council members would be Sr. Antonia Holthouse, Sr. Carmelita Myers, Novice Mistress, and Sr. Beatrice Schneider, Secretary. Members elected by the Community were Sr. Perpetua Reinart, Sr. Rita Sparber, Sr. Gregory Findley, Sr. James Poirot, and Sr. Celestine Pond.[20]

Other routine matters addressed at this first meeting chaired by Mother Benedicta were the following:

a) admission of two new Final Professed Sisters to the Corporation,
b) reading the annual report of past activities of Council. During the course of this meeting, Mother Benedicta made the following announcement:

"Our old Constitutions are to be read yearly until we get the new one. Bishop Fletcher said that we are still living by the old ones until he gets to finish (reading) the others."[21]

In closing, Mother Benedicta thanked Sr. Amora for her dedicated work for the Community as past Subprioress. The Sisters responded with a round of applause.

One of the first things Mother Benedicta did after being installed as Prioress, was to engage a business manager for the Community. After consultation with Bishop Fletcher and the Council, Mother Benedicta engaged the retired Colonel James N. Olhausen, as the first lay business manager to handle the business affairs for the Community.

Colonel Olhausen served admirably in this position for the next 16 years in handling the financial and legal matters for the Community, until his declining health forced him to resign in 1973. SEE PROFILE IN APPENDIX.

New Office Book

Since 1955, the Community had prayed The Divine Office in English from the Monastic Diurnal, containing the Day Hours, published by the Liturgical Press, St. John's Abbey, Collegeville, Minnesota. As result of the promulgation of the Constitution on the Sacred Liturgy, the first document completed by the Fathers of Vatican II, the Sisters of Holy Angels adopted in 1966, the new translation of the Divine Office. This new office book contained Lauds, Vespers and Compline. Sister Celestine Pond, Subprioress, who was also the Community choir director and liturgist, assisted the Community in making the transition.

Foreign Mission Activity

In response to the appeal by Pope Paul VI, for religious communities in the United States to send representatives from their members as missionaries to South America. Mother Benedicta, with Council approval, agreed to send one Sister to the mission being established by the American Benedictines in Bogota, Columbia. Sr. Jerome Locken was selected to go to the mission, along with Sisters from Cottonwood, Idaho; Crookston, Minnesota; and Richardton, South Dakota. Sr. Jerome had a degree in secondary education and also one in pharmacy, so she was doubly qualified to represent the Jonesboro Benedictines.

Bishop Fletcher came to Jonesboro on September 8, 1966, to officiate at a departure ceremony for Sr. Jerome and presented her with a missionary crucifix. In Bogota, Sr. Jerome taught in the high school for boys during the week, and on weekends, she opened a dispensary to provide needed medical supplies to the impoverished people. St. Bernards and the Jonesboro physicians were generous in providing medical supplies for Sr. Jerome to take to Bogota.[22]

Sr. Jerome served in that mission until she had a major stroke, after which she returned to the Motherhouse. However, Sr. Jerome recovered from this first stroke, but later had a second major stroke, which incapacitated her until her death in 1993.

Since there was no consensus among the Sisters on a location for the new Motherhouse and since Bishop Fletcher did not favor building in Hardy because of the distance from St. Bernards Hospital and Arkansas State College, he recommended that the Sisters look at properties closer to Jonesboro. The November 24, 1966 Council Minutes states the following:

"The (Council) members went to look at two pieces of property for possible future Motherhouse locations. One is the Riga property (Sr. Petra's parents). Both are within a reasonable distance from Jonesboro, and each drew favorable comments. No decision was made, as each Sister will have to see them and decide for herself."[23]

St. John's Seminary Closes

Sisters from Holy Angels served in the culinary department at St. John's Seminary from 1911 until 1967, when the Seminary closed. The Seminary was forced to close due to financial difficulties and declining number of students. After cooking and caring for the dining rooms for the Priests and Seminarians for 56 years, the services of the Sisters would no longer be needed. However, Bishop Fletcher requested that two Sisters be allowed to stay for a time, to cook and care for the few priests who would continue to live at the Seminary. Sr. Annella Willett and Sr. Theodore Roos stayed on until 1969, when the facility was turned over to lay employees. In expressing gratitude to the Sisters, Bishop Fletcher stated, "Sisters from Holy Angels Convent cooked and took care of the dining room at the Seminary. This was certainly a great contribution to the Seminary, and one for which not only I, but also all the old alumni, will be particularly grateful and can testify to the self-sacrifice and devotion of the Sisters. They certainly made a very important contribution to the Seminary." [24]

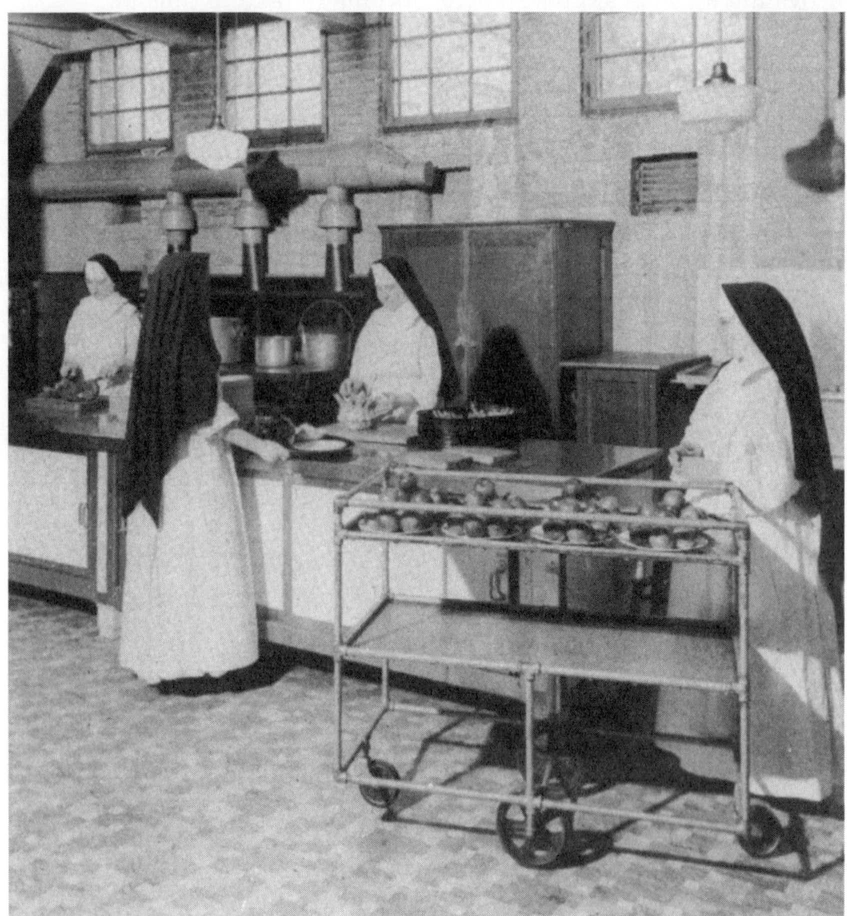

St. John's Seminary — Culinary Department 1967 (Sisters unidentified)

Winslow Property

With plans going forward to build a new Motherhouse, the Sisters voted on June 25, 1967, to sell the property and buildings at Winslow, Arkansas. Clara Muxen had bequeathed this property to the Olivetan Benedictine Sisters, Inc, in 1964, in exchange for caring for her until her death. The Trade School of the Ozarks had formerly been located in the buildings on this property. The property, located in Washington and Crawford Counties, included approximately 142 acres, and was sold in August 1967 for $25,070. Colonel James Olhausen, Community business manager, handled the business transaction and deposited the money in Community savings to build the new Motherhouse.

Habit Change

Discussions continued to arise concerning a change in religious garb or habit. Mother Benedicta conferred with Bishop Fletcher about the matter. At the June 11, 1967, Council Meeting, Mother Benedicta announced. "Some Sisters have expressed their concern with regard to the agitation for a change in habit. The Bishop is not against changing the forehead band but does not want the hair to show. One stipulation he did make, is that the Sisters should try a few experiments first, only at the Motherhouse, before deciding anything. He also said no Sister has to change." [25]

Therefore, during the summer of 1967, Mother Benedicta had the sewing department make up several samples of street-length habits of the same material as the traditional habits. Three styles were made: 1) two piece, over blouse, 2) fitted bodice, 3) one piece with modified scapular, and one piece with jacket. A white roll collar would be worn with all selections. A white "unicap" would be worn instead of the headband and circular collar. This "unicap" was a small white cap with a brim that overlapped the veil. The habit committee modeled three styles from which the Sisters could choose during this trial year.

At the Corporation Meeting on July 4, 1968, the Sisters voted by secret ballot on habit style. According to the record, an overwhelming number of Sisters voted for the different changes in habit. [26] Therefore, the sewing department enlisted volunteers to help with the sewing and the new-style habits began to be worn as they were completed.

Sisters modeling new habit choices: L – R: Sr. Lillian Marie Reiter, Sr. Mary Anne Nuce and Sr. Celestine Pond.

New Administrator

After hearing repeated concerns expressed by the doctors and hospital personnel, and receiving confirming documentation, Mother Benedicta and the Hospital Governing Board recommended that John W. Foley resign in 1967 as Administrator of St. Bernards. Following this, Mother Benedicta and Sr. Thomasine Walterscheid consulted the National Catholic Hospital Association in St. Louis for advice on Administrators. Fr. Flannigan, the Executive Director recommended that St. Bernards hire John B. Warner as Consultant to assist in selecting the next Administrator. Mr. Warner made monthly visits to Jonesboro to assist St. Bernards in an advisory capacity until his death of a heart attack in 1996.

After lengthy reviews of applicants, Colonel H.C. Knowlton was hired as the second lay administrator of St. Bernards. He had previously served as Adjutant General of Walter Reed Hospital in Washington, D.C. During his tenure, Colonel Knowlton emphasized employee education, training and recognition. He also improved salaries and employee benefits. [27]

Pastoral Care Department

Since the beginning of St. Bernards, the Sisters emphasized caring for the whole person and the importance of physical, emotional and spiritual health. By 1967 fewer Sisters were available for work in the hospital, so to continue providing this spiritual care for patients at St. Bernards, Mother Benedicta Boeckmann founded the Pastoral Care Department.

The Chaplain and the Sisters in the Pastoral Care Department work together to give hope and purpose in life to the people who come in contact with St. Bernards. In addition, St. Bernards hosts the monthly luncheon meeting of the Ministerial Alliance of greater Jonesboro to encourage ministers of all churches to be partners in providing spiritual support for the members of their respective denominations. [28]

Disaster Strikes

On May 15, 1968, a major tornado struck Jonesboro. Because of the training and preparations made in the early 1960s by the Civil Defense Team, St. Bernards Hospital in Jonesboro was able to respond to the emergency. South Jonesboro, particularly the area formerly called Nettleton was the hardest hit. The Sisters were awakened in the convent and as many as possible went to the hospital to help. Some called off-duty doctors and nurses, some listed names of those injured, and others helped relatives locate loved ones.

During this catastrophe, 34 people were killed and 479 people were injured. The Sisters opened up the convent dining room and provided meals for those people until the Red Cross set up other arrangements in the neighboring hall of Blessed Sacrament Church. [29] Victims that outnumbered the facilities of St. Bernards were sent to a hospital previously alerted in Memphis and in other cities. Before they were transported, doctors provided stabilized care for patients and readied them for transportation to other hospitals.

Throughout this time, sadness overshadowed the Community due to the trend of Sisters requesting dispensations from their Vows. The trend that began in the late 1950s and early 1960s, to request dispensations from both Temporal and Perpetual Vows, continued to increase. Mother Benedicta and the other Community members were saddened about the number leaving. Bishop Fletcher was saddened too, as he reluctantly gave approval for dispensations. The Sisters continued to struggle with the changes promulgated by Vatican II, and many decisions were made in haste.

Spiritual Renewal

To strengthen the Spiritual life of the Community, Priests from St. Meinrad Archabbey and from Subiaco Abbey were engaged to give summer workshops. For the Spiritual Renewal Program of the summers of 1967, 1968 and 1969, Mother Benedicta engaged Fr. Bernards Sause, OSB, a Canon Lawyer of St. Benedict's Abbey, Atchison, Kansas, as advisor. He was instructor at St. Benedict's during the scholastic year, so was available for the summers. According to records on file, Fr. Bernard gave a renewal program on Vatican II and assisted the Sisters in beginning the revision of their Constitutions during 1967, 1968 and 1969. [30] After the revised edition of the Constitutions were completed, they were submitted to Bishop Fletcher for his approval.

As mentioned earlier, the affiliation of Convent Maria Stein, Pocahontas (later Holy Angels Convent, Jonesboro, Arkansas) took place on January 15, 1893. According to Sr. Agnes in Green Olive Branch, Holy Angels did not have the original authentic documents of affiliation on file. Fr. Bernard contacted the Olivetan Abbot General, Romualdo M. Zilianti, OSB. The answer was dated, July 27, 1968.

"Very Reverend Father Bernards A. Sause, OSB
Holy Angels Convent
P.O. Drawer 130
Jonesboro, Arkansas 72403

Very Reverend Father,

Your letter of the fourth of the current month (July) has reached me. You inform me that you wrote also last year, but unfortunately such a letter as you refer to did not reach me.

In conformity with your request, I shall have the necessary researches made and shall inform you as much as you desire. I shall see to it that the material regarding our spirituality will be sent to you. It will be necessary for you to have patience because researches of this kind call for a bit of time.

Our monastic life, at least in Italy, is developing much like yours of the Benedictines of the American Cassinese Congregation, united to the contemplative life.

We have schools, institutes, hospitals and parishes. In the delay of communicating to you what you have asked for, I request to greet these good fellow-Sisters whom we Olivetans have always considered as constituting a part of our spiritual family.

I greet you cordially,
Affectionately and fraternally,
Romualdo M. Zilianti
(signed) Abbot General" [31]

During the summer of 1969, Mother Benedicta Boeckmann was elected to a second three-year term. Sr. Geraldine Homer, however, asked to be relieved of the duties of Subprioress. She had become involved in Catechetical work at the Eaker Air Force Base in Blytheville and felt she needed to devote full time to that ministry. Consequently in 1969, Sr. Celestine Pond was named Subprioress for the Community.

At that time, Sr. Celestine was also named Formation Directress, Liturgist and Choir Directress. She had just completed her Master's Degree in Organ from DePaul University in Chicago.

Benedictine Manor

By 1968, the old frame buildings at St. John's Place in Hot Springs, owned and operated by the Jonesboro Benedictines since 1913, had deteriorated badly. Mother Benedicta and the Council agreed to demolish the frame buildings and erect a new residential facility to be named Benedictine Manor, for retired persons and travelers.

Bishop Albert L. Fletcher conducted groundbreaking ceremonies May 29, 1968. During the ceremonies he stated, "Benedictine Manor was absolutely needed, as it was being erected in the name of the Lord." Lee Green, executive vice-president of the Hot Springs Chamber of Commerce said, "The Manor was a tremendous thing for Hot Springs and we are pleased to have it." [32]

Dedication of Benedictine Manor, took place on October 5, 1969, with Bishop Fletcher again officiating at the ceremonies. Vernon B. Warr, acted as Master of Ceremonies and summed up the contributions the Sisters had made to the Hot Springs community over the past 56 years. Mother Benedicta and a large delegation of Sisters from Jonesboro attended the ceremony, as well as a number of priests. Tours of the facility and refreshments followed the dedication. The Jonesboro Benedictines operated this facility until 1994, when it was sold due to financial constraints and new federal guidelines requiring costly renovations.

Change in Names

As result of Vatican II directives, another change occurred at Holy Angels in 1969. The new directive allowed a person to make religious profession of vows using their baptismal name, instead of receiving a monastic name. That practice was based on Scripture, which cites instances, when God calls a person to a new work, He gave them a new name. Such as in the Old Testament, He changed Jacob's name to Israel. In the new Testament, when God called Saul, He changed his name to Paul.

The new theology, cited in the Vatican II document, stressed that the commitment to follow Christ made at baptism is a lifetime commitment, so a person could retain their baptismal name when making religious profession. At Holy Angels, those Sisters who had already made religious profession years earlier, could revert to their baptismal name during the summer of 1969. Some Sisters did, while others who had been in vows for a number of years retained their monastic name. From 1969 on, those making religious profession had the option to retain their baptismal name or receive a monastic name.

As the 1960s drew to a close, religious communities across the nation continued to experience a loss of members. Although concerted efforts were made to stem the trend, the unrest continued. Some Sisters felt changes were being made too slowly, while others felt the religious spirit was being lost because too many changes had been made.

In remarks to the Sisters during the close of visitation on June 4, 1966, Bishop Fletcher stated, "Be not the first on whom the new is tried and not the last to lay the old aside." He used this philosophy in guiding the Jonesboro Benedictines throughout the years of renewal. [33]

CHAPTER 13
1970-1979

Decisions, Decisions

The 1970s were marked with major decisions that affected the future of the community. It was an era of community meetings, questionnaires and voting. While decisions made during the 1960s pertained primarily to rules and regulations regarding Community living, the 1970s expanded to include not only where the Community would live, but also, the building layout, accommodations and furnishings for the new Motherhouse.

Throughout this time, there was continued unrest in the Community, as a number of Sisters requested dispensations from their vows and left. Sisters struggled over the changes brought about by renewal in its earliest stages. Each member was trying to understand what to keep, and what to let go. A few Sisters wanted to experiment by living as a small group in an apartment in Jonesboro, rather than at the Motherhouse. However, the majority of Sisters did not favor this idea, so it never materialized.

Those who wanted to live in an apartment away from the Community eventually asked for dispensations and left. The majority of Sisters held firm to the traditions of Community, while placing emphasis on prayer and sacrifice. Mother Benedicta and the Council faced numerous challenges on what to do to stabilize membership and also to attract new vocations. Bishop Fletcher continued to urge the Sisters to make a decision about relocating the Motherhouse. He maintained if the community would decide on a location for the new Motherhouse, it would bring a sense of stability and hope for the future of the community.

While the community investigated several available properties around Jonesboro, the Frank Riga Family stepped forward and offered 160 acres, about 5 1/2 miles north of Jonesboro on which to locate the Motherhouse. The stipulation being that the community would in turn care for Rita Ann, a handicapped daughter, who would not be able to care for herself after the death of her parents.

Property Transactions

After prayer and numerous Community meetings, the Sisters decided to accept the property offered by the Frank Riga Family. Bishop Fletcher's advised that the Community first check on the soil content and the availability of utilities, before any decision was finalized. According to minutes from the Corporation meeting held on September 18, 1970, an overwhelming majority of Sisters voted to accept the Riga property on which to build their new Motherhouse.

Mother Benedicta signed a letter of agreement on February 8, 1971.

"Mr. & Mrs. Frank H. Riga
Route 1, Box 254
Jonesboro, Arkansas 72401

Dear Mr. & Mrs. Riga:

This is to acknowledge receipt of deed to Olivetan Benedictine Sisters, Incorporated, covering the Northeast Quarter of Section 20, Township 15 North, Range 4 East, in Craighead County, Arkansas. We are grateful to you for this generous contribution.

We have long had plans for the construction of a new Motherhouse. These plans have not yet become a reality due, in part, to our inability to acquire suitable real estate upon which to build.

Your most generous gift has provided that real estate and it is our intention to build our new home on this land.

In return, we agree to provide care and support for your daughter, Rita Ann, after the death of her parents.

Sincerely yours in Christ,
(signed) Mother M Benedicta
Boeckmann, OSB" [1]

However, the Bishop stipulated that two separate documents be drawn up, one to accept the property, and the other, to care for Rita

Ann, the daughter. Records in the archives attest that this was done according to stipulation.

After the Community made the decision to build their new Motherhouse on the Riga property north of Jonesboro, the Sisters had to decide what to do with the property in Fulton County near Hardy. The original cost of the 170 acres was $25,000, and another $10,048 was spent on improvements, which total $35,048 since purchase in 1967.

On December 9, 1971, the Community voted to sell the Hardy property and use the proceeds to build the new Convent. Chapter minutes reveal that the majority of Sisters voted to sell all the property, since they now had selected another location for the new Motherhouse. Mother Benedicta asked Colonel Olhausen, business manager for the Community, to handle the transaction.

Colonel James Olhausen had the property appraised and then put it on the market. He was able to sell the property in April 1972 for $70,000 to Cooper Communities, Inc. The proceeds were deposited in Community savings toward building the new Motherhouse. [2]

Hospital Change

While this was happening in the Community, another development occurred in the administration of the hospital. Differences arose between Colonel Knowlton and the philosophy of St. Bernards. After thorough investigation, Mother Benedicta and the hospital Governing Board accepted the resignation of Colonel Knowlton in April 1971 and shortly after, James G. Henson of Memphis, Tennessee was hired as administrator.

Mr. Henson had a brief tenure as administrator, however, and in the spring of 1972 Mother Benedicta and the Hospital Governing Board accepted his resignation. On July 3, 1972, Mr. Ben E. Owens was hired as the fourth lay administrator of St. Bernards. Mr. Owens, a native of Alicia, Arkansas, graduated from Arkansas College in Batesville and did graduate work in Hospital Administration at Columbia University, New York and in St. Louis,

Missouri. He had served in the U.S. Air Force before serving as vice-president of White River Medical Center in Batesville.[3] The Board envisioned great promise in Mr. Owens, and this insight proved true, as Mr. Owens successfully led St. Bernards into the 21st Century during the succeeding years.

Third Term

Mother Benedicta's second term expired in June of 1972, so a canonical election was scheduled at the close of the summer retreat. Before the election, Bishop Fletcher announced that because the building project was underway for the new Motherhouse, he would grant a dispensation from the Constitution and allow Mother Benedicta to have a third term if the Sisters so decided.

On June 6, 1972, Mother Benedicta Boeckmann was elected to a third, three-year term as Prioress. During the afternoon Corporation meeting, she was again elected as President of the Corporation. Mother Benedicta announced that Sr. Celestine Pond, would be re-appointed as Subprioress.[4] At a July 13, 1972 Corporation meeting, Mother Benedicta announced that the temporary, five-year approval of the Constitutions, given by Bishop Fletcher, in 1968 would expire in 1973. A committee would be formed to receive suggestions to revise the Constitution according to the new directives promulgated by Vatican II.[5]

New Bishop

Shock waves reverberated throughout the Convent, as well as throughout the Diocese, when on July 4, 1972, the news was received that Pope Paul IV, had accepted the resignation of Bishop Albert L. Fletcher (now 75 years old), and Rev. Andrew J. McDonald, of Savannah, Georgia was appointed as the new Ordinary for the Diocese of Little Rock. Installation in Little Rock was scheduled for September 7, 1972.

As Ordinary and spiritual director for the community for over 25 years, the community had grown to depend upon Bishop Fletcher and his guidance, especially through the turbulent 1960s and the beginning 1970s. Now, the Sisters were questioning how the new bishop would relate to the Community. Time would tell as history unfolded.

New Convent on the Way

Architect's rendition of new Holy Angels Convent — 1972.

After extensive consultation, Mother Benedicta and the Council engaged the architectural firm of Stuck and Associates of Jonesboro to build the new Convent. Mr. Sid Frier, AIA, one of the main architects with the firm, worked closely with the Sisters in designing the contemporary Convent of 15 separate buildings, joined by breezeways or hallways, encircling the Chapel in the center of the complex.

Committees were appointed to offer suggestions on different aspects of the living quarters. There was a committee of Sisters for the Chapel, the bedrooms, the business offices, kitchen and floor coverings, etc. After various meetings and voting concerning color of bricks, paint, covering, closet space and numerous other details, Ramsons Construction Company of Jonesboro was hired to erect the new one-story Convent.

Ground Breaking

According to records in the Archives, groundbreaking ceremonies for the new convent were held on July 11, 1972. Bishop Albert L. Fletcher and Mother Benedicta turned the first shovels of earth on the tree-shaded area. A large delegation of Sisters, who were home from the missions during the summer months, was present for this historic event.

For the third time in succession, the Sisters had selected high ground on which to erect their Motherhouse in Arkansas. First, on "Catholic Hill" in Pocahontas, one of the highest elevations in Randolph County; secondly, downtown Jonesboro located on Crowley's Ridge and now, an even higher elevation on the Ridge, five miles north of Jonesboro, near the KAIT-TV Station.

During this same time, while the new Convent was being built north of town, members of the hospital administration were busy making renovation plans to renovate the old 1929 Convent building and make it an Annex for the medical center. The original 40-bed brick hospital building and the Chapel erected in 1905, plus the 1898 Convent building would be razed. Construction time for the new Convent was estimated at 18 months, however, due to incessant rains, construction was delayed and extended over a period of two years.

Second Tornado

Before the new Convent was completed, a second tornado struck Jonesboro on May 27, 1973. With the experience of caring for the injured during the 1968 tornado, St. Bernards was well prepared. Billy Joe Emerson with his ambulance service and two-way radio system was first on the scene of the devastation south of town. Sr. Elaine Willett who had been assigned as Supervisor of the Emergency Room only two weeks earlier, had surveyed supplies and was prepared for the emergency.

Emergency rooms were open so supplies were available to those who needed them; many of the Sisters went over from the Convent to help. Sr. Elaine stated, "The Sisters did little things that meant so much to the people. They comforted people. They waited and prayed with them. They brought a blanket or a cup of coffee. The presence of the Sisters had a calming effect on the injured and their families. That night we treated more than 200 patients in the E.R. Department. Because we were better prepared and equipped than in 1968, when the first tornado struck Jonesboro, we could handle the emergency more efficiently."[6] Only three deaths occurred due to the 1973 tornado, while forty-three people died as a result of the 1968 tornado.

ASU Nursing Program

When Arkansas State University opened their nursing degree program, Sr. (Gregory) Patricia Lee Findley, M.A. was asked to join the faculty. However, she would not be able to do so, wearing the habit. In response to a request made by Mother Benedicta to Senator Jerry Bookout, Bill #199 was introduced in the 1973 Arkansas 69th General Assembly. This Bill passed would allow Sisters to wear their regular uniform (religious garb) while teaching at the University. The Senate Bill was entitled, "An Act to provide that any teacher may wear religious clothing while teaching in the public schools and State institutions of this State; and for other purposes." Arkansas State University hired Sr. (Gregory) Patricia Lee Findley, M.A., as instructor in the nursing program. She was named Assistant Professor of Nursing.[7] Later on, Sr. Elaine Willett was also hired to teach nursing skills to first year students in the Associate Degree Nursing Program.[8]

Constitution Revision

Since the five-year temporary approval of their Constitutions would expire in 1973, the Sisters voted on a Constitution Committee to organize the suggestions sent in and to lead the discussions. The Constitution Committee was comprised of the following: Sr. Claudia Bischsel, Sr. Henrietta Hockle, Sr. Julia Pruss, Sr. Cabrini

Arami, Sr. Beatrice Schneider and Sr. Pieta Decker. Sr. Henrietta was elected chairperson of the committee. The document temporarily approved now needed to be updated according to the directives issued by Vatican II, before submitting to the Ordinary for final approval.

Due to ill health of Fr. Bernard Sause, OSB, Atchison, who assisted the Community in drawing up the earlier revisions, Mother Benedicta engaged Fr. Adelbert Buscher, OSB, a canonist from St. Meinrad Archabbey, Indiana to advise the Community in making the needed changes in the Constitution in light of the Vatican II documents.

Fr. Adelbert flew to Little Rock in April 1974, where he held a preliminary meeting with the committee at Holy Souls Convent to outline the agenda for the summer sessions with the Community. Other members of the committee came to Holy Souls, along with Mother Benedicta. Fr. Adelbert outlined a new format containing the four parts to be used, "1) The Holy Rule; 2) the Spiritual Document; 3) Juridical Section; and 4) the Book of Customs. This would be presented to the Community at the General Chapter on June 10, 1974."[9]

With the guidance of Fr. Adelbert, the Community completed two separate documents, entitled Joyful Response. The first volume, approved by Bishop Andrew J. McDonald, DD, and published in 1975, contained Part II, "A Declaration on Benedictine Spiritual Life," and the Part III, "Juridic Elements." The second volume containing Part IV, the "Customary," was completed, approved and published in 1976.

In April 1974, the McNabb Funeral Home in Pocahontas made a substantial offer for approximately two acres of land facing Anna Street. A notice from Mother Benedicta, dated, April 4, 1974, announced at the Motherhouse and mailed to all the mission Sisters, stated the following: "Sometime ago, we agreed to make a subdivision called the 'Benet Addition,' which consisted of seven lots (along the back side of the property). This reduced the Convent property to 13 acres. The sale of this additional plot will still leave the Convent with 11 acres of property for their home. The disposal of this two-acre plot will also materially reduce maintenance cost of the Convent property at Pocahontas."

According to Chapter minutes, of April 16, 1974, the Sisters voted to sell the parcel of land to McNabb Funeral Home for $20,000.

Holy Angels Convent — 1974.

Nearing Completion

As workmen were completing the new Convent complex north of town in the summer of 1974, preparations were being made to relocate. Sr. Bernardine Grueninger drew the designs for the new chapel windows, which were sent to Laukhuff Stained Glass Company in Memphis for executing. The stained glass windows in the present chapel would be used as a dividing wall by the new library. Sr. Bernardine also painted a new set of Stations of the Cross, as the ones in the present chapel would not fit in the new contemporary-style chapel. The present ones would be weatherized and used outdoors. In addition, Sr. Bernardine also painted a small glass panel for each of the bedroom doors. The designs on these widows included Biblical sayings or excerpts from the Rule of St. Benedict.

Mr. Robert Schoenborn, head maintenance man, was busy with building the new altars for the chapel, both the altar of Sacrifice and the Eucharistic altar. He also made some small half-size pews to accommodate the new seating arrangement in the chapel. He also reupholstered the chairs for the dining room and made furniture for the bedrooms. Mrs. McDaniel, wife of the general contractor and professional interior decorator, assisted by making draperies for the new convent and by offering suggestions concerning arrangement of furniture.

According to oral history, by August 1974, after the mission Sisters left, the "home Sisters" began the mammoth task of packing. Before long, boxes and boxes lined the hallways throughout the Convent. By September, the Sisters began taking the first loads out to the new site. Sr. Claudia Bischsel, librarian, was assisted by Sr. Louise Frankenberger in moving the library. Sr. Christopher, Sr. Brenda and Sr. Annella Willett came home from Benton on weekends to also help with moving the library. The boxes of books were marked and referenced for placing in the new library.

All the Sisters contributed in some way to this giant undertaking of the moving process. Some of the mission Sisters, who were able to take off for weekends, came to help. Packing the furnishings from various departments, such as from Chapel, sewing room, and kitchen all needed extra help. Sr. Helen Swirczynski came home from Hot Springs to assist Sr. Frowina Hacker in packing kitchen utensils and appliances. Together they decided on arrangements in the new kitchen.

By October, actual moving of furnishings began in earnest. Mother Benedicta, assisted by Sr. Celestine, contributed greatly to this giant undertaking. A number of other Sisters, including Sr. De Porres Polk and Novitiate members, assisted in numerous ways. Mr. Schoenborn with John Gamble, plus a student from ASU, loaded the vehicles and the Sisters made the trips back and forth. Every available vehicle the Convent owned was used to transport furnishings. One large moving van was also engaged for the workmen to transport the larger items.

The Sisters themselves took care of moving a greater part of the library books and clothing. They would pack the vehicles in the evenings, and then transport them early the next day. As many trips as possible were made each day from morning until evening. Some Sisters stayed out at the new site to help direct the unloading and arrange the furnishings, while others went back for another load.

The TV road, now, County Road 766, was still graveled and quite rough. When it rained it became muddy and made loading and unloading more difficult. A number of humorous "tales" were related concerning the trips back and forth. According to oral history, one such incident was told about a cabinet falling off the pick-up truck when going to the new site. When the loss was discovered, the truck retraced its path and the Sisters found several men guarding the cabinet. The men helped reload the "runaway" cabinet so it could be transported to the new Convent.

On another occasion, the front of the station wagon lifted off the ground because the back was overloaded. When several "extra" Sisters were asked to sit in the front seat, the wheels touched the ground and the trip was safely made to the new location with cargo intact. Many such incidents were related as the moving process continued.

One mission Sister commented on her first visit to the new Motherhouse, "The new Convent looked so much like home because most of the furnishings from the old Convent were transported to the new location."

The only new furniture secured for the new convent was an easy chair donated by a generous benefactor for each Sister's room. A beautiful pipe organ for the new Chapel was also donated by the Karl Pfeiffer Family in Piggott. The furnishings from the old Convent that could not be used at the new location were disposed of at a giant sale.

Chapel Bell

The contractor told the Sisters the bell tower at the new location would not hold two bells, so a decision needed to be made. A new bell had been cast in 1962, by VanBergen Bell Foundries, Inc. of South Carolina, to commemorate the 75th anniversary of the founding of the Community. This bell had been dedicated in honor of St. "Walburga" to memorialize the thirty years Mother Walburga served as prioress.

The old bell cast in 1907 by Stuckstede BFCD Foundry, St. Louis, and hung in the chapel since 1907, was inscribed, "Dedicated in honor of St. Benedict." This bell had called the Sisters to prayer four times a day for the succeeding 67 years. Since the bell tower at the new site could not accommodate both the old and new bell, it was decided to give the old bell to a church that may need a bell. Since it was blessed, it could not be sold.

Rev. Lim Parks, who was rector of St. Mark's Episcopal Church at the time, made arrangements to procure the bell. A parishioner of St. Marks Church made a donation of $750 to the Convent in lieu of the bell. It is presently displayed in a memorial garden on the grounds of St. Mark's Church. Electric bells are now used to call the Episcopal parishioners to worship.

Holy Angels Convent Bell cast in 1907.

Cemetery

Grounds for a Cemetery at the new location had already been blessed and named Our Lady of Mount Olivet. Sr. Melanie Rintsch, who had died on March 13, 1974, and who had requested to be buried there, was the first Sister interred in the new Cemetery. Twenty Sisters had been buried in St. Paul's Parish Cemetery in Pocahontas, while a total of 110 Sisters had been buried in Holy Cross Cemetery, the Jonesboro Blessed Sacrament Parish Cemetery. According to records, the Community agreed on August 6, 1978, to pay $3,000 to the Parish Cemetery fund to be invested to provide perpetual maintenance of the Sisters graves in that Cemetery.[10]

The day before the dedication, on October 11, Sr. Victoria Meier died, therefore, she was the first Sister to die at the new location. Her body was laid to rest, next to the body of Sr. Melanie the day after the dedication.

Dedication of Holy Angels Convent October 12, 1974. Pictured L – R: Bishop Emeritus Albert Fletcher, DD, Fr, Paul Hadusek, OSB, Chaplain, Bishop Andrew J. McDonald, DD, Alan Patteson, Jr. Master of Ceremonies, Mother Benedicta Boeckmann, OSB, and Abbot Marian Omeara, OSB, St. Pius X Monastery, Pevely, Missouri.

A Dream Comes True

The great day of dedication arrived—October 12, 1974. Nature joined in the celebration, as October that year had decked the trees in the surrounding countryside with a myriad of fall colors. It was a memorable day for all who attended, but especially for the members of the Olivetan Benedictine Community, who would now call the new place home.

Alan Patteson, Jr. officiated as Master of Ceremonies at the Dedication. After blessing the building, Bishop McDonald remarked, "Just after I came to Arkansas, I was shown the plans for the new convent and I thought—Arkansas sure has some dreamers. However, through their faith, their courage, and their sacrifice, the

Olivetan Benedictine Sisters of Jonesboro have proved that dreams do come true at Holy Angels Convent."[11]

Indeed the dream had come true and the Sisters thanked God for His blessings. In blessing the new Chapel, Bishop McDonald remarked that the old Chapel was a Holy Place because of the many years of prayers offered there. That was the place where many Sisters had made their vows and celebrated their jubilees, so there was a sadness on the part of many to leave it. However, the Bishop challenged the Sisters to now, make the new Chapel Holy by their prayers.

Interior of New Holy Angels Chapel.

Mother Benedicta will be remembered for her leadership in the mammoth task of relocating the Convent in 1974 and for guiding the Community through the "troubled waters" of the renewal process. The Community had changed during the years of her tenure since 1966. Now the membership was smaller, but the Sisters who had remained throughout all the changes were determined to continue their commitment to live religious life in Community as Olivetan Benedictines.

Eleventh Prioress

Since Mother Benedicta's third term would expire in the summer of 1975, the community again prepared for a canonical election. This was the first time Bishop Andrew J. McDonald, DD, would preside at a Canonical election for the Olivetan Benedictine Sisters.

On June 6, 1975, Sr. Julia Pruss was elected the eleventh Prioress of the Olivetan Benedictine Community. Mother Julia, the first Prioress born in Arkansas, was a native of Marche, where she grew up. She held a Master's degree in education and taught in elementary and secondary schools for 35 years, most of which were spent in St. Paul's, Pocahontas. SEE PROFILE IN APPENDIX.

The same afternoon of her election, during the annual Corporation meeting, Mother Julia was voted President of the Corporation by the 94 Chapter members. One of her first decisions was to appoint Sr. Cabrini Arami as Subprioress. As a teacher, Sr. Cabrini had worked with Sr. Julia for many years in Pocahontas. Mother Julia then appointed Sr. Benedicta Boeckmann as the Formation Directress.

That summer, the Third Session of the General Renewal Chapter was held to finalize the first volume of Joyful Response, the document containing Part II, "A Declaration on Benedictine Spiritual Life," and Part III "Juridic Elements." After Bishop McDonald approved the document, it was sent to the Star Printing Company in Wynne, Arkansas. The document was published under the date of June 13, 1975 and the Sisters were happy to receive their individual copies. The Community still had one more document to complete the following summer, the "The Customary." The Committee continued to work on this document and welcomed suggestions during the year.

During the Chapter Meeting on June 2, 1976, Mother Julia announced that Cathedral Parish in Little Rock was selling the property of the old St. Andrew's School, where our present day care and music studio were located. She asked the Sisters to consider keeping these apostolates open in Little Rock. If so, we need to purchase a house somewhere in Little Rock. [12]

The Community voted to continue these apostolates, so Mother Julia and Sr. Cabrini went to Little Rock to make arrangements, as Sr. Philippa had located a piece of property she felt would be adequate. By August 1976, the Community purchased a house and a half-acre of land in the Geyer Springs area in St. Theresa's Parish in south Little Rock. The house was not large enough for both the day care and the music studio, so a three-bedroom mobile home was purchased and moved to the property. As of this date, Sr. Dominica continues to operate the day care in the house, while Sr. Philippa conducts the music studio in the mobile home. The Sisters also have their living quarters in the mobile home.

New Office Books

During 1976, information was published about a new edition of Christian Prayer: The Liturgy of the Hours, which arrange the Divine Office according to the revised norms, as approved by the Bishops of the United States. Since the Holy Angels Community had been praying the Divine Office from the 1966 text, the Sisters expressed interest in securing the new edition. After several Community discussions on the different texts available from The Liturgical Press and from Catholic Book Publishing, the Council voted on October 26, 1976, to purchase the books from Catholic Book Publishing Company.

This text from Catholic Book Publishing also included a music supplement, which the Sisters favored. By ordering the books before November 30, the Community would receive a 25% discount. Instead of paying $16.50, the books would cost $12.50 each. The new office books would be given to the Sisters as Christmas gifts that year.[19] Sr. Celestine again assisted the Sisters in making the transition to the format of new books.

At the Chapter Meeting on June 14, 1977, Mother Julia announced that Colonel Olhausen decided to retire as business manager, since the building program had been completed. However he would continue working on a part-time basis without accepting a salary. He offered to continue assisting the Community in financial matters as long as his health would permit and then he would help locate a replacement. [13]

Channel 8 Television Station contacted Mother Julia about jointly erecting a sign on the corner of Highway 141, to direct visitors to the two locations on this county road. The television station had secured the site free of rent. On June 23, 1977, Mother Julia presented this matter to members of the Chapter. By a voice vote, the Community

Sr. Bertha Frei praying by the reliquaries in the alcove outside chapel.

decided to share the cost of erecting the sign.

Because of the remote area, there was concern about the security of the Convent premises, Mother Julia and the Council decided to enclose the entire premises with a chain-link cyclone fence. A local business, the Dacus Fence Company, received the contract and installed the fence. The fence included a back entrance gate on Rolling Ridge Road, now known as CR#753, which is kept locked and used only in emergencies.

A New Mission

At a Chapter Meeting on April 17, 1978, Mother Julia read a letter from Fr. William Kane, pastor of Holy Redeemer Parish in El Dorado, requesting Sisters. The Philippino Sisters who were stationed there were not working out satisfactorily, because of language difficulties. They were scheduled to leave at the end of the school year. Bishop McDonald also sent a letter in support of Fr. Kane's request for Sisters.

After Community discussion, Sr. Geraldine offered to go to

El Dorado as Religious Education Director if the Community would vote to accept it. Mother Julia announced a vote would be taken from the home Sisters and await the votes from the mission Sisters before they were totaled.[14]

By April 26, the votes to accept El Dorado as a mission were received from the mission Sisters so they were tallied along with votes cast earlier by the home Sisters. Of the 81 Chapter members eligible to vote: 66 voted Yes to accept El Dorado; 12 voted No; two did not vote; and one vote was invalid. Early the following week, Mother Julia went to Pocahontas to talk to Sr. Pauline Morath, who was principal of the elementary school and sixth grade teacher. She asked her if she was happy there or would she request a change for the following scholastic year. Sr. Pauline said, "I am happy here and am not looking for a change." Mother Julia told her that she was considering another mission for her for next year.

Being in the same profession class, Sr. Pauline said, "Mother Julia, you and I were trained the same way. I told you I was happy here, but if you need me someplace else, I will be willing to go." Then Mother Julia proposed that she go to El Dorado with Sr. Geraldine. Sr. Pauline then said she would gladly go wherever she was needed.

By August, Sr. Geraldine Homer and Sr. Pauline Morath were missioned to Holy Redeemer Parish in El Dorado; Sr. Geraldine as Director of Religious Education and Sr. Pauline as Principal of the school.

Election Again

However before appointments were made for the following scholastic year, it was time again for a Canonical election during the summer of 1978. Mother Julia Pruss had completed her first three-year term, so she scheduled an election on June 17. Bishop Andrew McDonald presided at this Canonical election in which Mother Julia was elected to a second-three year term. At the afternoon Corporation meeting, she was re-elected President of the Corporation, and then reappointed Sr. Cabrini Arami to serve as

Subprioress of the Community.

Other Developments

By August, a swimming pool was being dug on the back side of the Convent grounds. This addition had been in the plans when the Sisters relocated to their new Motherhouse north of town. The Sisters had missed their pool which they left in town behind the tall wooden fence.

At the August 6, 1978, Council Meeting, Mother Julia announced that a neighbor, Herman Tinsley was digging a pond across the road from our property. Mr. Schoenborn had approached him about the cost of digging the pool for the Convent. It would be cheaper to do it while the heavy machinery was in the area. The total cost of installing a steel-lined, regulation-size swimming pool was estimated around $20,000. Mother Julia stated, the cost would offset expense over the years for water therapy for Sr. Eymard Lemmer and others who may be in need of it. In addition, all the Sisters could benefit from water exercises. The Council voted in favor of the proposal. [15]

Another development in 1978 was the addition of the new marble statue of the Risen Christ for the altar at the cemetery entrance.

Hubert Felderhoff of Muenster honored his three sisters—Sr.Amora, Sr. Lutgardis and Sr. Mildred—by donating the Carrara marble statue to replace the deteriorating statue of Christ's Agony in

Entrance gate showing the statues of the four welcoming angels.

Sr. Fidelis Rohmer praying by cemetery altar.

the Garden. This plaster statue had been located at the end of the hallway of the second floor of the old Convent, but had been weatherized before it was placed outdoors. However, it did not survive the elements and had to be replaced. The Felderhoff family also donated the four Carrara marble statues of angels located by the entrance gate.

Another area affected by the weather was the Chapel skylight, which leaked badly each time it rained. The Sisters went scurrying for pans and buckets to line the middle aisle below the skylight. After repeated attempts to repair it, the company finally had to replace it to provide the needed protection.

At the June 9, 1979 Chapter meeting, Fr. Adelbert Buscher, OSB, presented to the Community for consideration the possibility of aggregating with the Benedictine Confederation. However, after further discussion, nothing more was done in this regard. The Sisters decided to remain as they were at present time, as they understood it, with Spiritual Affiliation with the Olivetan Benedictine Federation.

As the 1970s drew to a close, the growth of St. Bernards, which had now become known as St. Bernards Regional Medical Center, paralleled the growth of Jonesboro itself. The hospital that opened in a rural community in 1900 now stood, on the occasion of its Diamond Jubilee, in the midst of the largest population centers of northeast Arkansas.[16]

The Community was becoming more stabilized, as the request for dispensations from vows had lessened. The Community received new members, but due to changing times, some of these did not persevere. Due to the decline in membership, some of the Missions previously staffed by the Community had to be relinquished.

After living at the new Motherhouse now for five years, it was becoming more like home. Sr. Elaine Willett and her mother had planted daffodils in the woods around the Convent prior to completion of the Convent. Both Sr. Edigna and Sr. Matilda Sparber planted roses around the buildings to enhance the property.

According to oral tradition, Sr. Matilda Sparber was a skilled wine maker. She had a recipe to make rose wine out of the petals. When the Sisters relocated to the new Convent in 1974, a closet full of wine was brought along. The wine was served periodically on Sundays and on special feastdays throughout the year. Sr. Matilda continued this art of wine making until her health declined and no one else has since taken up the tradition.

The documents of the Constitution and Customary, completed during the 1970s, provided direction and help in living religious life. Over three-quarters of a Century since its founding in 1887, the Community had survived and weathered the turbulence of changes in Religious life that occurred after the promulgation of the

Documents of Vatican II. With a renewed emphasis on the Liturgy of the Hours and Community living, the Sisters looked forward to the unfolding of the next decade.

CHAPTER 14
1980-1989

Sesquimillenium of Benedictinism

Slowly and quietly the decade of the 1980s slipped into place. However, excitement soon permeated 1980, as Benedictines throughout the world commemorated the Sesquimillenium of Benedictinism—the 1500th anniversary of the birth of St. Benedict. According to the dialogues of St. Gregory the Great, Benedict was born around the year 480 of a prominent Italian family in Nursia, located in central Italy.

Benedict studied in Rome, but became disillusioned with the political and social corruption of the time. He retired to a cave in the hills, a place known as Subiaco, to live a life of prayer and solitude. However, soon other young men followed him and begged him to lead them in their quest for holiness. Benedict later wrote a Rule, which he called "for beginners," but it has continued to be a guide and followed to present time by those who truly seek God.

To celebrate this special anniversary of the founding of the Benedictine Order, the American Benedictines held a symposium on Benedictine Life at St. John's Abbey in St. Joseph, Minnesota, and Cardinal Basil Hume, OSB, former Abbot of Ampleforth, England, presented a lecture at this special event. All Benedictines, from both male and female communities, were invited. Mother Julia Pruss and Sr. Henrietta Hockle attended this Symposium in June.

At Holy Angels, the Sisters renewed their efforts to live the Benedictine life to its fullest. Symposium papers given at different locations were shared at Community meetings. Mother Julia proposed that the Community purchase for each Sister the Sesquimillenium, pewter medal of St. Benedict, cast by Conception Abbey for the Jubilee Year. The image of St. Benedict was on one side and the word "Peace" was on the reverse. This medal was worn throughout the Jubilee year by all the Sisters, in lieu of the original Benedictine medal. By wearing this medal, the Sisters witnessed to each other and to visitors the importance of this Jubilee Year in the history of the Benedictine Order and the universal Church.

A special celebration was held on June 9, at Holy Angels to commemorate this Jubilee year. According to the minutes of the June 1, 1980 Corporation meeting, All former Sisters were invited for a Mass at 10:30 a.m. followed by a meal and tour of the facilities. They were invited to join the Community at Vespers at 3 p.m., which closed the celebration.[1]

Sisters spend time in private prayer in chapel.

Another "first" occurred in 1980, when a Sister from the Olivetan Benedictine Community in Pusan, Korea, made a request to transfer her stability to the Jonesboro Benedictine Community. She had come to Holy Angels earlier to learn English, and had been there for a year and a half, when she decided to make this request to transfer her vows.

After receiving the necessary permission from the Holy See and from the Ordinary of the Diocese, Bishop McDonald, and her own Superior in Pusan, Sr. Cordis Kim, made her request. At the Chapter Meeting on June 5, 1980, the Community voted to accept

Sr. Cordis into the ranks of the Olivetan Benedictine Community at Holy Angels.[2]

During this same time, new applicants requested admission to the Community. Some of the Sisters who had left the Community earlier requested readmission but only several returned. This trend of requesting dispensation from vows slowly dwindled to an occasional request. This trend was not unique to Holy Angels, as Religious Communities throughout the country experienced this same evolvement after the promulgation of the "Decree on the Appropriate Renewal of Religious Life," the first document resulting from Vatican II.

Center of Care

The development of new technologies that had begun at St. Bernards following World War II continued throughout the 1980s. Construction and renovation of facilities continued to enhance the delivery of medical services. The old 1929 Convent building at 223 East Jackson Street had been converted into St. Bernards Annex. The Area Health Education Center (AHEC) Program started in 1975 expanded in 1980 to include a residency program.

The Accreditation Council for Graduate Medical Education approved an application to offer a three-year Family Practice Residency Program at St. Bernards, with Dr. John R. Williams as its first director. The renovated Annex provided space for this new program in northeast Arkansas. After completing the residency program, a number of the graduates established their practice in the Jonesboro area.[3]

Promise Kept

A significant milestone of progress occurred in 1981 when County Judge Roy (Red) Bearden kept the promise made to the Sisters to blacktop the gravel road that runs from Hwy. 141 past the Convent, (now known as Hwy. CR766). After having driven the rough gravel road for the past six years since moving to the present site, the Sisters were grateful to the County Judge for keeping his promise. The Convent cars had all taken a toll from the rough roads, so now some of the vehicles had to be replaced. The area residents were also grateful to have the Sisters as influential neighbors.

Twelfth Prioress

Since the second three-year term of Mother Julia Pruss was drawing to a close in June 1981, a Canonical election was scheduled. On Saturday, June 6, 1981 Sr. Mary John Seyler of Muenster, Texas was elected as the twelfth Prioress of Holy Angels Convent.

Mother Mary John was the second Prioress to be elected from Texas. The first was Mother Perpetua Reinart of Lindsay, who served as Prioress of the Community from 1943 to 1954. Mother Mary John had received a Bachelor's of Arts degree from Avila College, Kansas City, Missouri and a Master's degree in religious education from St. Mary's University, San Antonio, Texas.

As the elected Prioress of the Community, Mother Mary John was also the President and Chairperson of the Governing Board of St. Bernards. This added responsibility necessitated a "crash course" in health care ministry for each new Prioress, and Mother Mary John was no exception. SEE PROFILE IN APPENDIX.

The traditional Corporation meeting was held that same afternoon of the election, to name a President. Mother Mary John was nominated and elected by unanimous vote as President of the Olivetan Benedictine Corporation. However, Mother Mary John did not name a Subprioress at that time, but the Corporation members elected Sisters to fill the two vacant positions on the Council. Sr. James Poirot and Sr. Celestine Pond were elected.[4] About two weeks later, Mother Mary John announced that Sr. Yvonne Lerner was named Subprioress for the Community. Sr. Eileen Schneider was appointed Formation Directress and Sr. Benedicta Boeckmann was named Directress of the Pastoral Care Department at St. Bernards, which she had established in 1967 while she was Prioress.

Expansion

Although closets were included in the bedrooms and in different areas around the Convent, Sisters continued to express the need for additional storage space. Mother Mary John addressed this need at the August 14, 1981 council meeting.[5] She presented the architect's drawing of a possible long addition to the side of the kitchen/dining room area. Council members approved this addition and recommended that an outside door be installed to allow for vendors to deliver supplies directly to the respective storage area.

During the Spring of 1983, Mother Mary John was also instrumental in having a restroom installed close to the left side of the Chapel entrance. This was a welcome addition, not only for the Sisters, but for visitors who may be attending Mass in the Convent Chapel.

Gifts to Community

At the August 14, 1981 council meeting, Mother Mary John informed the Sisters about the gift of farmland, willed to the Community, near Jonesboro from the Sellmeyer Trust Estate. Colonel Olhausen was handling the paperwork so the transfer could be finalized.[6]

Previously, a large gift of farmland, city buildings and bank stock had been willed to the Olivetan Benedictine Sisters by Maurice P. Welsh, who died October 4, 1946. However, the revenues from these holdings were willed to his niece Margaret Welsh Fairhead throughout her lifetime. Only after her death, December 22, 1981, did the Community receive title to the revenues.

The March 12, 1982 council minutes reveal that "Most of the Welsh Estate is in farm land, with three buildings in town included in it."[7] Mother Mary John stated, the estate included a 250 acre farm west of Jonesboro which had been farmed by a Mr. and Mrs. Leonard for the past 30 years. They now wished to retire and buy the brick-veneer, two-bedroom house, along with ten acres of land.

The August 13, 1982 council minutes reveal that the Community had been the beneficiary in the Wrape Foundation.[8] The Community received periodic donations, designated to the education fund, until the total gift had been received.

On August 30, 1982, the Community discussed this proposition. Colonel Olhausen, who made a presentation, had previously had the house and ten acres appraised. He recommended that the Community sell, but not for less than $35,000. He also reported that the Leonards are willing to pay cash and the transaction would not hinder another tenant from renting the remaining 240 acres.[9]

This same information was sent to the mission Sisters and they were asked to return their votes. By September 4, 1982, Council members counted the votes which showed the majority of Chapter members voted to sell the portion of the estate that included the farm house and ten acres of land.[10]

Finance Advisory Commission

Due to receiving additional properties willed to the Olivetan Benedictine Sisters, Inc., Mr. Jack Deacon, attorney, recommended that a Finance Advisory Committee be engaged to assist the Business Manager. Colonel Olhausen strongly favored this recommendation, as he expressed the desire to retire due to increasing health problems.

Mother Mary John presented this matter to the Council and in turn, the members voted to act on this recommendation. The July 9, 1982 council minutes confirmed that Mother Mary John asked Phil Jones, a local accountant, and Ralph Halk, a retired banker and investment officer, to serve on this committee. Both agreed to serve, but she asked for suggestions for a third member. Later, Robert Davidson, Sr., a local insurance carrier, agreed to join the committee.[11]

Oblate Program

After extensive research, Holy Angels Convent established an Oblate Program in the Spring of 1983. The April 8, 1983 council minutes reveal that Sr. Yvonne Lerner, Subproioress, recommended that the Community begin an Oblate Program. After explanation and discussion, the Council approved the idea to start such a program. Sr. Yvonne was named the first Directress of the Oblate Program. Although one Sister was named Directress, Mother Mary John asked all the Sisters to become involved by their prayers and input. [12] Sr. Yvonne visited a number of parishes and received the pastor's permission to explain the program to those interested.

Sr. Yvonne Lerner with a group of Oblates in convent courtyard.

The Oblate program continued to grow, as new members were enrolled and Oblations made at the Motherhouse each year. Sr. Yvonne promoted the program by holding areas meetings. In addition she conducted a spring day of Recollection and a weekend summer Retreat at the Motherhouse for the Oblates. Sr. Yvonne remained as Directress of the Oblate Program until her untimely death on September 7, 2000. By the time of her death, the number of Oblates had grown to approximately 60 members. After Sr. Yvonne's death, Sr. Mary John Seyler, who had completed her second terms prioress in 1987, was named Directress of the Oblate Program.

New Business Manager

Since Colonel James Olhausen's health was rapidly deteriorating, he was no longer able to assist in the management of financial matters for the community. At the June 3, 1983 council meeting, Mother Mary John proposed that the Community ask Ralph Halk, member of the finance committee, if he would be willing to serve in this capacity. The Council unanimously agreed that he should be engaged if possible. When Mother Mary John approached Halk, he cautiously agreed to serve in this capacity to the best of his ability.[13] SEE PROFILE IN APPENDIX.

This was a timely arrangement, as Colonel Olhausen died on August 9, 1983. The Community, as well as businessmen throughout northeast Arkansas, mourned the loss of this highly esteemed businessman. Later a plaque was erected in the Centennial Grotto, which states, *"Dedicated to the memory of Col. James N. Olhausen—Business Manager of Holy Angels Convent, who served faithfully and well from 1967 to 1983. We honor his integrity, his love for our Community, and his steadfast example of representing the highest ideals of a Christian Business Man."*

Schoen Lake

Mother Mary John loved nature and was an advocate for preserving native wildlife on the Convent grounds. She had the property posted and restricted for this proposes to prevent poachers from intruding. During the Spring of 1982, Bob Schoenborn, head maintenance, recommended that a pond be dug on the property to help with drainage, as well as balancing wildlife in the area. Mother Mary John obtained a consensus among the Sisters, so arrangements were made to have a pond dug. In addition to other benefits, a pond would also provide recreational opportunities for Sisters who enjoyed fishing. Herman Tinsley, the same neighbor who had earlier dug the swimming pool, received the contract to do the work.

Down the hill, to the right side of the main entrance of the Convent, a 2 1/2 acre pond was dug. According to oral history, Tinsley raised Australian Blue Heelers to help in herding his cattle. He frequently spoke of these smart dogs. On one of his trips to the Convent grounds to check on the digging of the pond, he was with

Sr. Alberta Krebs enjoying an afternoon of fishing at Schoen Lake.

Mother Mary John down by the excavation. He told his Blue Heeler to go back up to the truck (parked by the shop on top of the hill) and fetch some pliers. He had his tools spread out in the back of his truck. Within a few minutes, the dog returned with pliers in his mouth. Smart dog!

The pond was later named "Schoen Lake," in honor of Robert Schoenborn, a long time maintenance supervisor, who had spent 21 years in dedicated service to the Community. Schoenborn died an untimely death on March 12, 1990, when he suffered a massive coronary while working at the Convent. After the lake filled, following successive rains and draining the surrounding areas, the Arkansas Game and Fish Commission stocked the pond with various species of fish. The Sisters enjoyed many pleasant hours around the lake, and sometimes their efforts provided a tasty Friday meal.

During conversation later with Schoenborn, Mother Mary John thanked him for recommending the pond, and said, it was one of the best things he did for the Sisters. In his humble, subtle, humorous way, with downcast eyes, he said, "I don't think so; I think the construction of that extra restroom (outside Chapel) was the best."

Continuing Education

As part of continuing education, Mother Mary John continued the custom of engaging priests from Subiaco to give conferences at the Motherhouse. The minutes of the February 12, 1982 council meeting stated that Fr. David Flusche, OSB, Subiaco conducted this program which extended through several years. He also made periodic visits to the missions to give conferences and spiritual direction to the Sisters.

DCWR hosted at Holy Angels

On October 31, 1981, Holy Angels Convent hosted the Diocesan Assembly of Women Religious. This marked the first time the Diocesan organization held their annual assembly in northeast Arkansas. Sr. Geraldine Homer, DCRW President, organized the day and chaired the sessions. This occasion provided an opportunity for a number of Sisters from throughout the Diocese to visit and tour the new facilities of Holy Angels Convent.

Mission to Mexico

From stories about missionaries told by Sr. Fridoline Buck, her first grade teacher, Sr. Elaine Willett had always been interested in being a missionary. In 1982, Pope John Paul II issued a letter requesting Communities to send religious as missionaries to foreign lands. When Mother Mary John presented this letter to the Council members, she asked if they knew of anyone interested. Sr. Elaine spoke up and said she would be interested in going to Mexico if it would be possible.

After further inquiries, in August 1983, Sr. Elaine visited the Missionary Benedictine Sisters in Mexico City. Sr. Petra Riga accompanied Sr. Elaine and stayed in Mexico with her for a few months. The Mexican Sisters welcomed them and offered them the choice of working in some of their missions. By September 1983, Sr. Elaine and Sr. Petra went to El Ojite, an Indian Village in the State of Hidalgo, Mexico. In September 1985, Sr. Elaine moved to another Indian Village in the same Parish.

Although at the time Sr. Elaine did not have a good working knowledge of speaking Spanish she had audited Spanish classes at ASU while teaching in the nursing program (1981-1983). She continued to learn more Spanish, while working in Mexico. During the first two years they worked with five Mexican Sisters in their parish of 40 Indian Villages. This included Religious education, sewing, first aid and various medical themes.

During the second two years, Sr. Elaine's work centered more around Catechetical work and the medical needs of the people. She treated illnesses with her supply of medicines and would also deliver babies when the midwives were not available, or when they needed help with problem pregnancies. After four years in Mexico, Sr. Elaine returned to Holy Angels, to be named Formation Directress for the following five years.

Newsletter

At the same April 8, 1983 council meeting, Mother Mary John also proposed the possibility of re-establishing the publication of a newsletter. Mother Philippa had issued "Tidings from Home," a mimeographed newsletter to all the Sisters, but it was discontinued after she left office.

The newsletter, Mother Mary John now proposed, would also be sent to close relatives, friends and Oblates. She explained that would provide a good way to keep the Oblates, relatives, friends and benefactors in touch with the Community. After discussing cost estimates, the Council approved that the newsletter be re-established for a period of one year, before any final decision was made.[14]

According to Council Minutes of August 5, 1983, Sr. Louise Frankenberger was named the first editor of the newsletter, entitled "Holy Angels Echoes," which recalled the name of the school newspaper of the former Holy Angels Academy.[15] Sr. Beatrice Schneider, Secretary at the time, assisted in the typing and publication. For a few years this publication was mimeographed at the Motherhouse but later printed professionally.

This publication has continued and circulation has grown to over 1300 recipients who have expressed interest in the Sisters of Holy Angels Convent. In 1993, the three times a year publication was increased to a quarterly basis. Also in 1993, Sr. Geraldine Homer succeeded Sr. Louise as Editor. Since 2001, Sr. Henrietta Hockle serves as editor of this publication.

Title Change to St. Bernards

Because of the increase in business matters that needed to be addressed by the Hospital Administrator, Consultant, Mr. John Warner, recommended that the Hospital Administrator be named President of St. Bernards Medical Center, while the Prioress retain the title of Chair of the Board. He explained functions would remain basically the same but this would give the Hospital Administrator a better image in dealing with other large institutions. The bylaws of St. Bernards would need to be changed to reflect this change in title.

Mother Mary John presented this matter to the Council on September 9, 1983 and asked for advice. Council members deferred a decision on this matter until they could review the bylaws. According to the bylaws, this change may be made by the Council. Minutes of the April 13, 1984 council meeting recorded members voted to change the title of the Hospital Administrator to President/CEO of St. Bernards. The Prioress would continue to hold the title of Chair of St. Bernards Governing Board. [16]

Re-election

On June 7, 1984 Mother Mary John was elected to a second three-year term. At the Annual Corporation meeting held the following day, the Sisters voted to stagger the positions on the Council in such a way that two vacancies would fall in a year other than the year of election of the Prioress. This was done by electing one to serve a three-year term, and the second to a two-year term. Since this would break the pattern, no future changes would need to be made in length of terms on the Council. Sr. Julia Pruss was elected to the three-year term and Sr. Pauline Morath to the two-year term. [17]

Innovations

During 1984, the Council drew up short- and long-range goals for the maintenance and improvement of facilities of Holy Angels

Convent. One of the most significant changes that evolved from this effort was computerizing the business office functions.

Some of the long-range goals included: change the flooring around Chapel from Infirmary entrance to dining room and recreation room, to vinyl from carpet, to enable those in wheelchairs

The last six Swiss Sisters remaining in 1984. Seated, L – R: Sr. Veronica Studer, Sr. Irmena Tiefenaur and Sr. Bernadette Kaufman. Standing, Sr. Angela Weber, Sr. Theresina Grob and Sr. Caroline Basrmettler.

and walkers to more easily reach their destinations; Replace crumbling sidewalks; implement energy-saving measures by converting to heat pumps; place double-glass windows in more exposed areas; and repaint walls. A number of other topics were recommended for the long-range goals.

A company in Pocahontas had perfected a heat pump for heating and cooling that would save on electricity. Mr. Halk and Mr. Schoenborn both recommended that the Community install one and try it before purchasing others. At the December 14, 1984 council, members approved the expenditure of $17,000 for the purchase, drilling and installation of one heat pump. At first, this proved satisfactory but because of frequent needed service from the company in Pocahontas, the heat pump was later discontinued and replaced by equipment that could be serviced by the Convent maintenance staff. [18]

Pocahontas Property

A special Chapter meeting was held on February 2, 1985 to discuss the sale of Lots 1, 3, 4 and 5 of the Benet Addition to St. Paul's Parish that had petitioned the Sisters twice about the purchase. Since these lots had not yet been purchased by individuals, they were available for sale. Mission Sisters were sent the minutes of the meeting and ballots for voting. The total Community tally revealed that the majority of Sisters voted to sell the portions that were requested by St. Paul's Parish at the market value of $3,500 each.

Apostolates

During the annual Chapter meeting on June 11, 1985 the community discussed the declining number of Sisters available to serve in mission apostolates. To assist the Prioress in making the proper decisions concerning staffing, Mother Mary John proposed that each Sister draw up a list and prioritize the ones they preferred to keep as long as possible. This list would serve as a guide for making future decisions. The lists were tallied and the following reflect the consensus of the Community:

Missions to Retain

St. Paul's, Pocahontas
Blessed Sacrament, Jonesboro
Our Lady of Holy Souls, Little Rock
Sacred Heart, Muenster
Our Lady of Fatima, Benton
Benedictine Manor, Hot Springs
St. Michael's West Memphis
Holy Rosary, Stuttgart
St. Mary's, Paragould
Day Care/Music, Little Rock
Holy Redeemer, El Dorado
Immaculate Conception, Blytheville
El Ojite, Mexico [19]

Due to the declining health of Sr. Dolores Brady, long-time music teacher in Blytheville, and no replacements available, the music department in Blytheville was closed in January 1986. Materials were shared with Sr. Philippa Wavrick and Sr. Celestine Pond, the other music teachers. The house which was owned by the Community was then sold. Sr. Dolores retired to the Motherhouse and assisted in providing some of the music for liturgical celebrations for the community.

Water Storage Tank

The Farrville-Philadelphia Water Association contacted Mother Mary John about placing a water storage tank on the Convent property. She presented this matter to the Council on August 8, 1986. Mother Mary John explained that the proposed area would be a piece of property 100'x 100' on the crest of the hill off Rolling Ridge Road, now Hwy: CR753. Mr. Halk and Mr. Schoenborn were in favor of giving the land to the Association for this purpose.

In exchange for the land, the Association would provide a larger water line and one or two hydrants on Convent property. After further discussion, a voice vote was taken, and all Council members voted "yes." Mother Mary John asked if this matter should be taken to the Chapter for vote, since it involves a land transaction. According to the Constitution, Juridic Elements J-12 #6, "acts of extraordinary administration" is a matter for Chapter decision. Although this small portion of land was not deemed "extraordinary administration" at the August 8 council meeting, the members recommended that the Community should be polled.[20] Therefore, the Community was polled at a Chapter meeting on August 20, 1986, and ballots were mailed to the missions sisters. Later, the returns revealed that the majority of Sisters favored this decision.

Medical Expansion Center

In the middle of the 1980s St. Bernards dramatically expanded its services. Heart surgery was a significant factor in its progress.

The Winter 1984 edition of *The Banner* stated, "History was made at St. Bernards and a new era was entered when a surgical team performed the facilities first coronary bypass surgery this year." [21] Later that same year, the Sleep Disorder Center was opened on the third floor of the annex building. And in 1987, in response to a growing need in northeast Arkansas, St. Bernards established a Women's Diagnostic Center.

After numerous studies, the Arkansas Health Agency identified northeast Arkansas as a high incident area for cancer. By the fall of 1987, the Governing board considered a Cancer Treatment Center as a high priority. Plans were made to have a capital campaign to raise funds to erect such a center. "To speed up construction, funding was sought to cover about half the anticipated $3.8 million cost of the project." Mr. Owens announced that, "When construction begins it will include the entire complex of the treatment center and a parking deck. The multi-level parking facility will accommodate 700 cars. Access to the primary medical center structure will be covered with walkways. The construction project is expected to take 18 months."

In 1989, St. Bernards established a Hospice Program to provide comfort and care for individuals who were in the last phases of life. The program was certified by Medicare and the State of Arkansas June 16, 1989. In conjunction with administration of St. Bernards, Flo Jones, an R.N., was instrumental in establishing this program.

Centennial Preparation Committee

Since the foundation of the Olivetan Benedictine Community in Arkansas was begun on December 13, 1887, when the first four Sisters arrived in Pocahontas, the centennial year was nearing. A Centennial Preparation Committee was formed on June 11, 1985, and the following Sisters were elected to serve on this committee: Sr. Philippa Wavrick, Sr. Geraldine Homer, Sr. Henrietta Hockle, Sr. Mary Anne Nuce and Sr. Deborah Schump.

Major activities and expenditures were discussed which included both Spiritual and temporal. The celebration was scheduled to begin a year prior to the Centennial and close on the actual date of foundation of the Community. A committee chaired by Sr. Mary Anne Nuce published a Centennial Birthday Calendar. Birthdays of the Sisters and Centennial events were included in this calendar. The following is a list of the activities held during the year.

Centennial Events and Dates

November 28, 1986	—	PRE-CENTENNIAL BAZAAR in Jonesboro Bell Community Center
December 13, 1986	—	FOUNDERS DAY Opening of our Centennial, the 99th Anniversary of Foundation in Arkansas–Mass and Dinner–Bishop and Community
March 21, 1987	—	FEAST OF ST. BENEDICT Mass and Dinner–Special Guests: Hospital Administration, Governing Board, Foundation Board, Convent Advisory Finance Committee
July 4, 1987	—	SISTERS OF HOLY ANGELS DAY Community Celebration
July 11, 1987	—	SOLEMNITY OF ST. BENEDICT Mass and dinner–Special Guests: Abbot Primate and all Benedictines
July 18, 1987	—	OPEN HOUSE General Reception–Special Guests: Parishes, Hospital
August 6, 1987	—	FEAST OF TRANSFIGURATION - Final Vow Day–Mass and Dinner Special Guests: Relatives of honorees, All relatives of Sisters
October 2, 1987	—	FEAST OF HOLY ANGELS Community Feastday
October 12, 1987	—	ANNIVERSARY OF CONVENT DEDICATION Mass and Dinner–Special Guests: Oblates and all Former Members
November 27, 1987	—	DIOCESAN CLERGY / RELIGIOUS DAY Mass and Dinner– Special Guests: Priests, Deacons, Seminarians, and Religious in Diocese
December 13, 1987	—	CLOSING OF CENTENNIAL the 100th Anniversary in Arkansas–Mass and Dinner–Bishop and Community [22]

A commemorative Centennial booklet was also published and distributed to guests throughout the Centennial year. Parishes and individual sponsors contributed towards the cost of publication. The booklet contained an historical sketch written by Sr. Henrietta Hockle, plus an official picture of each Sister, numerous activity pictures, quotations from the Rule of St. Benedict, a necrology of all deceased Sisters, plus, listing of Parish and individual sponsors. Centennial Booklet Committee members consisted of the following: Sr. Louise Frankenberger, Sr. Georgia Felderhoff, Sr. Eileen Schneider, Sr. Miriam Burns, Sr. Beatrice Schneider and Sr. Henrietta Hockle.

Exterior of Centennial Grotto erected in honor of deceased Sisters.

A Centennial Grotto, donated by St. Bernards Hospital, was erected on the Convent grounds in memory of all the Sisters who dedicated their lives to the health care ministry. The Grotto houses a stained glass panel, depicting the Virgin Mary. The original bell, cast in 1890, that hung in the Convent Maria Stein Chapel in Pocahontas was brought over and erected in the Grotto.

The dedication plaque that hangs in the Grotto states, *"This Grotto is given in respect and gratitude for the Sisters who founded St. Bernards Regional Medical Center. By their courage, work and generosity of spirit they proclaimed, 'When you did it to the least of these you did it to me.' In this Centennial Year we honor their memory and all other Sisters whose destiny it has been to seek and find how to truly serve the Master of us all. Wherever the art of medicine is loved, there is also love of humanity, the greatest of all the Commandments."*

A bazaar was successful in raising $28,301.46 which was spent toward Centennial celebration expenses.

Interior of Centennial Grotto — Stained glass replica of the Virgin Mary. The Grotto also houses the original bell from chapel in Convent Maria Stein in Pocahontas.

Thirteenth Prioress

In June of 1987, Mother Mary John Seyler's second term in office drew to a Close, so a Canonical election was held on June 13, 1987. Sr. Cabrini Arami was elected the thirteenth Prioress of the Community.[23] Mother Cabrini Arami, the third Prioress elected from the "Lone Star State," was born and reared in Montague, Texas. She entered Holy Angels Convent in 1949. SEE PROFILE IN APPENDIX.

Shortly after the election, Mother Cabrini named Sr. Julia Pruss as Subprioress for the community. She announced that since she had served as Subprioress, when Sr. Julia was Prioress, she thought they could work well together. Sr. Elaine Willett was recalled from her ministry in Mexico and named Formation Directress. Mother Cabrini dedicated her efforts to continue the projects begun during Mother Mary John's tenure, both in the Community and in the hospital. She fostered the religious spirit and encouraged faithfulness to private prayer and recitation of the Divine Office. In addition to the annual retreat, Mother Cabrini also scheduled each summer a workshop on different aspects of Benedictine Spirituality. Mother Cabrini emphasized spirituality as a major component to the apostolates in which the Sisters were involved.

One of the first tasks of Mother Cabrini was to prepare for the Tri-Annual General Chapter to be held during the summer of 1988. A committee was formed to organize the agenda and lead the discussions. Revisions needed to Joyful Response, the Constitution and Customary were to be reviewed at this time.

Sr. Elaine scheduled Vocation Awareness Weekends to promote vocations to the community. A new informational vocation brochure was published to interest young ladies in the Benedictine way of life at Holy Angels.

Historical Marker

To commemorate the Centennial of the establishment of the Community in Arkansas, Sr. Louise Frankenberger proposed the erection of an historic marker on the Pocahontas property, where the Community first located. The Council considered this project during the October 9, 1987 council meeting, but Mother Cabrini advised the Sisters to wait until all the bills were paid from the yearlong Centennial celebration before any decision was made.[24]

Sr. Louise contacted her nephew, Albert Frankenberger, a local architect, for a cost estimate of a plaque. She reported, if purchased through the architect, a plaque 14" x 18" would cost approximately $600, with Frankenberger's work for designing it donated. The cast bronze plaque was erected in 1988, paid for in part by memorials given in honor of the late Eugene B. Wittlake, Ph.D., who had been Curator at the ASU Museum. Dr. Wittlake and his wife had been long-time friends of the Olivetan Benedictine Sisters. Frankenberger attached the plaque to the wall at the entrance to the Convent grounds in Pocahontas on December 13, 1988, the 101st Anniversary of the founding of the Community. The historic marker states:

> A tribute to the intrepid faith of the noble women who settled at this site on Pocahontas, Arkansas on December 13, 1887. The indomitable spirit of these Sisters continues to live in their contribution to Christian Education and to the Care of Suffering Humanity. Their followers serve Northeast Arkansas in schools and at St. Bernards Regional Medical Center in Jonesboro, Arkansas. In this same courageous spirit, we dedicate this site anew in 1987 through our continued efforts to serve the citizens of this area. OLIVETAN BENEDICTINE SISTERS—on the occasion of their Centennial Year. 1887–1987."

Social Security

A major decision affecting the future of the Community was made in October 1987. The Community met in Chapter on December 12, 1987, to consider the feasibility of joining the U.S. Social Security retirement system. Although this topic was researched and analyzed during Mother Mary John's tenure as Prioress, it did not come before the Community for a vote until 1987. "Using computer-designed models, Ralph Halk, business manager, indicated the most beneficial route for the Community to follow. Halk recommended that the Community pay taxes, five years back on all the Sisters who are presently working members of it. The Sisters would retire for purposes of this program at age 62, beginning to draw a monthly check at that time for the rest of their life." However the Sisters could continue working as long as they wish and were able. This monthly Social Security check would just be an added income. [25]

"Qualification for benefits is determined by a combination of age, tax-covered quarters, and taxes paid in on the individual. The first payment for the five back years, plus the first quarter of 1988, would be due January 31." Discussion ensued in which Halk responded the questions from the Sisters. A secret ballot indicated that the majority of Sisters voted in favor of joining the Social Security program beginning in 1988. This decision, made at the close of the Centennial year, marked one of the wisest made during the first one hundred years of the Community. Halk took care of the financial transactions to enroll all the Sisters eligible to participate. A separate retirement fund was established to hold and invest any funds received from this source.

Marian Year

Pope John Paul II declared 1988 as a Marian Year to commemorate and honor Holy Mother of God. The northeast Arkansas deanery held its closing event for the Marian Year at Holy Angels Convent on Sunday, August 29, 1988. Parishioners from Parishes throughout northeast Arkansas participated in this closing event held at 4 p.m. in Holy Angels Convent Chapel.

Cancer Treatment Center

By 1989, campaign chairman Wallace Fowler announced that the drive for the Cancer Treatment Center had been successful in raising over half of the anticipated $3.8 million cost of the project. Mother Cabrini and members of the Hospital Governing Board participated in the groundbreaking ceremonies held at 1 p.m. on January 21, 1989. The Governing Board voted to name the building the "Ben E. Owens Cancer Treatment Center," in recognition for his visionary leadership.[26] Mayor Hubert Brodell declared the following Tuesday, January 27, 1989, as "Ben E. Owens Day," and a reception was held at ASU Convocation Center to honor him.

Medical Arts Building

By the spring of 1989, the Jonesboro physicians expressed the need for increased office space. The March 10, 1989 council minutes stated "With 162 physicians on staff, St. Bernards needs additional office space. The Community was asked to approve the erection of a

Medical Arts Building at 800 South Church and leasing suite to the physicians." After receiving the appropriate Canonical permission, the Community voted to approve the construction of such a building. The first tenants to occur the new building were the Internal Medicine Physicians, who reserved the entire fourth floor.

Fire Station

Since the Farrville-Philadelphia Fire Station was now within city limits due to the recent annexation, the rural station would have to relocate. Fred Armstrong, member of the rural fire station commission, told Mother Cabrini if the city purchased the old site they would be interested in purchasing an acre of land from the Sisters. The property on the front corner of Rolling Ridge Road (Hwy. 753) and Hwy. 766 would be most suitable. If the city purchased the old site, the rural station would have to relocate.

At the annual Corporation meeting on June 15, 1989, Mother Cabrini presented this matter to the Chapter members for consideration. *Benefits*—fire service would be near if needed, fire insurance would drop, and property value would increase. *Disadvantages*—possibility of fire sirens becoming a problem and loss of privacy. The general consensus was not to sell. However, Mother Cabrini said if she is approached again about the matter, she would poll the Community before giving an answer.[27] Later, the rural fire commission built their fire station off Hwy. 351, so nothing more was said about the matter.

Apostolic Works

"From the earliest foundations of the Olivetan Benedictine Community, the service of the church in the active apostolate has been a major component in the life of its members. The chief works to which the Community has been dedicated have been Catholic education, Christ-like care of the sick and other apostolic works. In keeping with this heritage, the apostolic works of the Community are adapted to the needs of the Church and to the needs of the times, subject always to the approval of Church authorities and the authority of the Community."[28]

From the beginning of its history, the active ministry of the Community has been consistent with the above declaration from the Constitution, Part II, Benedictine Spiritual Life. Besides ministry in schools, hospitals and retirement centers, the Sisters served in the culinary department at St. John's Seminary, Little Rock. Other Ministries in which Sisters served were as follows: Sr. Annella Willett, Diocesan sponsored Social Service Outreach, Helping Hand, Little Rock; Sr. Yvonne Lerner, Parish Administrator at Arkadelphia, and later Diocesan Director of the Diaconate Program; Sr. Henrietta Hockle, Diocesan Superintendent of Schools; Sr. Geraldine Homer, Sr. Romana Rohmer and Sr. Miriam Burns, Catechetical Ministry.

As the decade of the 1980s drew to a close, there were fewer Sisters available to teach in the schools and to work in the hospital. Due to death, those leaving, and fewer numbers entering, membership had declined. At the beginning of the decade there were 84 Chapter members, but as the decade came to a close, there were only 65. The Community however, continued to respond, as far as possible, to the needs of the Church and the needs of the times. Sisters from Holy Angels Convent were sought, because they continued to reflect their Olivetan Benedictine heritage in their prayer and life style wherever they were assigned.

Wooden Repository used on Holy Thursdays in Chapel—The wooden repository was carved out of one walnut log by Lawrence Schneider and hand-painted by Sr. Bernardine Grueninger.

CHAPTER 15
1990-1999

Health Care Ministry Expansion

As the last decade of the Twentieth Century dawned, the Benedictine Community in Jonesboro was recognized as a beacon of hope in northeast Arkansas. After 90 years since its establishment, St. Bernards health care ministry had developed into a state of the art medical center for Christ-like healing to the community through education, treatment and health services. Services extended to 23 counties now, 17 of which were in northeast Arkansas and six in southern Missouri.

"Three major themes dominated the health care ministry in the 1990s. The first was the continuing expansion and development of increasingly sophisticated clinical services, which included among others, cancer treatment and radiation oncology. The Diagnostic and Treatment Center, which included the Ben E. Owens Cancer Treatment Center, opened in Summer of 1991, and was dedicated on June 7, when all new equipment was installed." [1]

In addition to the cancer program, other new services were opened during the decade. A Pain Management Center and an off site Pre-Admission Testing (PAT) unit were opened in Jonesboro. In addition, St. Bernards opened an Occupational Therapy/Physical Therapy Centers (OT/PT) in Blytheville, Paragould and Jonesboro. The business office, plus the purchasing, accounting and marketing offices were moved to an off site location. Physicians' office condominiums were developed in the Medical Arts Building at 800 South Church Street.

"Through the generosity of St. Bernards Auxilians, as well as citizens, firms and organizations throughout northeast Arkansas and southern Missouri, another dream for the improvement of patient care came true with the completion and opening of the

Auxiliary House on March 1, 1992." [2] This facility provides overnight accommodations for cancer patients while they are taking treatments. Members of the Auxiliary operate the facility by staffing and continue to contribute to the upkeep of the building.

Philanthropy to support these efforts and others became increasingly important and in the fall of 1993, St. Bernards Development Foundation announced the formation of "St. Bernards Advocates," a volunteer organization whose purpose is to aid St. Bernards in its pursuit of providing health care excellence. As a means of expanding community services, during this same year, St. Bernards established "Lifeline," a personalized help for people who needed immediate or emergency care.

Retirement Fund

While their health care ministry was making giant strides in the medical field, the Olivetan Benedictine Sisters made strides in preparing for the future of the Community by adopting policies to enlarge their retirement fund. The United States Catholic Conference of Bishops, along with the Conference of Major Superiors of Male Religious and the Leadership Conference of Women Religious (Tri-Conference), established a retirement program.

An annual collection would be taken up each December over a period of ten years in all Catholic dioceses throughout the nation. A National Religious Retirement Office would distribute these funds. Although the project was established in 1988, the first grants were not distributed until the following spring. The Olivetan Benedictines of Jonesboro received their first grant in June of 1989.

To continue to receive grants from this annual collection, a religious community would need to pass a formal resolution to keep the funds in a separate account and submit a formal application. "Conditions that qualified a Community to participate would be to establish a segregated fund for use exclusively for retirement purposes, whose investment objective is to obtain a fair return consistent with the preservation of capital." [3]

Since the Jonesboro Community had already established their

Retirement Fund in 1988, when they received their first Social Security check, now only a resolution was needed to verify this account. On March 9, 1990, the Council adopted a resolution to invest any funds received from the Tri-Conference Retirement Project, together with the present Community Retirement Fund.

"WHEREAS, Olivetan Benedictine Sisters, Incorporated, currently has an established segregated fund for use exclusively for retirement purposes, whose investment objective is to obtain a fair return consistent with the preservation of capital.

"Be it resolved that the Olivetan Benedictine Sisters, Incorporated, through this resolution passed and adopted by its Council on the ninth day of March 1990, agree to hold and invest any funds received from the Tri-Conference Retirement Project, together with our present Retirement Fund, and according to present policies as stated above."[4]

During each June in succeeding years, the Community has continued to receive a check from the National Religious Retirement Office. The business manager has faithfully handled the financial transactions for the application and the investment of funds.

Outdoor Stations of the Cross

By July of 1990, Sr. Marya Duscher and helpers completed the restoration of the Stations of the Cross that had been erected outdoors along the entrance driveway. First installed in the 1905 Holy Angels Chapel, these stations had been refurbished by Sr. Bernardine Grueninger and weatherproofed when installed outdoors in 1974 when

Sr. Marya Duscher refurbishing the outdoor Stations of the Cross which line the entrance drive.

the Convent was relocated to present site. Mr. Robert Schoenborn had erected wayside shrines in which to enclose them.

Now, due to deterioration caused by the weather, these nearly 100 year-old Stations of the Cross had to be refurbished again. Sr. Marya restored them to their original beauty by repainting and resealing them. To further protect them from the elements, Mr. Robert Schoenborn, head maintenance man at the time, attached a Plexiglas shield across the front of each shrine. These single-tiered shrines along the front drive provide a beacon of hope and encouragement to all who reflect on them to accept the crosses of life.

Business Transactions

On April 10, 1990, the Council passed two corporate resolutions. The first was to grant limited power of attorney to Carter Patteson for the purpose of supervising the business activities at the farms the Community owned in Eastern Craighead County, and with agencies who require his services in its behalf. The second corporate resolution was to reaffirm the authority of Ralph Halk to conduct business transactions on behalf of the Olivetan Benedictine Sisters.[5] This resolution was required so the business manager could continue to legally represent the Olivetan Benedictine Sisters, Inc. in all financial transactions.

Election Time Again

By June 1990, Mother Cabrini had completed her three-year term as Prioress of the Community, so a Canonical election was scheduled to be held on June 14, 1990 following the annual Retreat. Sr. Mary John Seyler and Sr. Romana Rohmer were elected as tellers and Bishop Andrew McDonald, DD presided at the election.

Mother Cabrini Arami was re-elected to a second three-year term and Sr. Julia Pruss was reappointed Subprioress for the Community. One of the first tasks of the Prioress was, again, to prepare for the Tri-Annual General Chapter that was to be held the following year. The following Sisters were elected to serve on the

Constitution Committee to prepare for the General Chapter to be held in June 1991: Sr. Georgia Felderhoff, Sr. Romana Rohmer, Sr. Eileen Schneider, Sr. Elaine Willett and Sr. Brenda Willett.

General Chapter 1991

Sr. Georgia, who chaired the committee to prepare for the General Chapter, asked the Sisters to review the Constitution, Joyful Response, and note any changes or additions that may be needed. The committee would accept suggestions from the Sisters and compile them for the Council to prioritize in preparation for the General Chapter. Fr. Nathaniel Reeves, OSB, a Canon lawyer from St. Meinrad Archabbey, was engaged to assist the committee with questions concerning Canonical matters.

Bishop McDonald opened the General Chapter on June 7, 1991 with the working sessions held the following day. Only minor changes were made in wording throughout Joyful Response, with the exception of a change in the Juridic Elements, J-73 Section E—Penalties and Appeals, which brought it in accord with the decree of the 1983 Code of Canon Law.

A second change which was determined by majority vote concerned the election to the Council. The new wording in the Customary C-16, reads as follows:

"An elected member serves a three-year term and is eligible for re-election only once. Any Council member who has served six years is not eligible for election to the Council until she has been off the Council for one term." [6]

Another significant change in wording concerned the custom of wearing crowns at Profession and Jubilee Ceremonies. Some of the Sisters stated that a "crown" had lost its symbolism and corsages would be more appropriate. After discussion, a vote was taken which showed that the majority of Sisters approved replacing crowns with corsages.

All changes were recorded and forwarded to the Bishop for his approval. Bishop McDonald approved the changes in the Constitution by letter dated July 12, 1991.

Benedictine Manor Advisory Board

Due to increased administrative and financial needs at the Community-owned and -operated retirement facility in Hot Springs, Mr. Halk recommended that an Advisory Board be established for it. In addition to Mother Cabrini Arami, Mr Halk and Sr. Brenda Willett, two laymen from Little Rock, Al Wrape and William O'Donnell, agreed to serve on this committee. In addition, another lay person would be selected from Hot Springs.

Benedictine Manor in Hot Springs sold and now called Crown Trace.

Because the Federal Government had begun a housing program for people of lower incomes, known as Christopher Homes, it was becoming increasingly more difficult for the Benedictine Manor to compete. The building was aging and some of the equipment needed to be replaced. Renovations needed to be made in order to maintain occupancy of the units. The Community needed to either expend considerable funds on this facility or relinquish it to a buyer.

By March 12, 1992, Mother Cabrini reported to the Council that she had been contacted by Al Wrape, who said he had conferred with Dennis Lee of the Social Service Department, Diocese of Little Rock. The diocese may be interested in purchasing and managing Benedictine Manor, and requested financial information, to aid in their decision. The diocese would continue it as a retirement center as stipulated in the deed by which the Community received the land. After further discussion, the Council agreed that a Chapter Meeting should be called to vote on this matter.[7] Mother Cabrini also sent a letter of explanation to all the mission Sisters with vote attached.

After the mission votes were returned and tabulated, along with votes cast at the Motherhouse, the results revealed that the majority of Sisters approved the release of financial reports to the diocese.

Salary Increase for Teachers

Bishop McDonald scheduled a meeting of a Steering Committee in 1991, comprised of superiors of each religious Community that had Sisters teaching in the diocese. This ad hoc committee would meet with the Bishop, Bill Hartman, Diocesan Comptroller, and with Sr. Henrietta Hockle, Superintendent of Schools, to revise the salary scale for the teaching Sisters. Some of the religious Communities had reported that they were now experiencing financial difficulties.

For the 1991-92 academic year, the present salary of $10,000 per Sister would be continued, plus housing and auto. The meeting would determine the scale for future years. Mother Cabrini and Sr. Julia attended this meeting, at which time, a scale was approved to increase both salary and retirement benefits in the following years.

Statue of St. Bernard Tolomei

With the erection of the new Cancer Treatment Center at St. Bernards, Mother Cabrini proposed to the Council on October 11, 1991, that the Community donate the purchase price of a statue of St. (Blessed) Bernard Tolomei for the new entrance on Jackson Street. The statue had been ordered from Italy and was being carved from "aurisina grana" fine stone. The statue was scheduled to be delivered in December 1991. This donation to the hospital from the Community would be made in honor of all our Sisters who had devoted their life to care of the sick in the hospital. The statue was six feet tall and cost $17,235.

Discussion brought out the hospital already had a concrete statue of St. Benedict located outside the Physical Therapy Department. However, after further discussion, the Council voted unanimously that the Community donate to the hospital the purchase price for the new statue.[8] The concrete statue of St. Benedict was later moved to the grounds of Holy Angels Convent, where it now graces a sunken garden along the entrance drive.

Maintenance

Since moving to the present Motherhouse in October of 1974, the eight flat-roofed areas between the buildings had continued to leak periodically whenever a heavy rain occurred. The builders had been called repeatedly to seal the areas, but nothing seemed to help and consistent leaks occurred. Mr. Halk sought bids to reroof all eight areas and shared the quotes with Mother Cabrini, who in turn presented it to the Council.

The proposal was to use a rubber material, which would be more leak-resistant to enable the rain to run off more readily. On May 10, 1991 the Council approved the quote to reroof all eight areas for a sum of $20,000. [9]

Insurance for Teaching Sisters

By the spring of 1993, the Diocese of Little Rock announced that a medical insurance program would be funded for each of the Sisters teaching in the Catholic schools. In addition to the monthly salary and retirement benefit, the Sisters in Catholic schools now would receive a medical insurance policy.

At a May 15, 1993 council meeting, Mother Cabrini announced that Christian Brothers would be the insurance carrier for the Arkansas Teachers, both lay and religious. Medicare would be the primary insurer for those who are age 65 or over. Bill Hartmann, of the diocesan office, would be the representative for processing claims.[10] This benefit was welcomed by all the religious Communities with teaching Sisters in the diocese, and the Jonesboro Community was no exception.

Community Living

In accordance with the Constitution, Juridic Elements #J-28, the

Council made semiannual spiritual evaluations of the life of the Community. During these sessions Mother Cabrini emphasized the importance of private prayer and encouraged the Sisters to be faithful to take time for this practice. All aspects of Community life were reviewed, including manual labor. In discussing the different works in the Community, Mother Cabrini was frequently heard to say, "All jobs in the Community are important. There is no small job."

One of the last items of business Mother Cabrini addressed in 1993, was the sale of the last lot in Pocahontas. According to the council minutes of May 15, 1993, Mother Cabrini stated, "There is interest in purchasing the corner lot of our Pocahontas property on the northwest corner. This is the last unsold lot from the strip across the north side. The Community approved this for sale some years ago."[11] The negotiations for this sale were completed successfully.

Sr. Helen Swirczynski meditating on the Second Station. — Jesus accepts the cross.

Fourteenth Prioress

As the summer of 1993 drew near, Mother Cabrini's second term came to completion. A Canonical election was scheduled for June 14 following the annual retreat. Sr. Pauline Morath and Sr. Mary John Seyler were the elected tellers and Bishop Andrew J. McDonald presided at the election.

On the morning of June 14 Sr. Henrietta Hockle was elected the fourteenth Prioress of the Olivetan Benedictine Sisters of Jonesboro. She was the first Jonesboro native to be elected in the 112 year-old history of the Community. Sr. Henrietta had been based in Little Rock, and had been serving as the diocesan Superintendent of Schools. She was not prepared for this sudden change and told the Sisters that she needed some time to decide what to do.

She asked Mother Cabrini to be the administrator in charge until she could transfer her responsibilities in Little Rock. Although, Mother Cabrini had hoped to go to Texas for a little vacation and to be with her aged mother, she graciously agreed to wait until Sr. Henrietta was able to return and take over her new duties.

Sr. Henrietta then returned to Little Rock that same afternoon discerning what to do first. SEE PROFILE IN APPENDIX.

Three days later on June 17, Sr. Henrietta wrote a letter back to the Motherhouse, and asked Mother Cabrini to read it to the Community. The letter stated her reason for discontinuing the European custom of addressing the Prioress as "Mother." Sister Henrietta wrote, "Sisters, I have consulted with Archabbot Timothy of St. Meinrad, Abbot Jerome of Subiaco, and Bishop McDonald, about my preference to be addressed as Sister. All three concur that this would be appropriate, since connotation of words change through the years, just as times change.

"Archabbot Timothy said it is now the general practice throughout the country for the Prioress to be addressed as Sister. The Canonical position to which one is elected is 'Prioress' not Mother. Abbot Jerome said the superior of religious women is elected for a designated term, so it would be less confusing. Bishop McDonald concurred and said he readily approved this preference."

Sr. Henrietta further wrote, "I realize this would need to be modified in our Constitution at the next General Chapter. However, for the time being, I honestly would prefer to be addressed as Sister. For those who feel uncomfortable with this change, please feel free to use the term 'Mother.' I am grateful to each of you for understanding my preference in this matter." [12]

At first, some of the Sisters found it difficult to change but eventually, most of them adjusted to this change of custom.

The majority of Sisters voted to make this change in wording at the next General Chapter. The statement reads, “The title ‘Mother’ or ‘Sister’ is the option of the incoming Prioress.” Sr. Henrietta conferred with several Sisters by phone about being Subprioress before Sr. Eileen Schneider offered to serve in that position. This was then announced to the Sisters at the Motherhouse. Sr. Henrietta transferred the responsibilities of the superintendent’s office in Little Rock to the newly hired Associate, Michael Rockers, who would then assume responsibilities. Sr. Henrietta then packed and returned to the Motherhouse on June 29.

On the morning of June 30, she announced to the Community that Sr. Julia Pruss would continue as Formation Directress and Sr. Romana Rohmer would be the Vocation Directress. In addition to Sr. Eileen as Subprioress, the following had agreed to serve as appointed members on the Council: Sr. Geraldine Homer, Sr. Georgia Felderhoff and Sr. Ann Marie Ferricher. [13] Sr. Geraldine was also appointed editor of the newsletter, *Holy Angels Echoes*.

Chapter Meeting

At the July 9, 1993 Chapter meeting, Sr. Benedicta Boeckmann was elected as the fourth Council member, to replace Sr. Carine whose second term had expired. She joined the three remaining Chapter members, Sr. Helen Swirczynski, Sr. Pauline Morath and Sr. Joanne Sandoval, along with the newly appointed members.

Members of a Constitution Committee were elected to make plans for the 1994 General Chapter. The following Sisters were elected: Sr. Georgia Felderhoff, Sr. Romana Rohmer, Sr Eileen Schneider, Sr. Elaine Willett and Sr. Brenda Willett. [14]

Spiritual Enrichment

One of the first matters to be addressed was to secure a priest for the Sacrament of Reconciliation and spiritual enrichment for the Community. Fr. Vinantius Preske, pastor in Weiner, had faithfully served the Sisters in this capacity for a number of years, but had been transferred. The Council recommended that Sr. Henrietta contact Abbot Jerome Kodell, OSB, Subiaco and to inquire if a priest could come one weekend monthly to provide this spiritual guidance.

The Community was blessed over the next six years to have a priest from Subiaco to spend one weekend each month to give the Sisters conferences and provide an opportunity for spiritual direction.

Benedictine Manor

At the July 9 Council meeting, Sr. Henrietta reported, "Before leaving for Texas, Sr. Cabrini recommended that Sr. Henrietta continue to pursue dialogue with the diocese about their interest in Benedictine Manor. Occupancy there was now only 50 or 60 percent and the cafeteria there was a liability, so something needed to be done." [15] The Council concurred with this recommendation.

At the August 13, 1993 Council meeting, Sr. Henrietta reported that two agencies, St. Joseph's Medical Center in Hot Springs and Mr. Davis, who heads the diocesan program for Christopher Homes, Inc. have both expressed interest in purchasing the Manor. [16]

The Community Finance Committee—Robert Davidson, Jim Osborn, Phil Jones, along with Ralph Halk—had met and determined it would be in the best interest of the Community to sell the Manor. By November, Mr. Halk asked for a Community decision on the matter so he would know how to proceed if he received a firm offer. [17]

At a November 9, 1993 Chapter meeting, the Community again discussed what to do about the Manor. The Community would need to invest a considerable outlay of funds or sell it to a buyer. According to the new federal guidelines, a sprinkler system and handicap conveniences in bathrooms would need to be installed. Additional signs, a new roof, and proper city zoning were also needed.

The possibility of selling the Manor was proposed and a vote was taken. A letter of explanation was sent to the mission Sisters along with a ballot. After votes from the mission Sisters were returned and tallied, along with those cast at the Motherhouse, results showed that majority of Sisters voted in favor of selling Benedictine Manor if a suitable buyer is located. [18]

Statue of Mary transferred form Benedictine Manor to Convent grounds.

New Business Manager

However, before the end of 1993, and a sale of Benedictine Manor would be negotiated. Mr. Halk announced that due to the deteriorating health of his wife, he would have to resign as business manager and spend more time at home. After faithfully and wisely managing the business affairs for the Community for the past ten years (1983-1993), this news came as a great disappointment to the Community. Mr. Halk did agree to continue on the Finance Committee and to help the next person selected as business manager.

Phil Jones, member of Community Finance Committee was instrumental in assisting Sr. Henrietta to engage Alan Patteson, Jr. as the next business manager. Patteson had recently retired after selling his family's Radio Stations KBTM am, and KJBR fm, and was open to taking a part-time position. He agreed to try it for one year to determine how it would work out for both the Convent and for himself.

Although Mr. Patteson would not officially assume responsibilities until January 1, 1994, he came during the month of December and worked closely with Mr. Halk to learn the business matters of the Community. He has continued the fine work that had been done by Colonel Olhausen and Ralph Halk. SEE PROFILE IN APPENDIX.

Diocesan Sesquicentennial

Pope Gregory XVI had established the Diocese of Little Rock on November 28, 1843, so a year-long sesquicentennial celebration was scheduled, beginning in the fall of 1993. All diocesan institutions were encouraged to participate in this historic event, and Holy Angels Convent was no exception.

Prior to the yearlong celebration, the diocesan office asked each Catholic institution to send in artifacts for an exhibit to celebrate the 150th Anniversary of the establishment of the Diocese of Little Rock. Sr. Louise Frankenberger, Sr. Julia Pruss and Sr. Beatrice Schneider served on a committee to gather artifacts from the Community for the diocesan exhibit.

The opening event was held on November 26, 1993. A fire was lit at Arkansas Post by Quapaw Indians, symbolizing the Light of Christ. After Bishop McDonald blessed the fire, it was carried to Plum Bayou, where the first church was erected. On November 27, the fire was carried to Little Rock by torch runners, where a sesquicentennial flame was lit on the grounds of St. John's, the diocesan pastoral center.

On November 28, the Sesquicentennial year was begun in every Catholic institution in the state. Sr. Brenda and Sr. Henrietta had gone to Little Rock the day before, to secure a light from the sesquicentennial flame to bring back to Holy Angels in time for the 11 a.m. Mass in the chapel. The sesquicentennial flame was kept lit in a sanctuary lamp throughout the sesquicentennial year and kept in a prominent place in the sanctuary.

Exterior of building showing new Norwegian Wood aluminum siding.

Building Repair

One of the first matters of business in 1994 was the needed repairs to the Convent complex. Due to deterioration over the years caused by the weather, the exterior walls of the Motherhouse and overhanging roofs were now in need of repair. Mr. Halk and Mr. Patteson together evaluated the problem and conferred with an architect about the best way to repair it.

After considerable investigation, it was decided that the rotting wood should be replaced and metal siding should be installed on all exterior walls. After further study a Council meeting was held on January 14, 1994 to report the findings. At this same meeting the Council discussed the change to have the power lines installed above ground and come in from the back of the property. The underground lines were deteriorating, since installation 20 years earlier, and were now breaking and causing frequent power failures. Both topics were approved by majority vote of the Council [19]

By April 1994 bids were submitted for installation of the aluminum siding and Bradley's Home Improvement Company of Jonesboro submitted the low bid. The Council selected a tan color named Norwegian Wood for the aluminum siding.

Alumnae Association/Homecoming

Due to interest of former students, Holy Angels Academy Alumnae Association was reactivated during the summer of 1994. Sr. Henrietta named Sr. Geraldine to be the coordinator for the Alumnae Association to plan the activities. With assistance of former members, an annual Homecoming celebration was held towards the end of June. Former Community members were also invited to attend this annual Homecoming/Reunion.

Classes celebrating their 50th and 60th anniversaries are honored each year. After the death of Sr. Geraldine in 2001, Sr. Henrietta was named the coordinator of the Alumnae Association.

Through these annual gatherings, the students and former members welcomed this annual opportunity to visit with each other and the Sisters again. A number of former members have kept in touch with the Sisters and have continued to contribute by making periodic donations to the Community.

General Chapter 1994

Bishop McDonald opened the General Chapter on June 9 with Mass. Sr. Georgia, chair of the committee introduced the first topic for discussion. Changes discussed and voted upon were all matters contained in the Customary. In addition to adopting the option concerning the manner in addressing the Prioress and the Interim Period, the majority voted to add the option of having a "proxy" for electing Council members. Up to this time, "proxy" was used only in the election of the Prioress. Other minor changes in wording were adopted by majority vote. All voted changes were later approved by Bishop McDonald.

Long Range Planning

In February of 1994, Mr. Ben Owens, President/CEO of St. Bernards and John Warner, hospital consultant, recommended

Pastoral Care Department in 1996, L – R: Sr. Benedicta Boeckmann, Fr. Nicholas Furhmann, OSB, Chaplain, Sr. Alberta Krebs, Sr. Marilyn Doss, Sr. Lenore Dust, Sr. Conrad Frankenberger, Sr. Damian Marie Atkinson and Sr. Cordis Kim.

that the Sisters submit a long-range plan to be included with the corporate plan for the Medical Center. Upon the advice of the Council, the Community engaged Paul Donnelly, Ph.D., a Catholic Hospital consultant from St. Louis, to assist in the planning procedure. [20]

On June 8 the Community assembled for the first day of the planning sessions. Dr. Donnelly stated, "The process of planning involves determining in advance what is going to be done by setting objectives and beginning to face the limitations of resources, Sisters as well as money." [21]

In addition to the sessions with the Community, Dr. Donnelly asked for the Council to act as a planning committee for the project. Each Council member worked with a subcommittee to refine the goals developed by the Community. They set priorities for the goals and listed the driving forces and strategies.

At the June 8, 1995 Annual Corporation meeting, the Community adopted by majority vote the following five goals to serve as a guide for the next five years.

"1. Maintain and develop human resources available to achieve the mission of the religious Community.
2. Maintain and improve the quality of religious life.
3. Continue to affirm and support the health care ministry.
4. Continue to affirm and support the education ministry.
5. Maintain financial resources available to support the religious Community and its ministries." [22]

Corporate Meeting 1955

At the annual corporation meeting on June 8, 1995, Sr. Henrietta asked for guidance again to prioritize Community ministries, since the last survey was done in 1985. The following list shows the results of this 1995 survey, from the most preferred ones to continue as long as possible.

MISSIONS PRIORITIZED

Missions which the Community now staffs and date it was begun.

"St. Paul's School, Pocahontas	1888
Blessed Sacrament School, Jonesboro	1889
Sacred Heart School, Muenster, Texas	1895
*Holy Rosary School, Stuttgart	1899-1943,1972-2001
Holy Souls School, Little Rock	1927
St. Michael's School, West Memphis	1959
Our Lady of Fatima School, Benton	1954
Little Agnes Day Care/Music, Little Rock	1961" [23]

*Due to the death of Sr. Geraldine Homer in 2001, the Community had no available replacement to send to Stuttgart. So for the second time in history, the Community withdrew from Holy Rosary School in Stuttgart.

Hispanic Ministry

During the summer of 1995, Fr. James Brockman, SJ, Director of Hispanic Ministry for the Diocese of Little Rock, contacted

Sr. Henrietta about engaging a member of the Jonesboro Benedictine Community to direct Hispanic Ministry in northeast Arkansas. Since Sr. Elaine Willett knew Spanish and had four years previous experience in Mexico, she agreed to accept this position. She signed a contract with the diocese on November 9, 1995 and developed the Hispanic ministry in northeast Arkansas.

Generous benefactors donated a building on Monroe Street in downtown Jonesboro, where a Hispanic Center was opened. With the help of volunteers, Sr. Elaine continues to provide programs for numerous Hispanic-speaking people who locate in northeast Arkansas.

Focus on Vocations

After the November 1995 National Bishops' Conference, Bishop McDonald asked all parishes and religious institutions in the diocese, to set aside a period each day for Exposition and Adoration of the Blessed Sacrament to pray for increase of vocations. The Sisters of Holy Angels agreed to have Exposition and Adoration ordinarily one half-hour before the daily Mass.

In addition to this, the Community agreed to have a Mass, offered on the first Saturday of each month, for the increase of vocations. The monthly Novena to the Infant Jesus of Prague was then discontinued as a Community devotion.

Sale of Benedictine Manor

By March of 1995 Mr. Davis notified Sr. Henrietta that the Diocese of Little Rock would not be able to purchase the Manor in Hot Springs. They could not secure a loan to make the needed repairs. In the meantime, a representative from Angeles Housing Concept, Inc. had made inquiry about purchasing the Manor.

In May 1995, Sr. Henrietta and Alan Patteson met with William Tuthill, president, and Craig Reinmuth, vice-president, of Angeles Housing Concepts to further dialogue about their interest. At this time they requested a copy of an updated Abstract and then they requested time to make a "due diligence" inspection.

Although the company continued to express interest in purchasing the Manor and continued contact with Patteson, it was not until January 4, 1996 that the sale was completed. The Community agreed to finance the sale with a ten-year 8% note, containing a final balloon payment. An initial down payment of $200,000 was made at closing. The Community has been grateful to Mr. Patteson for handling the transaction and grateful that the company has proved reliable in making scheduled payments.

Mosaic from Benedictine Manor relocated to entrance of Holy Angels Convent.

This property that had been under the direction of the Jonesboro Benedictines for 81 years, first as St. John's Place beginning in 1915, then as Benedictine Manor, dedicated October 5, 1968, was relinquished in 1996. After the new owners renovated and refurbished it, they named the facility "Crown Trace," and it is operating successfully. By the spring of 1996, discussion surfaced about St. Bernards building a retirement center here in Jonesboro.

Election 1996

By the summer of 1996, Sr. Henrietta's first term came to an end, so a Canonical election was scheduled for June 14, following the annual retreat. At a preliminary meeting the evening before Sr. Mary John Seyler and Sr. Cabrini Arami were the elected tellers. Bishop

Andrew J. McDonald officiated at the election on the morning of June 14. Sr. Henrietta was elected to a second-three year term.

That same afternoon at the annual Corporation meeting, the Sisters again elected Sr. Henrietta as president of the Corporation. Sr. Anne Marie Ferricher declined to accept a second term as an appointed Council member. Sr. Mary John Seyler was appointed to fill that position.

At the same time, Sr. Mary John was appointed Formation Directress. Sr. Julia Pruss had held that position until her death on April 18, 1996 from a massive coronary.

Sr. Mary Anne Nuce had filled this position on an interim basis since April. Sr. Mary John also taught Scripture Class at the ASU Newman Center for the following two years.

Due to declining health, Sr. Beatrice Schneider had to resign as secretary for the Community, so Sr. Henrietta appointed Sr. Lenore Dust to that position. She was also appointed Vocation Directress and visited area parishes on weekends. [24] She took along the new pictorial Storyboards, funded by St. Bernards to promote vocations. These Storyboards comprised six panels depicting the history of the Community, its prayer life, its ministries and Community living.

On July 9, 1996 a Chapter meeting was held to fill two positions on the Council. Due to the death of Sr. Vincent Hicks and the expiration of Sr. Benedicta's first term, two positions were open. Sr. Mary Anne Nuce was elected to fill Sr. Vincent's unexpired term and Sr. Benedicta was elected to a second three-year term. [25]

By the fall of 1996 discussion was held on the need to replace worn carpet throughout the convent. The Council voted to obtain bids and have the carpet replaced in the general business areas and hallways throughout the convent.

Entrance Sign

Through the generosity of benefactors, a new entrance sign was erected on the front park way to designate the location of the convent. Dewaine Beisner of Stuck Associates Architects designed the new sign and Olympus Construction Co. erected it. At a ceremony on January 3, 1996, Fr. Nicholas Furhmann, OSB, Chaplain, blessed the sign and Jerry Bookout, State Senator, spoke about the contributions the Sisters had made to northeast Arkansas. On this occasion, he also presented new state and U.S. flags to the Community which were raised on the new flagpoles along with the Community flag.

New entrance sign to Holy Angels Convent erected 1996 on Hwy. 766.

Property Agreement

When the Community accepted the land on which to build the convent from the Riga family, an agreement was signed on February 8, 1971 by Mother Benedicta to care for the handicapped daughter after the death of her parents. However, by October 22, 1998, the Council met in special session and voted unanimously to accept care of both the mother and daughter, Rita. The mother was in declining health and no longer able to care for herself or her daughter. They would live in the extension of the infirmary and receive care as needed. The mother died shortly after being relocated to the convent infirmary.

Pocahontas Property

By 1996 the property in Pocahontas was becoming a liability to the Community due to maintenance and upkeep of the building. The land had been given to the Benedictine Sisters by a hand written deed of Bishop Edward Fitzgerald, DD, dated May 16, 1888, shortly after the Sisters located in Arkansas. By 1996 only two Sisters were missioned there in the 24 room convent erected and funded by the Sisters in 1957. For over 100 years, the Community had continued the upkeep and maintenance of the property and building which was now in need of major repairs.

Sr. Henrietta announced that a discussion of the Pocahontas property would be on the Agenda for the 1997 General Chapter. "The National Religious Retirement Office (NRRO) had urged religious Communities to divest themselves of any unneeded non-income producing properties; in effect to do all they could to help themselves." [26]

Sr. Henrietta informed Bishop McDonald and Fr. Michael Bass, pastor of St. Paul Parish in Pocahontas, about the upcoming meeting. At the time, St. Paul parish did not express interest in the property.

At the June 13, 1997 General Chapter, the Sisters offered numerous ideas of what to do with the property. However after a lengthy discussion, the Sisters decided to delay any decision to the following year. A committee was formed to present ideas to the Community at the summer 1998 Annual Chapter meeting. The committee circulated lists of ideas to the Sisters throughout the year. Some suggested to use the building for a retreat house, a home for the needy, for pregnant mothers, as a food distribution center, or to sell it to a realtor.

However, at the Annual Chapter in 1998 no consensus was reached, so the Community decided to wait another year before making any decision. When visiting the Community on July 11, 1998 Bishop McDonald mentioned to Sr. Henrietta that a reversion clause had been noted in the deed from Bishop Fitzgerald, "that for any reason the property would not be used as a convent, it would revert to the Bishop of Little Rock." After Jack Deacon, attorney for the Community checked records in the Randolph County Courthouse, this was found to be accurate.

Although the Community had in previous years, received the Bishop's permission to sell small portions of the property, the remaining 11 acres, obviously, was not theirs legally to dispose of. Alan Patteson, business manager, Jack Deacon, Community attorney and Sr. Henrietta scheduled a meeting with Bishop McDonald to discuss what to do about the matter.

Since the Community could not utilize the property in any beneficial way, it was now becoming a liability. No decision materialized from this meeting and no assurances were given, but the Bishop agreed to study the matter. Early in 1999, Bishop McDonald met with the Pocahontas finance committee and proposed that St. Paul Parish assume responsibility for the property, and in justice, make a contribution to the Olivetan Benedictine Sisters' retirement fund.

By May 1999 Sr. Henrietta reported to the Community that St. Paul Parish agreed over a ten-year period to make a significant contribution to the Community retirement fund. St. Paul Parish would then assume responsibility for the property. The Community gratefully accepted this offer and an agreement was signed later that same year.

Personnel Changes

In the Spring of 1998, Father Warren Harvey, Diocesan Director of Ministry to Black Catholics, contacted Sr. Henrietta to request a Sister to help with that ministry in central Arkansas. Sr. De Porres Polk, LPN (Licensed Practical Nurse), who had served over 25 years in nursing at St. Bernards, was ready for a change in ministry so gladly responded to this request when approached.

Due to declining number of teachers, the Community withdrew from Our Lady of Fatima School in Benton at the close of the 1998 school term. Sr. Monica Swirczynski was appointed Secretary for the Community and to the Governing Board of St. Bernards Medical

Center. Sr. Lenore Dust was appointed to the Pastoral Care Department at St. Bernards. Sr. Yvonne Lerner was appointed Vocation Directress along with her ministry to the Oblates.

Anniversary Commemorated

In 1998 the Sisters commemorated the 150th anniversary of the birth of Mother Beatrice Renggli (1848-1998), the foundress of the Jonesboro Benedictine Community. Sr. Henrietta published a short biography of her life to commemorate this milestone. Cost of publication was funded by Mrs. Karl Pfeiffer of Piggott. A complimentary copy of this publication was sent to all the Benedictine houses in the United States, as well as to the Maria Rickenbach Convent in Switzerland, from where the Sisters first originated.

A monument was also erected in Pocahontas on the site of the original convent and dedicated on June 14, 1998. The plaque cast on the 100th anniversary of the foundation was relocated from the entrance gate and attached to this monument, along with a bronze plaque attesting Mother Beatrice as foundress. The wording on the centennial plaque was quoted in Chapter 14. The plaque honoring Mother Beatrice reads as follows: *"Commemorating the 150th Anniversary of the birth of our Foundress, Mother Beatrice Renggli, OSB — 1848–1998."*

Commemorative Monument in Pocahontas.

Web Site for Holy Angels

In December of 1998 the Council approved the Christmas gift money received by the Community would be used to purchase a Web site on the Internet to promote vocations. Mark Schneider with Internet Solutions, Inc. was engaged to install the hardware for the Internet and designed the Web site for Holy Angels Convent. Address: **olivben@olivben.org.** He included pictures from the Vocation Storyboards that depicted Prayer life, Community living, Ministry, and the Community Centennial History.

Novice Lisa McConnell signing First Profession document 1998 L – R: Fr. Camillus Cooney, OSB, delegate of Bishop McDonald, DD, Sr. Lisa and Sr. Henrietta Hockle, prioress.

St. Bernards Corporate Office

On January 6, 1999 Articles of Incorporation for St. Bernards Healthcare, Inc. were filed with the state. The process began for the establishment of the corporate office. The medical center was to be considered as the "flagship" of this enterprise. The other entities were St. Bernards Village, opened October 1998; Behavioral Health, acquired January 1997; Rural Clinics; Doctors Health Group;

Regional Healthcare Services; Jonesboro Real Estate Holdings; and the Heartcare Center opened in May 1999. More entities would be added later as the enterprise developed. Ben E. Owens would head the corporate office.

Fifteenth Prioress

As the summer of 1999 drew near, Sr. Henrietta's second term came to a close so a Canonical election was scheduled for June 18, following the annual retreat. At a meeting the evening before, Sr. Mary John Seyler and Sr. Georgia Felderhoff was elected tellers for the election. Bishop Andrew J. McDonald, DD, presided at the election. Sr. Eileen Schneider was elected the fifteenth Prioress of the Olivetan Benedictine Community. Sr. Eileen was the second Jonesboro native to be elected Prioress. She would lead the Community into the 21st Century. SEE PROFILE IN APPENDIX

Shortly after election, Sr. Eileen announced that Sr. Mary Anne Nuce would be the Subprioress for the Community. At a Chapter meeting on July 8, 1999 Sr. Eileen announced that the following Sisters were appointed to the Council: Sr. Mary Anne Nuce, Sr. Geraldine Homer, Sr. Judith Dalesandro and Sr. Miriam Burns. These would join the existing members whose terms had not expired: Sr. Carine Myers, Sr. Monica Swirczynski and Sr. Joanne Sandoval. Sr. Christopher Flowers was elected to fill the expired term of Sr. Benedicta Boeckmann.[27]

Later that same year Sr. Mary John was appointed to the Pastoral Care Department at St. Bernards, first to intern, then as Directress of the Department. Sr. Josita Lopez was appointed to work in Hispanic Ministry after completing a semester of course work at the Mexican American Cultural Center (MACC) in San Antonio.

To prepare for the 2000 Tri-Annual General Chapter, a Community meeting was held on December 28, 1999 to elect committee members to receive suggestions for the agenda. The following were elected to serve on this committee: Sr. Carine Myers, Sr. Mary John Seyler, Sr. Romana Rohmer, Sr. Yvonne Lerner, Sr. Brenda Willett. Sr. Mary John was then elected to serve as chair of this committee. She encouraged the Sisters to send in suggestions concerning topics they wish discussed at the 2000 General Chapter.

At this same meeting, Sr. Eileen announced that Bishop McDonald had designated Holy Angels Convent Chapel as a diocesan Pilgrimage Site during the 2000 Jubilee Year. At a future meeting, the Community would discuss what activities to schedule during the Jubilee Year. Sr. Eileen then asked for volunteers to serve on a committee to coordinate activities. [28]

As the 20th Century drew to a close, the Sisters of Holy Angels prepared, not only the Jubilee Year, but also for the dawn of the 21st Century. During the 1990s, advanced technology had been installed in the medical center and in the convent offices. Now with the approaching turn of the Century, there was concern about the electronic transfer to the year 2000. However, when the change occurred at midnight on December 31, no incident of malfunction occurred.

CHAPTER 16
2000-2003

Jubilee Year 2000

At the beginning of Advent for the Jubilee Year 2000, Pope John Paul II opened the Jubilee Year in Rome by breaking the seal on the Holy Door at St. Peter Basilica for the pilgrims who would journey to Rome. He also designated the Cathedral of every diocese as a place of pilgrimage. In addition, each bishop was granted permission to designate certain churches in their diocese, as places of pilgrimage. Bishop Andrew McDonald, DD, designated Holy Angels Convent Chapel, as one of the 15 official Pilgrimage sites in the Diocese of Little Rock.

As stated in the last chapter, Sr. Eileen asked for volunteers to serve on a steering committee to coordinate activities. At a Chapter Meeting on December 28, 1999 the Sisters selected October 1, 2000 (Sunday nearest to Feast of Holy Angels) as the official date for the Community celebration during the Jubilee Year. All Parishes would be invited. A Mass would be celebrated at 2 p.m. which would be followed by a reception and tour of the convent. Those who could not attend on this date, would be invited to join the Sisters at the 11 a.m. Mass on the first Sunday of any month during the Jubilee Year.

Official Jubilee Symbol for the Year 2000

"Arrival time for the Pilgrims was scheduled for 9:30 a.m., with coffee and refreshments available. Then a tour of the convent would be given before visitors would join the Sisters at the 11 a.m. conventual Mass, followed by dinner. After the meal, a slide presentation would be presented on the history of the Community." [1]

The committee formed to coordinate the activities was headed by Sr. Yvonne Lerner, who served as liaison to the diocesan office. A brochure with information about pilgrimages to Holy Angels during the Jubilee Year was mailed to every parish. Sr. Marya Duscher designed the cover for this brochure. Sr. Judith Dalesandro directed tours for the pilgrims and Sr. Josita Lopez was in charge of food service. Sr. Henrietta Hockle wrote a brief history to be distributed to the pilgrims before they left. A number of delegations from different parishes made a pilgrimage to Holy Angels during the Jubilee Year.

Sisters at prayer in chapel.

St. Bernards Enterprise

As the Community celebrated Jubilee Year 2000, St. Bernards Enterprise, headed by Ben E. Owens, continued to evolve. The Corporate offices were completed in the Annex buildings former auditorium of the Academy. After the corporate officers relocated to the new location, the medical center director and staff occupied the existing administrative offices. The new corporate structure was designed to provide a "fire wall" separating the different entities to provide legal protection for the enterprise.

The medical center was considered the "flagship" of the enterprise. Scott Street was administrator of the medical center until 2001, when Chris Barber was named to that position. In 2002 Chris Barber was named the Corporate Executive Officer of St. Bernards Medical Center.

St. Bernards Medical Center — new entrance on Jackson.

Entities included in the Enterprise were listed in the previous chapter when the corporate office was established in January 1999. Additional entities were added as they evolved. St. Bernards leased CrossRidge Community Hospital in Wynne and established a management arrangement of Walnut Ridge Community Hospital and Lawrence Hall Nursing Home. St. Bernards also has an affiliate arrangement through Volunteer Hospitals of American (VHA) with Piggott Community Hospital. Through a joint venture with physicians, St. Bernards opened the Jonesboro Outpatient Surgery Center in 2003, and collaborated with Arkansas State University to open a Sports Medicine Center on ASU Campus that same year. As chairperson of St. Bernards Governing Board, Inc., Sr. Eileen appointed members to serve on these different boards including some of the Sisters.

Celebrating 125 Years

To commemorate the 125 years since the first group of Swiss Sisters left Maria Rickenbach in 1874, to come to America, the

Benedictine Houses in the United States hosted Swiss Sisters from their original foundation. In July 2000, Mother Andrea Kappeli, OSB, Prioress of Maria Rickenbach and Mother Anita Baumann, Prioress from Mechtal Monastery (as interpreter) toured the American foundations, beginning with the original foundation, St. Scholastica Monastery at Clyde.

Holy Angels Convent was privileged to host the Swiss Sisters on July 5 and 6 which coincided with St. Bernards centennial celebration. The Jonesboro Community had lost its last Swiss "connection" on October 3, 1996 with the death of Sr. Theresina Grob, the sole remaining Swiss Sister.

At a special noon luncheon Sr. Eileen welcomed the Swiss Sisters, after which Mother Andrea answered questions from the Sisters through an interpreter. A Swiss flag was hung in the Community dining room to honor the visitors from the foundation in the country of its "roots." Later that same day the visitors joined in the centennial celebration of the hospital.

Sr. Eileen Schneider, Prioress, Mother Andrea Kappeli, Mother Anita Baumann and Sr. Mary Anne Nuce, Subprioress in front of Swiss flag.

Centennial of St. Bernards

July 5, 2000 marked the 100th anniversary since the establishment of St. Bernards. The centennial of health care service to the citizens in northeast Arkansas and southern Missouri was marked with special events and distinguished visitors. To reflect the mission of the Olivetan Benedictine Sisters, St. Bernards provided a two-day outreach event, entitled, "Mission Serve," to provide medical and social services to over 4,000 needy and indigent people in northeast Arkansas and Southern Missouri. The Arkansas National Guard set up a field hospital on Craighead County Fairgrounds and handled the logistics for the event. Members of the medical profession donated their services, and businesses contributed funding to make this outreach possible. Numerous citizens volunteered to assist in this gift to the community.

Banner advertising St. Bernards Free Health Clinic

On July 5, 2000, the actual day of the 100th anniversary, a centennial picnic was held on the grounds of Bell Community Center for employees and past employees. Sr. Eileen Schneider, Prioress, welcomed the gathering of employees plus visiting dignitaries. Joining Sr. Eileen on the platform was Ben E. Owens, President/CEO of St. Bernards, along with state and county representatives who spoke to the gathering. In addition, Mayor Hubert Brodell read a proclamation designating July 5, as "St. Bernards Day," in northeast Arkansas. Owens presented a copy of A Century of Serving, a history of St. Bernards Medical Center written by Sr. Henrietta Hockle, to the Swiss visitors as well as to the state and local dignitaries.

"As St. Bernards marked its 100 years of service, it assessed and reconfirmed the values that were the basis of its founding in 1900. The defining values of St. Bernards are:

1. A commitment to promote and defend the dignity of every person.
2. An approach to care that is holistic and includes the spiritual needs of each person.
3. A commitment to offer health care to all persons in need." [2]

The Sisters used this occasion to express gratitude to God, and to all those who contributed when there was a need in the past, and to all those who support St. Bernards today. The purpose of the founding Sisters of St. Bernards in 1900 was, and continues to be now 100 years later, to provide Christ-like healing to the community through education, treatment and health services. [3]

The closing of St. Bernards Centennial Year was held on December 8, with the blessing and dedication of the newly renovated chapel, Pastoral Care Department and Chaplain's Office. On this occasion Ben E. Owens, President/CEO of St. Bernards expressed gratitude to the Sisters for the sacrifices they made over the past 100 years. He quoted the closing lines from Robert Frost's poem, *The Road Not Taken,* by reading, "Two roads diverged in a wood, and I, I took the one less traveled by, And that has made all the difference." Mr. Owens stated, "A hundred years ago, the early Sisters took the road less traveled by when they opened the hospital, and that has made all the difference in northeast Arkansas." [4]

Personnel Change

Since the beginning of the Community in 1887, until the year 2000, a Sister had always been in charge of food service at the convent kitchen. Lay employees had been hired to assist in the convent kitchen since the early 1970s. Due to the shortage of personnel, during the summer of 2000, a lay supervisor was hired to be in charge of the convent food service and kitchen. Sr. Mary Anne Nuce, Subprioress, was assigned to be the liaison between the supervisor and the Community. Sr. Mary Anne worked closely with the lay supervisor to coordinate meals for special Community feastdays.

Community enjoying meal in dining room.

Reassessing Long Range Plans

In January 2001, the Olivetan Benedictine Sisters again undertook long-range planning initiatives to reassess the goals and directional statements that had been adopted in 1995. John C. Render, Ph.D., consultant from Hall, Render, and Lyman in Indianapolis, Indiana, was engaged to assist in this endeavor.

Because the Community agreed to continue support for the health care ministry at St. Bernards, something needed to be done to strengthen this endeavor. With fewer Sisters available to work in the hospital, a decision was made to create a position for Mission Effectiveness to ensure the continuation of the goals established by the founding Sisters. Mr. Render recommended that this position be filled, at least at first, by a member of the religious Community.

After consultation with Ben E. Owens, President/CEO of St. Bernards and the Community Council, Sr. Eileen Schneider, Prioress, appointed Sr. Mary John Seyler to the position of vice-president of Mission Effectiveness. She retained her position as Directress of Pastoral Care for St. Bernards Medical Center. In her new duties, "Sr. Mary John was responsible for leading and supporting all levels of awareness and ongoing articulation of the identity, mission, vision and core values of St. Bernards Healthcare as an expression of the spiritually centered healing ministry."[5]

Promoting Vocations

To continue the promotion of vocations, Sr. Eileen appointed Sr. De Porres Polk, as Directress of Vocations in the fall of 2000. Since the death of Sr. Yvonne Lerner, this post had been vacant. However, due to Sr. De Porres' heavy schedule with the ministry to Black Catholics in central Arkansas, Sr. Judith Dalesandro was appointed to this position in 2001, as the first full-time Vocation Directress. Later, she was assigned additional duties.

By using the Internet installed in January 1999, Sr. Judith corresponded by e-mail with interested persons who sought information about the Community. She invited interested prospects to visit the Community. This effort, plus the Community prayer and correspondence by a number of Sisters, resulted in growth in the Community.

In the Spring of 2002, Sr. Carmelita Myers was appointed as interim Directress of Formation. Two new members were accepted in the Community, as Postulants, on Easter Monday, 2002. Only one Junior Sister remained in the Novitiate at that time, who made Perpetual Vows in August 2002.

During the summer of 2002, Sr. Georgia Felderhoff was appointed Formation Directress. At the end of summer two additional Postulants were accepted. On the eve of the Feast of the Holy Angels, the Postulants accepted in April, were admitted to the Novitiate to begin their Canonical Year of Formation.

Canonical Election 2002

During June 2002, Sr. Eileen Schneider's first term was drawing to a close so a Canonical election was scheduled for June 18. Fr. David Bellinghausen, Prior of Subiaco Abbey, serving as Bishop J. Peter Sartain's delegate, officiated at the election. Sr. Eileen was re-elected for a second three-year term as Prioress of the Community and Chair of St. Bernards Governing Board of Trustees. She was also elected President of the Olivetan Benedictine Corporation, Inc.[6]

At a special Chapter Meeting held on June 19, 2002, Sr. Eileen announced that she had re-appointed the same officials, Sr. Mary Anne Nuce, Subprioress; Sr. Monica Swirczynski, Secretary; Sr. Joanne Sandoval, Treasurer. The same appointed council members were reappointed: Sr. Mary Anne Nuce, Sr. Cabrini Arami, (who replaced Sr. Geraldine Homer in 2001), Sr. Judith Dalesandro and Sr. Miriam Burns. Elected Council members whose terms had not expired were: Sr. Carine Myers, Sr. Monica Swirczynski and Sr. Joanne Sandoval. Sr. Christopher Flowers, whose term had expired, asked not to be re-elected. An election was held and Sr. Georgia Felderhoff was elected to fill this position.

Library: Seated L – R: Sr. Louis Frankenberger, Sr. Angeline Massery and standing: Sr. Brenda Willett, librarian.

At this same meeting, members of a Constitution Committee were elected to prepare for the General Chapter the following summer. These Sisters were elected: Sr. Mary John Seyler, Sr. Romana Rohmer, Sr. Mary Anne Nuce, Sr. Brenda Willett and Sr. Elaine Willett.[7] Later the committee elected Sr. Mary Anne as chair of the committee, who accepted suggestions and recommendations for any changes needed in the Spiritual, Juridic and Customary sections contained in the Constitution.

General Chapter 2003

The 2003 General Chapter was held on June 18 and 19. Abbot Jerome Kodell, OSB of Subiaco, delegate of the Bishop J. Peter Sartain, DD, opened the General Chapter and addressed the Sisters about the question of joining an American Benedictine Federation for Women. Although, he said he found it helpful to belong to the Swiss American Federation for Men, he recommended that before any decision is made, the Sisters make a list of all the questions they may have about a Federation. He then recommended that this list be sent to each of the Presidents of the four existing Federations.

In addition, the Community recommended that a letter be sent to the Olivetan Benedictine Abbot General, Michelangelo Tribili, OSB, to inquire if joining an American Benedictine Federation would jeopardize in any way their Olivetan affiliation.

At this General Chapter, Sr. Eileen encouraged the Sisters to submit questions and asked for volunteers to serve on a committee to compile the list and send to each of the Federation Presidents. Sr. Eileen also asked for a second committee to draw up a Vocation/Formation Handbook to guide the Vocation/Formation Directresses and the Community in the acceptance procedure and formation program. [8]

During the second day deliberations of this General Chapter, the topic arose concerning the length of the Novitiate. Sr. Eileen asked for discussion on the length of the Novitiate. She stated, "The way the Constitution is written at present time, Section J-68, places a burden on the superior." [9]

"J-68 Upon completion of the Novitiate, if the Novice requests it, and an absolute majority of the Chapter have judged her suitable, she will be allowed to make temporary profession. Still, if a doubt remains regarding her readiness, the Prioress can extend the time of probation but not more than six months." (CIC 653.2)

Sr. Eileen asked the Community to consider extending the time of the Novitiate to 18 months. This would then take the burden off the superior from making that decision. After much discussion, the majority of Sisters voted to change the time of the Novitiate to 18 months. The first 12 months would be considered the Canonical year, while the remaining six months, the Novice would continue in training before making First Profession.

Federation Inquiry Committee

Shortly after this meeting, the following Sisters volunteered to serve on this committee: Sr. Mary John Seyler, Sr. Romana Rohmer, Sr. Mary Anne Nuce, Sr. Miriam Burns, Sr. Cecilia Shannon and Sr. Lisa McConnell. After receiving responses, the Committee noted that the Community would have to discontinue its affiliation with the Olivetan Benedictine Congregation if it would affiliate with an American Benedictine Federation. The community consensus was to keep the Olivetan Affiliation but this matter will be decided during the 2004 General Chapter.

Formation Handbook Committee

Shortly after this meeting, the following volunteered to serve on the Formation committee: Sr. Petra Riga, Sr. Monica Swirczynski, Sr. Georgia Felderhoff, Sr. Eileen Schneider, Sr. De Porres Polk, Sr. Elaine Willett, Sr. Judith Dalesandro, Sr. Damian Marie Atkinson, Sr. Marilyn Doss and Sr. Josita Lopez.

This committee contacted the Benedictine Community in Fort Smith for a copy of their Formation Handbook and used some of the ideas to draw up a Vocation/Formation Handbook for Holy Angels Convent. The project was completed by the summer 2003 and the new handbook was implemented by the Community.

Due to one of the Novices having a terminal illness from cancer, Bishop J. Peter Sartain, DD, granted her permission to make vows early during her Canonical year. Sr. Micaela Carucci made

Profession of Vows on July 27 and died a little over a month later on September 5, 2003.

Membership in the Community has fluctuated throughout its history, but at this time, it is in a growth mode. There have been interludes of "lean years," but as of December 2003, the Formation Program in the Novitiate includes four Novices and five Postulants.

Postulants with Formation Directress. L – R: Postulant Therese Dunn, Postulant Hai Nguyen, Sr. Georgia Felderhoff, Postulant Jana Oelkers, Postulant Tanya Cenac and Postulant Rita Falconer — 2003.

Due to God's blessing, prayer and effort by the entire Community, the Jonesboro Benedictines have continued throughout their history to build their physical and spiritual foundation on high ground. Although the Community made a number of changes and adaptations, recommended by the Vatican II documents, it has remained on high ground by retaining its Olivetan Benedictine heritage. It has continued the monastic recitation of the Liturgy of the Hours, devotion to the Eucharist, a Community life style, and has retained a recognizable "habit" or religious garb.

Since its founding in 1887 this community parallels the growth and decline of membership in religious orders throughout the country. From its earliest beginning in 1887 of four members, to nearly 200 at its peak in the mid-60s, to its present membership of

52, the monastic traditions have been lived.

Sr. Patricia Wittberg, OLC, associate professor of sociology at Indiana University, offers this theory, "The growth and decline of religious orders occurs in 250-year cycles." [10] Although the Jonesboro Benedictine Community has not been in existence for that length of time, it has gone through a similar cycle.

Roger Finke, Ph.D., an associate professor at Purdue University, makes an interesting case when he states, "Vatican II made far more revisions than were desirable for strengthening religious orders." [11] Only history will verify this statement for future generations.

Regardless how history in future years will tell the story of religious orders in the United States, the Jonesboro Community has experienced some of the same effects of the changes promulgated by Vatican II, especially by the "Decree on the Appropriate Renewal of Religious Life." However, the Benedictines in northeast Arkansas have continued to seek high ground on which to carry out their mission of "Ora et Labora," (prayer and work) throughout its history.

To paraphrase Robert Frost in "The Road Not Taken," the Jonesboro Benedictines have taken the road less traveled by, and that has made all the difference in lives of thousands of people, whose lives they have touched throughout these 116 years.

The mission of the Jonesboro Benedictines is the same today as it was 116 years ago, when the founding Sisters first came to Arkansas, to seek God and to serve others. The Benedictine motto, "That God may be glorified in all things," is aptly expressed in the Community mission statement:

> "We are a Community of monastic women who seek God through prayer and work in the Olivetan Benedictine Heritage. Accordingly, we proclaim Jesus Christ and the Gospel message through our service to each other in Community, hospitality, health care, education and other apostolic works." [12]

APPENDIX
Leadership Profiles

Superiors of Holy Angels

MOTHER M. BEATRICE RENGGLI, OSB, Founding Prioress 1887-1892

Mother Beatrice is recognized as the Foundress and first superior of Holy Angels Convent. It was originally known as Convent Maria Stein when she and three other sisters first came to Arkansas and settled in Pocahontas in 1887. She was born on January 1, 1848 at Entlebuch, Canton Lucerne, Switzerland and was christened Rose at her baptism. She was the seventh child of James and third of the second marriage.

After her father James Renggli died in 1858 and her mother remarried, the ten year old Rose went to live with her mother's brother, the Pastor of Entlebuch. Her half-sister, Catherine, who was her uncle's housekeeper took a great interest in the gifted child and provided food, clothing and the money necessary toward her education. The Reverend uncle, too, watched carefully over his brilliant niece, enriching lessons of the classroom with instruction in French and Latin in his home.

At the age of 17, Rose expressed a desire to become a Sister. Her uncle aided her in selecting a convent of her choice, Maria Rickenbach, which she entered in 1865. She made her first vows on August 21, 1867 and received the name Sister Beatrice.

Because the neighboring monks at the Monastery of Engleberg had started a foundation in America, Abbot Anselm encouraged the superior of Maria Rickenbach to do the same. The missionary monks needed help in teaching the children of German immigrants who settled in Missouri.

After much discernment prayer, Sister Beatrice was chosen, along with four others to go to America to open a convent at Conception, Missouri. They arrived in America on August 31,1874 and traveled to Missouri. Sister Beatrice was chosen the first superior of Convent Maria Stein and came to Pocahontas, Arkansas on December 13, 1887, along with three other sisters. Mother Beatrice served as superior until 1892. She continued to be actively involved in Community operations and served as advisor to future superiors. When St. Bernards was opened in 1900, she served as bookkeeper for both the hospital and the convent. She was involved in all subsequent building projects. Mother Beatrice died at the age of 94 on September 7, 1942.

MOTHER M. ALOYSIA UNTERBERGER, OSB, Prioress 1892-1894, 1909-1915, Administrator of St. Bernards 1900-1914

Father Weibel appointed Sister Aloysia Unterberger the second superior of Convent Maria Stein in 1892. She was later elected by the sisters to be superior in 1909. Sister Aloysia was born in 1864 in Canton Unterwalden, Switzerland and was christened Christine at her baptism.

After completing grammar school studies in Canton Unterwalden, Switzerland, she continued advanced studies to become a teacher. Christine also studied nursing before responding to the call to come to America to enter Convent Maria Stein. She became interested in becoming a Sister and serving the needs of the immigrants settling in the heartland of United States.

Christine made first profession of vows at Convent Maria Stein on February 28, 1890 and received the religious name of Sister Aloysia. At first, Sister Aloysia was assigned to teaching duties and being the superior of the school in Paragould. However, two years later, Father Weibel appointed her the new superior of Convent Maria Stein to follow Mother Beatrice. Mother Aloysia held this position for the next two years and then later in 1909 was elected for two terms of three-years each and served until 1915. Following this she also served the Community as Subprioress.

Since Sister Aloysia had had nurses' training in Switzerland, she was assigned to be the first superintendent of St. Bernards Hospital. She continued to serve in this capacity when she was elected prioress in 1909, and remained in charge of the hospital while serving as superior of the convent until 1914, when Sister Hilda Gabler was named superintendent.

During Mother Aloysia's administration as Prioress, the Sisters staffed both St. John's Hospice in Hot Springs and the culinary department of St. John's Seminary in Little Rock. She was also instrumental in establishing the Nurses Training School at St. Bernards Hospital in 1914. After leaving office, Sister Aloysia continued her interest in St. Bernards and supported it until her death on January 6, 1928. She witnessed nearly three decades of growth in the hospital since it opening July 5, 1900.

MOTHER AGNES DALI, OSB, Prioress 1894-1897

Mother Agnes Dali, the third prioress of Convent Maria Stein, was the first elected superior of the Olivetan Benedictines in North America. The first two had been appointed. She was born in Neudorf, Canton Lucerne in 1839. At her baptism, she was christened Anna. Anna grew up with three siblings.

At the age of 21, Anna entered the convent of Maria Rickenbach in Switzerland and received the name of Sister Agnes. On May 5, 1862, she made first vows before Mother Gertrude Leupi, one of the foundresses of the institution. Sister Agnes was talented in art so the superior recognized this and sent her to study under ecclesiastical artists in Switzerland. When she returned, she was placed in charge of the liturgical arts department of the convent. She also served as novice mistress for several years.

Coming to America in 1874, Sister Agnes spent 13 years at Maryville, Missouri. Ten of those years she was superior and novice mistress and then she was sent to teach at the Grande Ronde Indian Reservation in Oregon for three years. When she returned to Maryville in 1887, she was sent along with three others to begin a third foundation at Convent Maria Stein in Pocahontas, Arkansas.

After arriving in Pocahontas, she opened the first school for blacks on January 2, 1888. The first day 36 students were registered. The school was forced to close five years later due to prejudice against the black race. In addition to teaching the black children in Pocahontas, she later taught in the parish schools of Jonesboro and Paragould. She was elected superior in 1894. During her administration plans were made to relocate the Motherhouse to Jonesboro. Sister Agnes died on June 10, 1915.

MOTHER M. CECILIA HUBER, OSB, Prioress 1897-1900

Mother Cecilia was elected the fourth prioress of Holy Angels Convent in 1897. She was born on March 27, 1870 in Rorschach, Canton Saint Gallen, Switzerland. At her baptism she was christened Maria Lidwina.

Maria attended school in her hometown, and then entered the Institute at Menzingen where she earned her teacher's certificate. She returned to Rorschach and taught school there for several years. She became interested when she heard of others going to America to join a religious order and teach the children of Swiss immigrants. She responded to the invitation by Father Weibel, who was recruiting aspirants for Convent Maria Stein in Pocahontas, Arkansas. Early in 1891, she traveled with a group going to America to enter various convents. Maria and three companions entered Convent Maria Stein.

On August 9, 1891 along with her companions, Maria was invested as novice and received the religious name of Cecilia. She made first profession of vows on August 28, 1892, with final profession in 1896. After completing her religious training, Sister Cecilia was assigned to teach in a number of parish schools that were staffed by the Community. She taught in Arkansas, Missouri, Illinois and Texas. During many of these years, she served as mission superior and principal of the school.

Although, St. Bernards did not open during Mother Cecilia's term of office as Prioress, it was during her term that plans and preparations were made for the opening of the hospital. She worked tirelessly with Father Weibel and Dr. C. M. Lutterloh to reach this goal. After completing her term of office in 1900, she was again assigned to work in the mission schools by teaching and being principal. Throughout her lifetime, she continued her interest and support of St. Bernards. Mother Cecilia died on September 13, 1943.

MOTHER M. EDWARD END, OSB, Prioress 1900-1903

Mother Edward was elected the fifth prioress of Holy Angels Convent in 1900. She was born on December 18, 1870 in Boswiel, Canton Aragau, Switzerland. At her baptism she was christened Marie.

Marie attended the local school in Boswiel. After completing her studies in the primary school, she continued in the Institute, as she wanted to be a teacher. At an early age she expressed interest in consecrating her life to God as a missionary and after obtaining her teacher's certificate, she responded to a request to join a group going to America.

In 1889 she joined 16 other young aspirants headed for Convent Maria Stein in Pocahontas, Arkansas. She was invested as a Novice in 1890 and received the name of Edward. After completing the novitiate training, Sister Edward made first vows. Profession was scheduled for 6 a.m. on May 28, 1891, because Reverend Anthony McQuaid was to say his First Mass in his hometown later that same day. Also, it was the Feast of Corpus Christi and there would be a procession with the parish. That same year, her younger sister Sophie entered the convent and became Sister Meinrada.

Sister Edward was prepared for the teaching ministry. She taught in different schools in Arkansas, Missouri and Illinois staffed by the Community. In the summer of 1900, she was elected Prioress and served one term of three years. After leaving office, she was assigned to be in charge of St. John's Hospice in Hot Springs.

Although plans and preparations had been made to open a hospital during Mother Cecilia's administration, it was after Mother Edward took office that St. Bernards Hospital was officially opened. Throughout her lifetime, Sister Edward continued her interest and support of St. Bernards. Sister Edward died on August 12, 1958.

MOTHER M. ANGELINA BOESCH, OSB, Prioress 1903-1909

Mother Angelina was elected the sixth prioress of Holy Angels Convent in 1903. She was born September 22, 1873 in Mulhausen, Germany. At baptism she was christened Emilia.

In the fall of 1890, Emilia, along with four other young ladies, responded to a request from Father Eugene Weibel for Postulants to come to America to serve in the mission fields. They were on their way to Convent Maria Stein in Pocahontas, Arkansas to teach children of the immigrants. They were invested in 1889 with the first class to receive their Monastic name at investment instead of at profession of first vows. Emilia received the Monastic name of Angelina, and had St. Angela Merci as her patron.

After making first vows, she was assigned to teach in St. Roman's School in Jonesboro, since she had already received her teaching certificate in Germany. In following years, she was also sent to Europe several times to recruit new members. In 1903, she was elected Prioress.

During Mother Angelina's six years as Prioress, St. Bernards continued to grow. Under her direction the hospital added 40 new beds and electric lights were installed in every room. Running water was added to the new convent and hospital complex. During her tenure, the new convent Chapel was erected in the area between the convent and hospital buildings. A grotto was erected on the grounds in honor of Our Lady of Lourdes.

After completion of her second term in office, Mother Angelina was returned to the educational apostolate. She was assigned to be the superior and teach in different parish schools staffed by the Community. Throughout her life, she continued her strong support for St. Bernards. Mother Angelina died on July 11, 1944

MOTHER M. WALBURGA HOEGGER, OSB, Prioress 1915-1945

Mother Walburga was elected the seventh prioress of Holy Angels Convent in 1915, and served for 30 years, the longest of any Prioress in the history of the Community. She was born in Canton Thurgau, Switzerland in 1873. At baptism she was named Pauline. No records exist of her parents or siblings.

After obtaining a teacher's license from Canton Thurgau in Switzerland on October 11, 1892, she responded to a request from Father Eugene Wiebel, who was recruiting volunteers for Postulants for Convent Maria Stein in Pocahontas, Arkansas. She volunteered along with three other young ladies from Canton Thurga to come to Arkansas to join the Community of Benedictines.

Pauline was invested in the Community in 1893 and received the name of Walburga. Sister Walburga made first vows in 1894. She was assigned teaching positions in various schools staffed by the Community. In 1909, she was recalled to the Motherhouse and appointed Subprioress to Mother Aloysia. From 1910 until 1915 she was also the Novice Mistress.

In 1915, Sister Walburga was elected Prioress and was re-elected for nine consecutive terms, for a total of 30 years as Prioress. This was permitted before changes in Canon Law which stipulated only two terms allowed for a major superior. When Sister Perpetua Reinart was elected Prioress in 1945, Mother Walburga served as her Subprioress until her death on July 12, 1950.

During Mother Walburga's administration, St. Bernards added the second building, which was fire proof. The expanded facilities contained a maternity floor and surgical departments. Bed capacity was increased to 115. Throughout her years in administration, Mother Walburga provided strong leadership and support for St. Bernards. Mother Walburga died on July 12, 1950.

MOTHER M. PERPETUA REINART OSB, Prioress 1945-1954

Mother Perpetua was elected the eighth prioress of Holy Angels Convent in 1945. She was the first American-born superior to be elected Prioress of the Jonesboro Community. She was born to Nicholas and Helena Neu Reinart in Roselle, Carroll County, Iowa on November 12, 1888, and the oldest of six children. At her baptism she was named Anna Susanna. Her mother died in giving birth to the seventh child. Her father married again and Suzanne had seven half-brothers and sisters.

Suzanna attended school taught by the Franciscan Sisters in Roselle, Iowa, until the family moved to Lindsey, Texas in 1900. The Sisters of Divine Providence taught in Lindsey. For some years, Suzanna thought of entering the Sisters of Divine Providence, but in 1908, the Olivetan Benedictine Sisters from Jonesboro were making plans to open a Novitiate in Muenster.

She was encouraged to enter there. She entered there, but plans for the Novitiate in Muenster did not materialize. Therefore, by December 1909, Susanna was on her way to enter the Novitiate in Jonesboro, where she joined a class of 15 young ladies from Switzerland. She made first vows in 1911 and received the name of Perpetua.

Sister Perpetua prepared for a career in teaching by attending the summer sessions at the Normal School of Little Rock College, Arkansas State College and the University of Arkansas. She also took special courses in business administration, which served her well during her many years in administration. Her teaching career extended from 1911 through 1961. However, she served as Subprioress to Mother Walburga from 1925 to 1945. She was elected Prioress in 1945 and served in this capacity until 1954. She retired to the Motherhouse and assisted in the library until her death.

During Mother Perpetua's administration, St. Bernards added a new addition with the emergency department and a psychiatric department. The number of beds increased to 150 during these years. Throughout her years of leadership, Mother Perpetua was a strong supporter of St. Bernards. The hospital continued to expand services to the people throughout northeast Arkansas. Mother Perpetua died on February 12, 1976.

MOTHER M. PHILIPPA WAVRICK, OSB, Prioress 1954-1966

Mother Philippa was elected the ninth prioress of Holy Angels Convent in Jonesboro in 1954. She was born in Burke, Idaho, the daughter of Godlieb and Bertha Bentelschies Wavrick. She was baptized Cecilia Ruth in St. Alphonsus Church in Wallace, Idaho. The Wavrick family moved to Arkansas from Wieser, Idaho and settled on a 680 acre farm in Hardy, Arkansas.

Cecilia's music education began at age three with her mother. At age six, Cecilia was enrolled in St. Mary's School in Paragould, Arkansas as a boarder with the Sisters. She continued to study music throughout grade school before entering Holy Angels Convent. She received the name Philippa at her investment and made professions first vows in 1930. After completing high school at Holy Angels Academy, she continued her studies in higher education.

Sister Philippa was sent to Chicago for studies in music at the American Conservatory of Music, with classes at Northwestern University and Marquette University in Milwaukee. She received both a B.A. degree and a M.A. in music and spent a lifetime teaching music. Sister Philippa was a noted organist and was appointed by Bishop John B. Morris, DD in 1941, as the main organist for all music activities at St. Andrew's Cathedral in Little Rock.

When Sister Philippa was elected Prioress in 1954, she returned to the Motherhouse to take up leadership of the Community. Mother Philippa worked closely with the hospital administration and was instrumental in making numerous improvements. During her administration, St. Bernards added a new laundry building and completed an enlarged pediatrics department. Two years later, three floors of the east wing were completed, in addition to the new surgical suite and a new dietary department and cafeteria were completed.

In 1961, Mother Philippa hired the first lay administrator, John W. Foley to be the administrator of St. Bernards Hospital. Throughout her administration, Mother Philippa provided strong support for the growth of St. Bernards. After Sister Philippa completed her administration as Prioress, she maintained a strong interest in St. Bernards. She returned to her music ministry in Little Rock where she is presently located.

MOTHER M. BENEDICTA BOECKMANN, OSB, Prioress 1966 - 1975

Sister Benedicta was elected the tenth prioress of Holy Angels Convent in June 1966. She was the fourth child born to Ferdinand and Johanna Dickneite Boeckmann of St. Elizabeth, Missouri, June 7, 1912. When she was eight years old, the family moved to Knoble, Arkansas.

Christine entered Holy Angels Convent on September 31, 1931 and received the name of Benedicta. She made perpetual vows on August 15, 1935. Sister Benedicta holds a Certificate of Administration of Nursing Homes from the Catholic Hospital Association Training Program.

Sister Benedicta served in many capacities throughout her religious life, the first 13 years being at St. John's Seminary in Little Rock. She was administrator during the last four years she was there. In 1946 Sister Benedicta was missioned at St. John's Hospice, where she served as administrator from 1948 to 1955. For the next five years she was in charge of the Juniorate at Holy Angels Convent. In 1960 she was missioned at New Iberia, Louisiana where she organized and administered a diocesan home for elderly citizens, known as Consolata Home. She served as administrator there until 1966 when she was elected Prioress.

To alleviate overcrowding at the convent and at St. Bernards, Mother Benedicta was instrumental in relocating the convent to north Jonesboro off Hwy. 141, on what is now known as Hwy. CR 766. The new Motherhouse was dedicated on October 12, 1974. Moving their convent marked a significant milestone in the history of the Olivetan Benedictine Sisters in Arkansas and made room for hospital expansion.

The following additions and improvements were made at St. Bernards Hospital during Mother Benedicta's administration. One floor was added to the East Wing of the hospital, which increased bed capacity to 274 beds. In addition, the new emergency room and ancillary facilities were added to the north wing of the main building. An Intensive Coronary Care Unit was added in 1974. Throughout her years in the Community, Sister Benedicta continues to provide strong support for the administration and the mission of St. Bernards.

After serving as Prioress, Sister Benedicta was named Director of Formation for the Community and served in this capacity for six years. In 1981 she was named Director of the Pastoral Care Department at St. Bernards, which she had organized while she was Prioress. She continues to serve part-time in the Pastoral Care Department and is devoted to visiting the cancer patients.

MOTHER M. JULIA PRUSS, OSB, Prioress 1975-1981

Sister Julia was elected the 11th prioress of Holy Angels Convent in June 1975 and served in that capacity until 1981. She was born October 28, 1927, the fourth child and only daughter of John and Angeline Niedzwiedz Pruss in Marche, Arkansas. She was baptized at Immaculate Heart of Mary Church, Marche and given the name of Jadwiga, (headwig) after the patroness of Poland. Two of her four brothers had preceded her in death when she died on April 18, 1996.

Headwig grew up in Marche and left home to enter Holy Angels Convent in August 1944. She completed her high school education at Holy Angels Academy and made first vows, receiving the name of Julia. She received a B.A. degree in History and a M.S.E. degree in education from Arkansas State University. She also attended Mount Marty College in Yankton and St. Meinrad's College in Indiana.

For over thirty-five years, Sister Julia taught in elementary and secondary schools, most of which were spent in St. Paul's, Pocahontas, Arkansas. She also taught religious education classes in Arkansas and in Texas. In 1975 she was elected the tenth Prioress of Holy Angels Convent. After leaving the Prioress's office, she again re-entered the teaching field until she was name Subprioress in 1987. She served as Subprioress for six years, and was named Formation Directress in 1993. She served in this capacity until her death from a weakened heart on April 18, 1996.

During Mother Julia's administration, the following improvements were made at St. Bernards. After the Sisters relocated their convent to their new location north of Jonesboro in 1974, the vacated buildings not deemed structurally sound were demolished.

The 1888 convent building, the chapel and original 40-bed hospital erected in 1905 were demolished. Renovation was begun on the 1929 convent building, which was then annexed to the hospital by a covered walkway. After renovation, this building, facing Jackson Street was named "Hospital Annex" and now houses AHEC Program, hospital offices and guestrooms. Sister Julia died of a heart attack on April 19, 1996.

MOTHER MARY JOHN SEYLER, OSB, Prioress 1981-1987

Sister Mary John was elected the 12th Prioress of Holy Angels Convent in 1981 and led the development of the Community until 1987. Sister Mary John was born December 23, 1931 to Agnes Fette Seyler and Ben Seyler in Muenster, Texas and was named Margaret Henrietta. She has two living sisters and one adopted brother.

Sacred Heart School in Muenster, her home town, and the Olivetan Benedictine Sisters who taught there made a lasting impression on Margie, that the only thing which will make a person happy is doing God's will. After ten years in Sacred Heart School, Margie left home to enter Holy Angels Convent in June 1947. She made first vows in 1949 and received the name Sister Mary John. Her degrees include a B.A. from Avila College, Kansas City, Missouri and an M.A. in religious education from St. Mary's University, San Antonio, Texas.

Sister Mary John's first teaching assignment was at Blessed Sacrament School in Jonesboro. During this period, her father died suddenly in September 1952, a fact which saddened her final profession in 1953. Her teaching career included schools in

Arkansas, Louisiana and Texas.

During Mother Mary John's administration as Prioress, the north wing of the hospital was renovated and also the emergency department was renovated to contain the administrative offices. In addition, the Annex Building (formerly the Academy building facing Jackson Street) was renovated to add personnel offices, the Health Education Center and Stroud Hall. By 1985, the Sleep Disorder Center, cardiovascular surgery units were established. In 1986, the Bone Bank was established and the Home Health building was acquired. The Employee Fitness Center was established and a family room was designated for families of I/CCU patients.

In 1987, construction projects include six holding areas for surgery, two out patient surgery units and a separate elevator for patients and staff. By 1982 the expansion project increased bed capacity to 325. In addition, a helicopter landing pad was built, the cafeteria was expanded, the gift shop area renovated and a unit for Magnetic Resonance Imaging was established.

After completing her second term as Prioress in 1987, Sister Mary John returned to Muenster in a dual role, caring for her mother while teaching at Sacred Heart School. Her chief hobby is gardening. After the death of her mother in 1995, she returned to Holy Angels Convent and served as Directress of Formation for the Community for three years and later appointed Directress of the Pastoral Care Department. In addition, in 1995, Sister Mary John was appointed vice-president of Mission Effectiveness for St. Bernards Healthcare, Inc.

MOTHER M. CABRINI ARAMI, OSB, Prioress 1987-1993

Sister Cabrini was elected the 13th Prioress of Holy Angels Convent in June 1987. She was born on May 22, 1930 to the late Angelina Vicari Arami and Amedeo Arami in Montague, Texas. She received the name of Bertha Mary at Baptism. She has one brother, Herman Arami of Montague, and one sister Velva Sloan of Arlington, Texas.

After completing high school, Bertha entered Holy Angels Convent in Jonesboro, Arkansas. She received the name Cabrini at investment and made profession of first vows in 1949. Sister Cabrini was interested in the education field, so prepared for the ministry of teaching. She received her B.S.E degree from Arkansas State University and her M.D. from the University of Arkansas in Fayetteville.

Sister Cabrini's first mission was Sacred Heart School in Muenster, Texas. Her teaching career spanned over 40 years and included teaching both elementary and secondary students. Teaching assignments included schools and Catechetical classes in Arkansas, Texas and Louisiana. She served as principal during many of these years. From 1957 through 1973 Sister Cabrini served as education coordinator for the Community. Sister Cabrini also served as Subprioress of Holy Angels Convent from 1975 to 1981.

During Mother Cabrini's administration as Prioress (1987-1993), the multilevel parking deck was built at St. Bernards. In addition, the Ben E. Owens Cancer Treatment Center was erected, including the Women's diagnostic center and the dialysis unit. Two out patient floors were designated on two-east, the microbiology pharmacy lab was expanded and the hospice program was begun.

A number of other changes were made, including the establishment of a pain management center, occupational therapy and a physical therapy center was established. A physician office condominium was erected on South Church Street, which also houses a retail pharmacy. Bed capacity was increased to 375 when a number of offices were moved to new locations on campus. The following offices were relocated to buildings outside the hospital including the purchasing, accounting and marketing departments.

Throughout her years as Prioress, Mother Cabrini continued to support the mission of St. Bernards. After completing her second term as Prioress in 1993, she returned to the teaching ministry in Muenster, Texas. Sister Cabrini later returned to the Motherhouse, where she now serves on the Board for St. Bernards Village.

SISTER M. HENRIETTA HOCKLE, OSB, Prioress 1993-1999

Sister Henrietta was elected June 14, 1993, as the 14th Prioress of the Olivetan Benedictine Sisters. She was the first Jonesboro native to be elected Prioress during the 112 year history of the Community.

She was born on April 8, 1927, the daughter of Joe and Minnie (Thielemier) Hockle. She was the second oldest of four daughters and was named Minnie Jo, after her parents at Baptism. After graduating from both the elementary and secondary Catholic schools in Jonesboro, she entered Holy Angels Convent and received the name Henrietta at investment and she made profession of first vows in 1945. Sister Henrietta obtained her B.A. degree from St. Scholastica College in Duluth, Minnesota and her M.A. and Ed.S. Degrees from Arkansas State University in Jonesboro.

Her chosen ministry was in the field of education, in which she served as teacher, as principal and as superintendent of Catholic Schools of Arkansas until she was elected Prioress in 1993. During her 17 year tenure as superintendent, Sister Henrietta became one of the founding members of the Arkansas Nonpublic School Accrediting Association, Inc. and was elected its first executive director.

During her administration as Prioress and Chairperson of the Board (1993-1999), Sister Henrietta provided strong support for St. Bernards Regional Medical Center. St. Bernards made the following additions during this time. The transitional care unit was opened and the SHARP-PHO, Inc. was established. Eleven rural health clinics and medical clinics were opened throughout northeast Arkansas. In collaboration with Mr. Ben E. Owens, a shared vision was realized in the dedication of St. Bernards new dialysis center in 1997, St. Bernards Retirement Village in 1998, and the new Heartcare Center in March 1999.

After completing her second term as Prioress, Sister Henrietta continues to serve as a member of St. Bernards Governing Board and affirms St. Bernards healthcare ministry by working part-time in the Marketing Department. In 2000 she published, *A Century of Serving*, a centennial history of St. Bernards Hospital.

SISTER EILEEN SCHNEIDER, OSB, Prioress 1999-

Sister Eileen was elected June 18, 1999 as the 15th Prioress of the Olivetan Benedictine Sisters of Holy Angels Convent. A native of Jonesboro, she is the third of 11 children of the late Lawrence and Eva Schneider. She was born July 23, 1933 and received the name of Kathryn Ann at baptism.

Kathryn Ann attended both Blessed Sacrament School and Holy Angels Academy. After graduation from high school, she worked in the Medical Records Department of St. Bernards for 3 1/2 years before entering Holy Angels Convent. She received the name of Sister Eileen when invested and she made profession of first vows in 1956.

Sister Eileen's chosen ministry was in the field of education. She received her B.S.E. degree from Arkansas State University and majored in Elementary Education. She completed the diploma program from the Theology Institute at St. Norbert's College, De Pere, Wisconsin. Sister Eileen taught primary grades in parochial schools in Arkansas and Louisiana for more than 30 years.

In 1981, Sister Eileen was appointed Formation and Vocation Directress for the community and served in this capacity until 1987. She also served as Vice President for the Diocesan Council of Women Religious for three years. She was appointed Subprioress for the Community and served on the Governing Board for St. Bernards Regional Medical Center from 1993 to 1999, when she was elected Prioress.

Sister Eileen collaborates with Mr. Ben E. Owens in restructuring the Corporate Structure of St. Bernards Healthcare, Inc. to strengthen the health care ministry in the 21st Century. She reaffirms the long-term goal adopted in 1994 by the Community, "*To continue to support the health care ministry.*"

COLONEL JAMES N. OLHAUSEN - Business Manager - 1967-1983

Colonel James N. Olhausen became the first lay business manager for Holy Angels in the fall of 1967. He was born in Ridgley, Tennessee and attended Southwestern in Memphis and Union University in Martin, Tennessee.

Olhausen married Ruth Carter on May 18, 1934, and had a daughter, Ann and a son, James, Jr. He received his commission in the U.S. Army in 1936 and received his training as an officer in Los Angeles, California. He was stationed at Pearl Harbor during the Japanese attack. Olhausen served in Europe and Korea and received numerous military honors. He was commissioned as a full Colonel before retiring in 1967.

After his retirement, he began looking for a part-time position. While visiting relatives in Tennessee, he saw an ad in the Memphis paper for a business manager for Holy Angels Convent. He interviewed for the position, and after consultation with Bishop Fletcher and the Council, Mother Benedicta Boeckmann hired him.

Throughout his nearly 16 years of service, Olhausen conscientiously administered the business affairs of the Community finances and land holdings. According to the inscription on the plaque displayed in the centennial grotto, "Colonel Olhausen represented the highest ideals of a Christian businessman." Due to debilitating health problems, he retired in June 1983 and died in August of that same year.

RALPH JULIAN HALK - Business Manager - 1983-1993

Ralph Julian Halk was engaged as business manager for Holy Angels Convent in June 1983. Upon the retirement of Colonel Olhausen, Halk had been recommended to Mother Mary John Seyler by the local business community. After consultation with Bishop McDonald and the Community Council, he was hired to handle the business affairs for the Community.

Halk was born in Cherry Valley, Arkansas, but shortly after, the family moved to Long Beach, California where he grew up. He graduated form the University of California Berkley and joined the Navy. He served as a Navy Communication Officer on the USS Booth during World War II. Halk married Ann Whitehead and they had four children, two sons and two daughters. After his tour in the Navy, Halk worked for the Stanford Research Institute before forming his own company in Silicon Valley.

At the age of 45, he retired and returned to his native state of Arkansas and taught business at Arkansas State University for the next five years, before being hired as business manager for Holy Angels. He served in this capacity admirably for the next ten years, handling the financial affairs and land holdings of the Community.

Due to his wife's deteriorating health problems, he retired in the fall of 1993. Because of his cheerful disposition and humor, even in stressful situations, he was affectionately called "Saint Ralph" by the Sisters. Ralph Halk died on June 11, 2003 after fighting a courageous battle with ALS.

ALAN GUY PATTESON, JR. - Business Manager 1993 -

Alan Guy Patteson, Jr., a native of Jonesboro, is the third layman to serve in the position as business manager for the Olivetan Benedictine Sisters of Holy Angels Convent. Upon the retirement of Ralph Halk, the Sisters were looking for someone to fill that position.

In partnership with his brother, Patteson had recently sold the radio stations KBTM-AM & FM. Although he was still involved in the family farm operations, ginning and land holdings, he was open to a part-time position. Phil Jones, a member of the Community Business Advisory Committee was aware of the need and recommended Patteson for the position.

After consultation with Sr. Henrietta Hockle, Prioress at the time, Patteson took the position on a "one-year" trial basis. Both he and Sr. Henrietta agreed to this arrangement. Patteson was ably qualified with his wealth of experience in business and he was active in the civic community and in his church as a member of Blessed Sacrament Parish. Patteson married Carol All Busch in 1952 and they have three daughters and two sons.

Patteson's civic activity includes: President of Jonesboro Chamber of Commerce, President Jonesboro Rotary Club; long service on the Boards of City Water & Light and St. Bernards. He was actively involved with library development and civil rights. He was a member of the Arkansas Library Commission, and chaired the Arkansas Human Relations Commission and the state National Conference of Christians and Jews. He also served on the boards of three financial institutions.

During his nearly ten years as business manager, Patteson has been instrumental in helping the Community divest itself of Benedictine Manor in Hot Springs, which sale converted a liability into income producing assets. Another successful transaction resulted from the transfer of the Pocahontas property to the diocese. St. Paul's Parish, the beneficiary of the property, is making periodic contributions to the Community retirement fund.

The Community is extremely grateful to Alan, as he requested to be called, for his dedicated service throughout these "yo-yo" years in the financial market.

MISSIONS SERVED

by Convent Maria Stein and Holy Angels Convent — 1888–2003

MISSION	LOCATION	DIOCESE	YEARS SERVED
St. Paul School	Pocahontas, AR	Little Rock, AR	1888 -
St. Paul (colored)	Pocahontas, AR	Little Rock, AR	1889-1900
St. Roman School / Blessed Sacrament	Jonesboro, AR	Little Rock, AR	1889 -
St. Mary	Paragould, AR	Little Rock, AR	1890-1991 *
St. Boniface	Fort Smith, AR	Little Rock, AR	1890-1903
St. John (later public)	Engelberg, AR	Little Rock, AR	1891-1968
Sacred Heart	Popular Bluff, MO	Springfield, MO	1891-1909
Immaculate Conception	New Madrid, MO	Cape Girardeau, MO	1891-1902
St. Edward	Little Rock, AR	Little Rock, AR	1891-1904
Sacred Heart	Muenster, TX	Dallas-Fort Worth, TX	1895 -
St. Anselm / St. Mary / St. Peter	Wynne, AR	Little Rock, AR	1895-1901 & 1949-1973
St. Francis	Forrest City, AR	Little Rock, AR	1896-1910
Guardian Angels	Oran, MO	Cape Girardeau, MO	1899-1901
Holy Rosary	Stuttgart, AR	Little Rock, AR	1899-1943 & 1973-2001
All Saints	Hoxie, AR	Little Rock, AR	1900-1903 & 1930-1934
Immaculate Conception	Higginsville, MO	Springfield, MO	1900-1901
Sacred Heart	New Brunswick, MO	Springfield, MO	1903-1905
St. Polycarp	Carmi, IL	Belleville, AR	1903-1908
St. John Nepomucene	Dahlgreen, IL	Belleville, AR	1903-1906
St. Joseph	Cairo, IL	Belleville, AR	1903-1908
St. Patrick	Cairo, IL	Belleville, AR	1903-1908
St. Joseph	White Church, MO	St. Louis, MO	1903-1906
St. John	Brinkley, AR	Little Rock, AR	1904-1929
St. Joseph	Cobdon, IL	Belleville, AR	1905-1912
St. Andrew Cathedral	Little Rock, AR	Little Rock, AR	1907-1961
St. Mary	North Little Rock, AR	Little Rock, AR	1907-1908
St. John	Hot Springs, AR	Little Rock, AR	1908-1922
St. Edward	Texarkana, AR	Little Rock, AR	1908-1922
St. Joseph	Rhineland, TX	Dallas/Fort Worth, TX	1908-1968
St. Mary of the Lake	Lake Village, AR	Little Rock, AR	1908-1910
Holy Family	Nazareth, TX	Amarillo, TX	1909-1914
St. John Seminary	Little Rock, AR	Little Rock, AR	1911-1967
St. Elizabeth	Eureka Springs, AR	Little Rock, AR	1911-1912
St. Paul's Hospice	Armstrong Springs, AR	Little Rock, AR	1911-1912
St. John's Place / Benedictine Manor	Hot Springs, AR	Little Rock, AR	1913-1996
St. Peter / Immaculate Conception	Blytheville, AR	Little Rock, AR	1915-1986
SB School of Nursing	Jonesboro, AR	Little Rock, AR	1919-1962
St. Anthony	Weiner, AR	Little Rock, AR	1921-1972 *
St. Bernard	Knobel, AR	Little Rock, AR	1924-1935
Our Lady of Holy Souls	Little Rock, AR	Little Rock, AR	1947-
St. Norbert	Marked Tree, AR	Little Rock, AR	1950-1957
St. Maria Goretti	Lake Arthur, LA	Lafayette, LA	1955-1975

MISSION	LOCATION	DIOCESE	YEARS SERVED
St. Michael	West Memphis, AR	Little Rock, AR	1956-
Our Lady of Fatima	Benton, AR	Little Rock, AR	1959-1998
Catechetical Center	Erath, LA	Lafayette, LA	1959-1962
Parish Hospital	New Iberia, LA	Lafayette, LA	1960-1975
Consolata Home	New Iberia, LA	Lafayette, LA	1960-1976
Carrol C. Hospital	Eureka Springs, AR	Little Rock, AR	1959-1968
Little Angels Day Care	Little Rock, AR	Little Rock, AR	1961-2004
M. Gazzola Hospital	Brinkley, AR	Little Rock, AR	1963-1977
Muenster Hospital	Muenster, TX	Dallas, TX	1963-1968
* Holy Redeemer	El Dorado, AR	Little Rock, AR	1978-1990

Although Community withdrew from school, Sisters continue to teach religious education in the parish on a part-time basis.

FOREIGN MISSIONS

Bogota, Columbia	1966-1979
El Ojite, Hidalgo, Mexico	1983-1987

SCHOOLS AT MOTHERHOUSE/HOSPITAL

St. Bernards School of Nursing,	Jonesboro, AR	1919-1962
Holy Angels Academy,	Jonesboro, AR	1930-1962

NECROLOGY

In Memory of our Departed Sisters
Sisters Buried in ST. PAUL'S CEMETERY, Pocahontas, Arkansas
(Data taken from grave stones)

NAMES	BIRTH	PROFESSION	DEATH
Sr. Frances Metzler	1879	1887	1890
Sr. Scholastica Stoeckle	1865	1890	1890
Sr. Adelheida Mueller	1869	1891	1894
Sr. Gregoria Straub	1872	1897	1897*
Sr. Boniface Jacobs	1873	1897	1897*
Sr. Edeltrudis Limacher	1879	1897	1897*
Sr. Benedicta Koett	1872	1891	1898
Sr. Mechtildis Schuehert	1868	1891	1899
Sr. Xaveria Yost	1878	1898	1900
Sr. Irmengard Reimer	1873	1899	1903
Sr. Catherine Gamma	1880	1908	1908*
Sr. Magdalene Kolley	1886	1902	1910
Sr. Frowina Sonderegger	1864	1890	1913
Sr. Placida Gerschwiller	1870	1894	1914
Sr. Georgia Maier	1876	1906	1918
Sr. Mathilda Weibel	1888	1908	1919
Sr. Raphael Kimmet	1868	1895	1922
Sr. Loretta Hanselmann	1897	1924	1924
Sr. Heinrica Weider	1852	1891	1927

Sisters Buried in HOLY CROSS CEMETERY (PARISH), Jonesboro, Arkansas

NAMES	BIRTH	PROFESSION	DEATH
Sr. Elizabeth Vogler	1879	1900`	1900
Sr. Mathilda Ming	1866	1891	1901
Sr. Antonia Gerhig	1959	1892	1902
Sr. Clara Haus	1841	1882	1902
Sr. Margaret Helg	1873	1899	1904
Sr. Lutgardis Gloor	1873	1903	1905
Frances Bricker	1893	***(Candidate)***	1907
Sr. Celestine Buergler	1886	1905	1908
Sr. Regina Mudd	1872	1903	1910
Sr. Gertrude Willsau	1862	1891	1911
Sr. Paula Gabler	1884	1904	1911
Sr. Theresina Stockman	1860	1891	1912
Sr. Evangelista Weber	1869	1891	1913
Sr. Berchmans Weber	1869	1891	1913
Sr. Agnes Dali	1839	1862	1915
Prioress 1894-1897			
Sr. Agatha Hanie	1879	1900	1917
Sr. Petra Spirig	1825	1906	1919
Sr. Gregory Kienzler	1879	1907	1919
Sr. Lutgardis Weber	1894	1911	1920
Sr. Anselma Wuersch	1868	1890	1920
Sr. Anna Brogli	1872	1903	1922
Sr. Frances Bossart	1871	1894	1923
Sr. Othmara Leuchinger	1869	1895	1926
Sr. Aloysia Unterberger	1864	1890	1928
Prioress 1892-1894, 1909-1915			
Sr. Benedicta Stuebi	1880	1902	1930
Sr. Helen Suter	1887	1911	1932
Sr. Petra Rohmer	1903	1924	1932
Sr. Callista Schwitter	1902	1924	1932
Sr. Camille Suter	1880	1908	1933
Sr. Juliana Wyss	1874	1898	1934
Sr. Evangelista Sandor	1902	1920	1934
Sr. Christine Oggenfuss	1878	1908	1936
Sr. Bathildis Keller	1891	1926	1937
Sr. Boniface Weiss	1873	1904	1937
Sr. Martina With	1865	1904	1937
Sr. Lidwina Reinhard	1879	1907	1940
Sr. Stephany Wilhelm	1870	***Oblate***	1940
Sr. Barbara Graf	1858	1895	1941
Sr. Otillia Bisang	1872	1898	1941
Sr. Huberta Tschudi	1899	1926	1941
Mother Beatrice Renggli	1848	1867	1942
Foundress - Prioress 1887-1892			
Sr. Rose Muheim	1871	1891	1943
Sr. Frederica Spirig	1877	1898	1943

**** Novice made Profession of Vows on deathbed.***

NECROLOGY continued...

In Memory of our Departed Sisters
Sisters Buried in HOLY CROSS CEMETERY (PARISH), Jonesboro, Arkansas
(Data taken from grave stones)

NAMES	BIRTH	PROFESSION	DEATH
Sr. Cecilia Huber	1870	1892	1943
Prioress 1897-1900			
Sr. Georgia Dust	1909	1929	1944
Sr. Angelina Boesch	1973	1892	1944
Prioress 1903-1909			
Sr. Dominica Weibel	1876	1900	1945
Sr. Romana Wuest	1868	1891	1946
Sr. Fidelis Roth	1899	1924	1947
Sr. Meinrada End	1864	1892	1947
Sr. Scholastica Eicher	1869	1894	1948
Sr. Dorothy Sidler	1897	1926	1948
Sr. Monica Barnwart	1874	1900	1948
Sr. Alberica Steffen	1879	1906	1948
Sr. Innocentia Kuenzli	1881	1904	1949
Sr. Hildergard Huerlimann	1861	1891	1949
Sr. Alphonsa Gruenenfelder	1878	1904	1949
Sr. Vincentia Baettig	1875	1898	1950
Sr. Celestine Worland	1874	1898	1950
Mother Walburga Hoegger	1873	1894	1950
Prioress 1915-1945			
Sr. Clara Raeber	1883	1910	1951
Sr. Anastasia Ruegg	1889	1908	1952
Sr. Johanna Willis	1864	1891	1953
Sr. Felicitas Hunkler	1872	1891	1954
Sr. Eugenia Brodell	1873	1890	1954
Sr. Wilhelmina Galatti	1883	1907	1955
Sr. Josepha Waespe	1871	1891	1955
Sr. Ignatia Rohmer	1883	1907	1955
Sr. Bernarda Hutter	1875	1900	1955
Sr. Thecla Lothenback	1903	1924	1957
Sr. Teresa Fetsch	1899	1916	1957
Sr. Edward End	1870	1891	1958
Prioress 1900-1903			
Sr. Fidelis Baumberger	1874	1903	1958
Sr. Edeltrudis Boeni	1876	1900	1959
Sr. Justine Rinki	1879	1906	1959
Sr. Lawrence Jennimann	1890	1907	1959
Sr. Mechtildis Stolz	1876	1903	1959
Sr. Stanislaus Niedzwiedz	1899	1925	1960
Sr. Elizabeth Gobel	1886	1906	1960
Sr. Maura Jorski	1890	1908	1961
Sr. Salesia Gesbach	1879	1907	1961
Sr. Magdalena Weber	1888	1912	1961
Sr. Celine Truebenbach	1908	1927	1961
Sr. Ida Egli	1878	1903	1962
Sr. Spes Dingler	1875	1903	1962
Sr. Paula Dietsche	1890	1915	1962

NECROLOGY continued...

NAMES	BIRTH	PROFESSION	DEATH
Sr. Remigia Dietsche	1892	1911	1963
Sr. Albertina Hutter	1900	1926	1964
Sr. Catherine Gruener	1881	1911	1964
Sr. Charitas Buergi	1882	1903	1964
Sr. Josephine Jud	1902	1926	1964
Sr. Hedwig Peterli	1873	1898	1965
Sr. Philomena Willimann	1879	1898	1965
Sr. Lioba Suter	1888	1915	1966
Sr. Loretta Nause	1906	1927	1966
Sr. Xavier Lange	1889	1911	1966
Sr. Columba Kuster	1886	1904	1967
Sr. Leonarda Foehn	1890	1910	1967
Sr. Pia Wyss	1875	1898	1967
Sr. Rosalia Braenddli	1877	1895	1967
Sr. Margaret Zubler	1874	1907	1968
Sr. Thomasine Walterscheid	1908	1929	1970
Sr. Canisia Senn	1904	1926	1970
Sr. Stella Kaiser	1888	1936	1970
Sr. Hilda Gabler	1887	1910	1970
Sr. Coletta Nieererer	1888	1924	1970
Sr. Antonia Holthouse	1885	1906	1971
Sr. Ursula Straessli	1886	1906	1973
Sr. Adela Spirig	1889	1911	1973
Sr. Edith Free	1899	1940	1974

Sister Buried in OUR LADY OF MOUNT OLIVET CEMETERY - Convent Grounds, Jonesboro, Arkansas

NAMES	BIRTH	PROFESSION	DEATH
Sr. Melanie Rintach	1900	1930	1974
Sr. Victoria Meier	1883	1910	1974
Sr. Clementine Riga	1992	1920	1974
Sr. Frances Hofbauer	1906	1926	1975
Sr. Adelaide Gschwend	1897	1900	1975
Sr. Leona Stegler	1892	1914	1975
Sr. Gonzaga Morant	1900	1926	1975
Mother Perpetua Reinart *Prioress 1945-1954*	1888	1976	1976
Sr. Bertha Frei	1892	1910	1976
Sr. Mildred Felderhoff	1904	1930	1976
Sr. Agatha Knauf	1897	1922	1976
Sr. Marcella Huser	1897	1924	1977
Sr. Lutgardis	1895	1923	1977
Sr. Modesta Fetsch	1894	1914	1977
Sr. Fridoline Busk	1875	1899	1977
Sr. Lucy Staubi	1886	1903	1979
Sr. Patricia Murray	1903	1923	1979
Sr. Raphael Studer	1899	1926	1980
Sr. Alexia Suter	1895	1911	1980
Sr. Edigna Sparber	1906	1925	1980
Sr. Gebharda Trueneger	1898	1924	1981
Sr. Claudia Bichsel	1895	1914	1981

NECROLOGY continued...

Sister Buried in OUR LADY OF MOUNT OLIVET CEMETERY - Convent Grounds, Jonesboro, Arkansas
(Data taken from grave stones)

NAMES	BIRTH	PROFESSION	DEATH
Sr. Bernardine Grueninger	1892	1924	1981
Sr. Theodora Roos	1900	1926	1982
Sr. Berchmans Buehler	1903	1924	1982
Sr. Gertrude Poole	1896	1914	1984
Sr. Bridget Murray	1899	1983	1984
Sr. Angela Weber	1904	1926	1986
Sr. Patricia L. Findley	1927	1947	1986
Sr. Caroline Barmettler	1905	1924	1987
Sr. Gerarda Carns	1905	1923	1987
Sr. Camille McNeil	1923	1945	1988
Sr. Irmina Tiefenauer	1898	1924	1988
Sr. Imelda Pels	1911	1929	1988
Sr. Clare Myers	1922	1942	1989
Sr. Bernadette Kaufmann	1900	1929	1989
Sr. Frowina Hocker	1900	1929	1989
Sr. Eymard Lemmer	1917	1935	1989
Sr. Dolores Brady	1901	1920	1990
Sr. Regina Willett	1898	1919	1991
Sr. Rita Sparber	1906	1925	1992
Sr. Jerome Locken	8-04-1911	1933	10-8-1993
Sr. James Poirot	1-25-1918	1936	2-11-1994
Sr. Veronica Studer	11-30-1904	1933	1-7-1995
Sr. Agnes Voth	3-28-1900	1918	1-12-1995
Sr. Aloysia Kleiss	1-15-1909	1929	11-18-1995
Sr. Vincent Hicks	10-03-1919	1952	11-21-1995
Sr. Gabriel Koechne	5-16-1907	1925	4-12-1996
Sr. Julia Pruss *(Prioress 1975-81)*	10-28-1927	1945	4-18-1996
Sr. Anna Knoff	5-8-1907	1925	7-18-1996
Sr. Matilda Sparber	6-20-1902	1926	7-30-1996
Sr. Theresina Grob	9-29-1904	1926	10-3-1996
Sr. Martina Bolds	9-13-1910	1944	10-11-1996
Sr. Jane Frances Dalmer	10-24-1917	1938	2-12-1997
Sr. Amora Felderhoff	10-22-1895	1915	10-20-1997
Sr. Annella Willett	2-05-1910	1932	2-16-2000
Sr. Yvonne Lernee	12-11-1939	1957	9-7-2000
Sr. Florentine Tempel	4-30-1916	1933	9-27-2000
Sr. M. Michael Lange	11-2-1912	1931	4-2-2001
Sr. Geraldine Homer	4-25-1915	1932	5-25-2001
Sr. Anselma Haverkamp	1-22-1898	1922	2-7-2003
Sr. Carmelita Creasy Myers	4-22-1921	1949	7-24-2003
Sr. Micaela Carucci	9-4-1955	2003	9-5-2003
Sr. Fidelis Rohmer	4-30-1920	1951	3-02-2004

Community Membership
2003

Holy Angels Community

Sr. Philippa Wavrick

Sr. Benedicta Boeckmann

Sr. Genevieve McConnell

Sr. Helen Swirczynski

Sr. Louise Frankenberger

Sr. Conrad Frankenberger

Sr. Alberta Krebs

Sr. Carine Myers

Sr. Petra Riga

Sr. Henrietta Hockle

Sr. Pauline Morath

Sr. Angeline Massery

Community Membership
2003

Holy Angels Community (continued)

Sr. Georgia Felderhoff

Sr. Mary John Seyler

Sr. Cabrini Arami

Sr. Monica Swirczynski

Sr. Dominica Wise

Sr. Romana Rohmer

Sr. Mary Anne Nuce

Sr. Fidelis Rohmer

Sr. Christopher Flowers

Sr. Celestine Pond

Sr. Alphonse Gain

Sr. Beatrice Schneider

Community Membership
2003

Holy Angels Community (continued)

Sr. Eileen Schneider

Sr. Elaine Willett

Sr. Lenore Dust

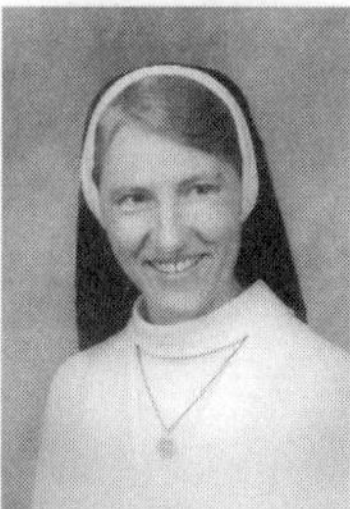
Sr. Jeanette Bayer

Sr. Lillian Marie Reiter

Sr. Brenda Willett

Sr. Cordis Kim

Sr. De Porres Polk

Sr. Cecilia Marie Shannon

Sr. Joanne Sandoval

Sr. Judith Dalesandro

Sr. Marya Duscher

Community Membership
2003

Holy Angels Community (continued)

Sr. Miriam Burns

Sr. Ann Marie Ferricher

Sr. Damian Marie Atkinson

Sr. Marilyn Doss

Sr. Josita Lopez

Sr. Laura Cathcart

Sr. Therese Johnson

Sr. Lisa O'Connell

Novice Elizabeth Love

Novice Virginia Baltz

Novice Chon Marie Nguyen

Novice Deborah Coffey

Community Membership
2003

Holy Angels Community (continued)

POSTULANT RITA FALCONER

POSTULANT THERESE DUNN

POSTULANT TANYA CENAC

POSTULANT JANA OELKERS

POSTULANT HAI NGUYEN

Reference Notes

Chapter 1

1. The centenary brochure of the Maria Rickenbach Convent, Garden Enclosed.published 1957, give an outline of this legend
2. Dowling, Sr. M. Dolores, OSB, In Your Midst, Clyde, Missouri: Monastery Press, 1988, p. 2
3. Ibid. p. 2-3
4. Ibid. p. 4
5. Ibid. p. 4
6. Ibid. p. 4
7. Ibid. p. 6
8. Partial German handwritten copy of these Statutes, Archives, Clyde, Missouri
9. Dowling, Sr. Dolores, OSB, p. 6
10. Malone, Edward, OSB, A History of Conception: Colony, Abbey and Schools, Interstate Printing Co., Omaha, Nebraska, 1971
11. From the German Chronicles of Maria Rickenbach, Vol. 4, Translated by Sr. DeSales Markert, OSB, St. Louis, Missouri, 1974
12. Excerpts taken from Journal by Sr. Beatrice Renglli, OSB, Archives, Holy Angels Convent, Jonesboro, Arkansas
13. Dowling, Sr. Dolores, p. 12
14. Ibid. p. 12
15. Renglli, Sr. Beatrice, OSB, Journal
16. Ibid.
17. Ibid.

Chapter 2

1. Excerpts taken from the Journal by Sr. Beatrice Renglli, OSB, Archives, Holy Angels Convent, Jonesboro, Arkansas
2. Ibid.
3. Ibid.
4. Ibid.
5. Dowling, Sr. Dolores, OSB, In Your Midst, Clyde, Missouri, Monastery Press, 1988. p. 18
6. Ibid. p. 20
7. Letters to Abbot Anselm, October, 1874
8. Dowling, op. cit. p. 22
9. Ibid. p. 24
10. Ibid. p. 27
11. Ibid. p. 33
12. Letters from Mother Anselma and Others (Archives at Clyde)

15\. Letter of July 8, 1880 in Early Chronicled History: Relationship Between Maryville and Conception, p. 102

16\. Dowling, Sr. Dolores, OSB, p. 35

13\. Ibid. p. 35

16\. Voth, Sr. Agnes, OSB, Green Olive Branch, Chicago, Illinois: Franciscan Herald, Press, 1973. p. 42

17\. Ibid. p. 42

18\. Ibid. p. 43

19\. Dowling, op. cit. p. 36

20\. Ibid. p. 40

21\. Ibid. p. 40

22\. Ibid. p. 47

Chapter 3

1. Weibel, Fr. J.E., 40 Years Missionary in Arkansas, St. Meinrad, Indiana, Abbey Press, 1968, p. 10-11
2. Ibid. p. 23
3. Voth, Sr. Agnes, OSB, Green Olive Branch, Chicago, Illinois, Franciscan Herald Press, 1973, p. 44
4. Weibel, op. cit. p. 41
5. Voth, op. cit. p. 46
6. Weibel, Fr. J.E., The Catholic Missions of Northeast Arkansas, Jonesboro, Arkansas, Arkansas State University Press, 1967, p. 39
7. Ibid. p.50
8. Voth, op. cit. p. 47
9. Fitzgerald, Bishop Edward, Letter to Abbot Frowin Conrad (Conception Missouri), Archives, Clyde, Missouri, August 23, 1887
10. Dowling, Sr. Dolores, In Your Midst, Clyde, Missouri, Monastery Press, 1988. p. 47
11. Hunkler, Sr. Felicitas, "The Beginning" Unpublished Document, Archives, Holy Angels Convent, Jonesboro, Arkansas
12. Renggli, Mother Beatrice, Unpublished Notes, Archives, Holy Angels Convent, Jonesboro, Arkansas
13. Voth, op. cit. p. 49
14. Ibid. p. 53
15. Ibid. p. 54
16. Ibid. p. 55
17. Renggli M. Beatrice, Letter to Abbot Frowin Conrad, June 18, 1888
18. Voth, op. cit. p. 57
19. Renggli M. Beatrice, Letter to Abbot Frowin Conrad, July 16, 1888, Archives, Holy Angels Convent, Jonesboro, Arkansas
20. Renggli M. Beatrice, Letter to Abbot Frowin Conrad, June 17, 1888, Archives, Holy Angels Convent, Jonesboro, Arkansas
21. Renggli, op. cit. Unpublished Notes
22. Voth, op. cit. p. 59
23. Renggli, op. cit. Unpublished Notes
24. Renggli, Ibid. Unpublished Notes

Chapter 4

1. Voth, Sr. Agnes, Green Olive Branch, Chicago, Illinois, Franciscan Herald Press, 1973. p. 79-80
2. Renggli, Mother Beatrice, Unpublished Notes, Archives, Holy Angels Convent, Jonesboro, Arkansas
3. Voth, op. cit. p. 81
4. Renggli, op. cit. Unpublished Notes
5. Voth, op. cit. p. 81-82
6. Brochure, Maria Stein Academy, Free Printing Press, Pocahontas, Arkansas, 1888
7. Hunkler, Sr. Felicitas, "In the Beginning", Unpublished Notes, Archives, Holy Angels Convent, Jonesboro, Arkansas
8. Voth, op. cit. p. 82
9. Ibid. p. 82
10. Weibel, Fr. J.E. Letter to Abbot Frowin Conrad. February 16, 1892, Archives, Conception, Abbey, Missouri
11. Voth, op. cit. p. 83
12. Ibid. p. 84
13. Fitzgerald, Bishop E. Letter to Fr. Weibel, June 2, 1892, Archives, Holy Angels Convent, Jonesboro, Arkansas
14. Hunkler, Sr. Felicitas, "In the Beginning", Unpublished Notes, Archives, Holy Angels Convent, Jonesboro, Arkansas

Chapter 4 *continued*

15. Voth, op. cit. p. 94
16. Stocker, Augustine, OSB, Letter to Mother Beatrice, February 26, 1912, Archives, Holy Angels Convent, Jonesboro, Arkansas
17. Zilianti, Romualdo M. OSB, to Fr. Bernards Sause, OSB, January 12, 1969, Archives, Holy Angels Convent, Jonesboro, Arkansas
18. Rooney, Abbot Marcell, OSB, Letter, March 11, 1997-
19. Unterberger, Sr. Aloysia, Letter, October 16, 1893
20. Hunkler, op. cit
21. Hunkler, op. cit
22. Voth, op. cit. p. 117
23. Ibid. p. 118

Chapter 5

1. Voth, Sr. Agnes, OSB, Green Olive Branch, Chicago, Illinois. Franciscan Herald Press, 1973. p. 120
2. Ibid. p. 120
3. Hunkler, Sr. Felicitas, "In the Beginning", Unpublished Document, Archives, Holy Angels Convent, Jonesboro, Arkansas
4. Voth, op. cit. p. 123
5. Hunkler, op. cit.
6. Newspaper Clippings - Undated and Pasted in Sequence in Scrapbook, Archives, St. Bernards Hospital, Jonesboro, Arkansas
7. Voth, op. cit. p. 123
8. Ibid. p. 127
9. Ibid. p. 127
10. Ibid. p. 128
11. Hunkler, op. cit.
12. Voth, op. cit. p. 128
13. Hunkler, op. cit .
14. Gabler, Sr. Hilda, Unpublished Document, Archives, Holy Angels Convent, Jonesboro, Arkansas
15. Hunkler, op. cit.

Chapter 6

1. Gabler, Sr. Hilda, "Service – Not Recognition," Unpublished Notes, Archives, Holy Angels Convent, Jonesboro, Arkansas
2. Yearbook, Directory of St. Roman's Church and St. Bernards Hospital, 1901, Archives, St. Bernards Hospital, Jonesboro, Arkansas
3. Gabler, op. cit.
4. Voth, Sr. Agnes, Green Olive Branch, Chicago, Illinois, Franciscan Herald Press, 1973, p. 132
5. Renggli, Mother Beatrice, Unpublished Notes, Archives, Holy Angels Convent, Jonesboro, Arkansas.
6. Voth, op. cit. p. 132
7. Hockle, Sr. Henrietta, Century of Service, Jonesboro, Arkansas Pinpoint Publishing, Inc., 2000, p. 6
8. Record Book, St. Anna's Infirmary, Archives, Holy Angels Convent, Jonesboro, Arkansas
9. Voth, op. cit., p. 133
10. Ibid. p. 133
11. Voth, op. cit., p. 134
12. Hockle, op. cit., p. 3
13. Voth, op. cit., 136
14. Ibid. p. 137

Chapter 6 *continued*

15. Ibid. p. 137
16. Boesch, Sr. Angelina, Undated Letter Found, Archives, Holy Angels Convent, Jonesboro, Arkansas
17. Voth, op. cit., p. 139
18. Boesch, Sr. Angelia, Letter to Bishop Morris, Undated, Archives, Holy Angels Convent, Jonesboro, Arkansas
19. Voth, op. cit., p. 141
20. Hockle, op. cit., p. 9

Chapter 7

1. The History of Catholicity in Arkansas, Published under the auspices of the Historical Commission of the Diocese of Little Rock, The Guardian, 1925, pages not numbered
2. Woods, James M., Mission and Memory, Little Rock, Arkansas, August House, Inc.,1993, p. 168
3. Voth, Sr. Agnes, Green Olive Branch, Chicago, Illinois, Franciscan Herald Press, 1973, p.142
4. Woods, Ibid. p. 168
5. Voth, op. cit. p. 141
6. Ibid. p. 142
7. Hockle, Sr. Henrietta, A Century of Serving, Jonesboro, Arkansas, Pinpoint Publishing, Inc. 2000, p. 12
8. Ibid. p. 12
9. Ibid. p. 13
10. Stuck, Charles A. The Story of Craighead County, The Hurley Company, Jonesboro, Arkansas 1960, p. 154
11. Council Minutes, February 16, 1916, Archives, Holy Angels Convent, Jonesboro, Arkansas
12. Council Minutes, October 29, 1916, Archives, Holy Angels Convent, Jonesboro, Arkansas
13. Hockle, op. cit. p. 16
14. Ibid. p. 15
15. Ibid. p. 16
16. Voth, op. cit. p. 143
17. Ibid. p. 143
18. Hockle, op. cit. p. 15
19. Voth, op. cit. p. 146
20. Ibid. p. 147
21. Council Minutes, Archives, October 6, 1919, Archives, Holy Angels Convent, Jonesboro, Arkansas
22. Voth, op. cit. p. 149
23. Keller, Fr. Gregory K., Letter, April, 29 1922, Archives, Holy Angels Convent, Jonesboro, Arkansas
24. Hoegger, M. Walburga, Notation on bottom of letter, Holy Angels Convent, Jonesboro, Arkansas

Chapter 8

1. Hockle, Sr. Henrietta, A Century of Serving, Jonesboro, Arkansas, Pinpoint Publishing, Inc. 2000. p. 20
2. Ibid. p. 20
3. Voth, Sr. Agnes, Green Olive Branch, Chicago, Illinois, Franciscan Herald Press, 1973, p. 160
4. Ibid. p. 150
5. Ibid. p. 150
6. Hockle, op. cit. p. 23
7. Ibid. p. 23
8. Voth, op. cit. p. 153
9. Ibid. p. 153
10. Ibid. p. 154
11. Ibid. p. 159

Chapter 8 *continued*

12. Voth, op. cit. p. 160
13. Ibid. op. cit. p. 161
14. Hockle, op. cit. p. 26
15. Ibid. p. 26
16. Ibid. p. 26
17. Hoegger, Mother Walburga, Day Book, Archives Holy Angels Convent, November 27, 1924
18. Document of Incorporation, Files, Archives, Holy Angels Convent, Sept. 30, 1928
19. Voth, op. cit. p. 166
20. Ibid. p. 172
21. Ibid. p. 17
22. Jonesboro Tribune, Dedication, Holy Angels Convent, Jonesboro, Arkansas, April 17, 1929, p. 1
23. Diamond Jubilee Brochure, Archives, Holy Angels Convent, Jonesboro, Arkansas, 1962
24. Voth, op. cit. p. 174

Chapter 9

1. Hunkeler, Sr. Felicitas, Unpublished Notes, Archives, Holy Angels Convent, Jonesboro, Arkansas
2. Voth, Sr. Agnes, Green Olive Branch. Chicago, Illinois, Franciscan Herald Press, 1973, p. 178
3. Hockle, Sr. Henrietta, A Century of Serving, Jonesboro, Arkansas. Pinpoint Publishing, Inc. 2000. p 33
4. Ibid. p. 33
5. Voth, op. cit. 175
6. Ibid. p. 17
7. Ibid. p. 176
8. Ibid. p. 177
9. Ibid. p. 177
10. Hockle, op. cit. p. 33
11. Ibid. p. 34
12. Ibid. p. 34
13. Ibid. p. 35
14. Voth, op. cit. p. 186
15. Hockle, op. cit. p. 37
16. Hoegger, M. Walburga, Diary, Archives, Holy Angels Convent, Jonesboro, Arkansas
17. Tempel, Sr. Florentine, Recollection Related to Author
18. Voth, op. cit. p. 198
19. Ibid. p. 199
20. Hoegger, op. cit. Diary
21. Voth, op. cit. p. 200
22. Ibid. p. 200
23. Ibid. p. 201
24. Ibid. p. 201

Chapter 10

1. Hockle, Sr. Henrietta, A Century of Serving, Jonesboro, Arkansas, Pinpoint Printing, Inc. 2000, p. 40
2. Voth, Sr. Agnes, Green Olive Branch, Chicago, Illinois, Franciscan Herald Press, 1973, p. 203
3. Ibid. p. 204
4. Ibid. p. 203
5. Lamp, Yearbook for Nurses, 1940, Archives, St. Bernards Hospital, Jonesboro, Arkansas
6. Voth, op. cit. p. 207
7. Certificate of Verification, November 22, 1922, Archives, Holy Angels Convent, Jonesboro, Arkansas

Chapter 10 *continued*

8. Hockle, op. cit. p. 42
9. Ibid. p. 42
10. Minutes of Annual Corporation Meeting, July 10, 1942, Archives, Holy Angel Convent, Jonesboro, Arkansas
11. Hockle, op. cit. p. 43
12. Hockle, Sr. Henrietta, Mother Beatrice Renggli, OSB, Biography, Creative Multigraphics, Inc., 1998, Jonesboro, Arkansas
13. Voth, op. cit. p. 205
14. Minutes of Annual Corporation Meeting, July 3, 1944, Archives, Holy Angels Convent, Jonesboro, Arkansas
15. Minutes of Annual Corporation Meeting, July 2, 1945, Archives, Holy Angels Convent, Jonesboro, Arkansas
16. Minutes of Council Meeting, July 16, 1945, Archives, Holy Angels Convent, Jonesboro, Arkansas
17. Voth. op. cit. p. 218
18. Minutes of Council Meeting, February 21, 1947, Archives, Holy Angels Convent, Jonesboro, Arkansas
19. Minutes of Council Meeting, June 6, 1948, Archives, Holy Angels Convent, Jonesboro, Arkansas
20. Voth, op. cit. p. 218
21. Ibid. p. 220
22. Ibid. p. 222
23. Hockle, Sr. Henrietta, A Century of Serving, Jonesboro, Arkansas, Pinpoint Publishing, Inc., 2000, p. 47
24. Ibid. p. 47
25. Voth, op. cit. p. 223
26. Ibid. p. 223
27. Census Records, Hospital Archives, 1949

Chapter 11

1. Hockle, Sr. Henrietta, A Century of Serving, Jonesboro, Arkansas, Pinpoint Printing, Inc., 2000, p. 50
2. Jonesboro Sun Newspaper, Archives, St. Bernards Hospital, Jonesboro, Arkansas, January 22, 1950
3. Jonesboro Sun Newspaper, Archives, St. Bernards Hospital, Jonesboro, Arkansas, July 4, 1950
4. Hockle, op. cit. p. 51
5. Voth, Sr. Agnes, Green Olive Branch, Chicago, Illinois, Franciscan Herald Press, 1973, p. 231
6. Community Prayerbook, St. Meinrad, Indiana, Abbey Press, December 2, 1950
7. Council Minutes, Archives, Holy Angels Convent, Jonesboro, Arkansas, April 26, 1951
8. Chapter Minutes, Archives, Holy Angels Convent, Jonesboro, Arkansas, November 1, 1951
9. Hockle, op. cit. p. 54
10. Constitutions of the Olivetan Benedictine Sisters, Archives, Holy Angels Convent, Jonesboro, Arkansas, December 6, 1952
11. Voth, op. cit. p. 219
12. Ibid. p. 237
13. Chapter Minutes, Archives, Holy Angels Convent, Jonesboro, Arkansas, July 2, 1954.
14. Voth, op. cit. p. 239
15. Chapter Minutes, Archives, Holy Angels Convent, Jonesboro, Arkansas, July 10, 1955
16. Voth, op. cit. p. 248
17. Tidings From Home, Vol. 2, No. 2, October 1955, p. 1
18. Council Minutes, Archives, Holy Angels Convent, Jonesboro, Arkansas, Nov. 26, 1957
19. Voth, op. cit. p. 250
20. Ibid. p. 255
22. Voth, op. cit. p. 254
23. Council Minutes, Archives, Holy Angels Convent, Jonesboro, Arkansas, November 28, 1959
21. Hockle, op. cit. p. 57

Chapter 12

1. The Documents of Vatican II, "Decree on Appropriate Renewal of Religious Life," promulgated, October 28, 1062, p. 468
2. Fletcher, Bishop Albert. L., Letter to Superiors, Archives, Holy Angels Convent, Jonesboro, Arkansas, June 18, 1962
3. Voth, Sr. Agnes, Green Olive Branch, Chicago, Illinois, Franciscan Herald Press, 1973, p. 264
4. Ibid. p. 279
5. Hockle, Sr. Henrietta, A Century of Serving, Jonesboro, Arkansas, Pinpoint Printing, Inc. 2000, p. 60
6. Document of Separating Corporation, Archives, Holy Angels, Convent, June 15, 1962
7. Hockle, op. cit. p. 62
8. Certificate of Separation, Archives, Holy Angels Convent, Jonesboro, Arkansas, June 16, 1962
9. Hockle, op. cit. p. 62
10. Ibid. p. 63
11. Voth, op. cit. p. 271
12. Jonesboro Sun, June 8, 1963, p. 1
13. Voth, op. cit. p. 275
14. Financial Records, Archives, Holy Angels Convent, Jonesboro, Arkansas, December 1964
15. Records, Archives, Holy Angels Convent, Jonesboro, Arkansas, June 15, 1965
16. Jonesboro Sun, December 19, 1965, p. 1
17. Purchase Agreement, Archives, Holy Angels Convent, Jonesboro, Arkansas, June 4, 1966
18. Records, Archives, Holy Angels Convent, July 2, 1966
19. Corporation Meeting Minutes, July 2, 1966
20. Ibid.
21. Ibid .
22. Voth, op. cit. p. 283
23. Council Minutes, Archives, Holy Angles Convent, Jonesboro, Arkansas, November 24, 1966
24. Fletcher, Bishop Albert L. Statement Archives, Holy Angels Convent, Jonesboro, Arkansas, 1969
25. Council Minutes, Archives, Holy Angels Convent, Jonesboro, Arkansas, June 11, 1967
26. Corporation Meeting, Archives, Holy Angels Convent, Jonesboro, Arkansas, July 4, 1968
27. Hockle, op. cit. p. 65
28. Ibid. p. 67
29. Ibid. p. 68
30. Records, Archives, Holy Angels Convent, Jonesboro, Arkansas, July 27, 1968
31. Zilianti, Romualdo M. Abbot, General, Letter, Archives, Holy Angels Convent, Jonesboro, Arkansas, July 27, 1968
32. Dedication Record, Archives, Holy Angels Convent, Jonesboro, Arkansas, October 5, 1969
33. Fletcher, Bishop Albert L., Oral History

Chapter 13

1. Boeckmann, Sr. Benedicta, letter, Archives, Holy Angels Convent, Jonesboro, Arkansas, February 8, 1971
2. Chapter Meeting, Archives, Holy Angels Convent, Jonesboro, Arkansas, December 9, 1971
3. Hockle, Sr. Henrietta, A Century of Serving, Jonesboro, Arkansas, Pinpoint Printing, Inc., 2000, p. 72
4. Corporation Meeting, Archives, Holy Angels Convent, Jonesboro, Arkansas, June 6, 1972
5. Corporation Meeting, Archives, Holy Angels Convent, Jonesboro, Arkansas, July 13, 1972
6. Hockle, op. cit. p. 74
7. Ibid. p. 68
8. Ibid. p. 69
9. General Chapter Meeting, Archives, Holy Angels Convent, June 10, 1974
10. Community Records, Archives, Holy Angels Convent, Jonesboro, Arkansas, August 6, 1978
11. Hockle, Sr. Henrietta, Promises Kept, Little Rock, Arkansas, Porbeck Printing Company, 1978

12. Chapter Meeting, Archives, Holy Angels Convent, June 2, 1976
13. Chapter Minutes, Archives, Holy Angels Convent, Jonesboro, Arkansas, June 14, 1977
14. Chapter Meeting, Archives, Holy Angels Convent, Jonesboro, Arkansas, April 17, 1978
15. Council Meeting, Archives, Holy Angels Convent, Jonesboro, Arkansas, August 6, 1978
16. Hockle, Sr. Henrietta, A Century of Serving, Jonesboro, Arkansas, Pinpoint Printing Inc., p. 70

Chapter 14

1. Corporation Meeting, Archives, Holy Angels Convent, June 1, 1980
2. Chapter Meeting, Archives, Holy Angels Convent, June 1, 1980
3. Hockle, Sr. Henrietta, A Century of Serving, Jonesboro, Arkansas, Pinpoint Printing, Inc, 2000, p. 81
4. Corporation Meeting, Archives, Holy Angels Convent, Jonesboro, Arkansas, June 6, 1981
5. Council Meeting, Archives, Holy Angels Convent, Jonesboro, Arkansas, August 14, 1981
6. Council Meeting, Archives, Holy Angels Convent, Jonesboro, Arkansas, August 14, 1981
7. Council Meeting, Archives, Holy Angels Convent, Jonesboro, Arkansas, March 12, 1982
8. Council Meeting, Archives, Holy Angels Convent, Jonesboro, Arkansas, August 13, 1982
9. Council Meeting, Archives, Holy Angels Convent, Jonesboro, Arkansas, August 30, 1982
10. Council Meeting, Archives, Holy Angels Convent, Jonesboro, Arkansas, September 4, 1982
11. Council Meeting, Archives, Holy Angels Convent, Jonesboro, Arkansas, July 9, 1982
12. Council Meeting, Archives, Holy Angels Convent, Jonesboro, Arkansas, April 8, 1983
13. Council Meeting, Archives, Holy Angels Convent, Jonesboro, Arkansas, June 3, 1983
14. Council Meeting, Archives, Holy Angels Convent, Jonesboro, Arkansas, April 8, 1983
15. Council Meeting, Archives, Holy Angels Convent, Jonesboro, Arkansas, August 5, 1983
16. Council Meeting, Archives, Holy Angels Convent, Jonesboro, Arkansas, September 9, 1983
17. Chapter Meeting, Archives, Holy Angels Convent, Jonesboro, Arkansas, June 7, 1984
18. Council Meeting, Archives, Holy Angels Convent, Jonesboro, Arkansas, December 14, 1984
19. Chapter Meeting, Archives, Holy Angels Convent, Jonesboro, Arkansas, June 11, 1985
20. Council Meeting, Archives, Holy Angels Convent, Jonesboro, Arkansas, August 8, 1986
21. The Banner, Hospital Newsletter, Archives, Holy Angels Convent, Jonesboro, Arkansas, Winter Issue, 1984
22. Hockle, Sr. Henrietta, A Century of Serving, Jonesboro, Arkansas, Pinpoint Printing, Inc., 2000, p. 87
23. Chapter Meeting, Archives, Holy Angels Convent, Jonesboro, Arkansas, June 13, 1987
24. Chapter Meeting, Archives, Holy Angels Convent, Jonesboro, Arkansas, October 9, 1987
25. Chapter Meeting, Archives, Holy Angels Convent, Jonesboro, Arkansas, December 12, 1987
26. Hockle, Sr. Henrietta, A Century of Serving, Jonesboro, Arkansas, Pinpoint Printing, Inc., 2000, p. 87
27. Corporation Meeting, Archives, Holy Angels Convent, Jonesboro, Arkansas, June 15, 1989
28. Joyful Response, Constitution of Olivetan Benedictine Sisters, (mimeographed), Apostolic Works, p. 22

Chapter 15

1. Hockle, Sr. Henrietta, A Century of Serving, Jonesboro, Arkansas, Pinpoint Printing, Inc., 2000, p. 90
2. Ibid. p. 91
3. Council Meeting, Archives, Holy Angels Convent, Jonesboro, Arkansas, March 9, 1990
4. Corporation Resolution, Archives, Holy Angels Convent, Jonesboro, Arkansas, March 9, 1990
5. Council Meeting, Archives, Holy Angels Convent, Jonesboro, Arkansas, April 10, 1990
6. Joyful Response, Constitution-1994 Revision, Customary, C-16, p. 61
7. Council Meeting, Archives, Holy Angels Convent, Jonesboro, Arkansas, March 12, 1992
8. Council Meeting, Archives, Holy Angels Convent, Jonesboro, Arkansas, October 11, 1991
9. Council Meeting, Archives, Holy Angels Convent, Jonesboro, Arkansas, May 10, 1991
10. Council Meeting, Archives, Holy Angels Convent, Jonesboro, Arkansas, May 15, 1993
11. Ibid.
12. Hockle, Sr. Henrietta, Letter, Holy Angels Convent, Jonesboro, Arkansas, June 17, 1993

Chapter 15 *continued*

13. Hockle, Sr. Henrietta, Announcement, Archives, Holy Angels Convent, Jonesboro, Arkansas, June 30, 1993
14. Chapter Meeting, Archives, Holy Angels Convent, Jonesboro, Arkansas, July 9, 1993
15. Council Meeting, Archives, Holy Angels Convent, Jonesboro, Arkansas, July 9, 1993
16. Council Meeting, Archives, Holy Angels Convent, Jonesboro, Arkansas, August 13, 1993
17. Chapter Meeting, Archives, Holy Angels Convent, Jonesboro, Arkansas, November 9, 1993
18. Council Meeting, Archives, Holy Angels Convent, Jonesboro, Arkansas, January 14, 1994
19. Ibid.
20. Council Meeting, Archives, Holy Angels Convent, Jonesboro, Arkansas, February 14, 1994
21. Planning Session, Archives, Holy Angels Convent, Jonesboro, Arkansas, June 8, 1994
22. Corporation Meeting, Archives, Holy Angels Convent, Jonesboro, Arkansas, June 8, 1995
23. Long Term Goals, Archives, Holy Angels Convent, Jonesboro, Arkansas, June 1995
24. Corporation Meeting, Archives, Holy Angels Convent, Jonesboro, Arkansas, June 14, 1996
25. Chapter Meeting, Archives, Holy Angels Convent, Jonesboro, Arkansas, July 9, 1996
26. National Religious Retirement Office–(NRRO), Letter, Archives, Holy Angels Convent, Jonesboro, Arkansas, April 1997
27. Chapter Minutes, Archives, Holy Angels Convent, Jonesboro, Arkansas, July 8, 1999
28. Chapter Minutes, Archives, Holy Angels Convent, Jonesboro, Arkansas, December 28, 1999

Chapter 16

1. Chapter Meeting, Archives, Holy Angels Convent, Jonesboro, Arkansas, December 28, 1999
2. Hockle, Sr. Henrietta, A Century of Serving, Jonesboro, Arkansas, Pinpoint Printing, Inc., 2000, p. 101
3. Ibid. p. 101
4. Echoes, Community Newsletter, Creative Multigraphics, Jonesboro, Arkansas, January 2001
5. Job Description for "Vice-President for Mission Effectiveness," Archives, Holy Angels Convent, Jonesboro, Arkansas, May 24, 2002
6. Chapter Meeting, Archives, Holy Angels Convent, Jonesboro, Arkansas, June 18, 2002
7. Ibid.
8. General Chapter, Archives, Holy Angels Convent, Jonesboro, Arkansas, June 18-19, 2003
9. Ibid.
10. Fialka, John J. Sisters, St. Martin's Press, New York, 2003, p. 326
11. Ibid. p. 328
12. Joyful Response, Constitution, Holy Angels Convent, Jonesboro, Arkansas, 2000

Index

On High Ground

E

F

G

H

I

J

K

L

M

N

O

P

R

S

T

W

Z

Sister Henrietta Hockle, OSB

About the Author

Sr. Henrietta Hockle, OSB, member of the Jonesboro Benedictines and native of that same city, was former Prioress of Holy Angels Convent and Chairperson of St. Bernards Governing Board. She has a background in education, having received her B.A. Degree from St. Scholastica College, Duluth, MN, and her M.A. Degree and Specialist Degree, Ed.S. from Arkansas State University, Jonesboro, AR.

She served as Superintendent of Catholic Schools of Arkansas for 17 years before being elected Prioress in 1993. Sr. Henrietta is listed in the *American Catholic Who's Who* for her contributions in the field of education.

She is past contributor to the Craighead County Historical Quarterly and in 1988 published *Gift and Promise*, a history of the Catholic Schools of Arkansas. In 1998 she published the history of *Mother Beatrice Renggli, OSB.*, Foundress of the Jonesboro Benedictines. In 2000 Sr. Henrietta published, *A Century of Serving,* a centennial history of St. Bernards Hospital. Currently, Sr. Henrietta is editor of the *ECHOES,* Community newsletter and is coordinator of the Alumnae Activities. Her hobbies include reading—especially biographies, flower gardening, bird watching, nature walks and needlework.

Father Hugh Assenmacher, OSB

About the Editor

Fr. Hugh Assenmacher, OSB, a Monk of Subiaco Abbey, is a native of Billings, Missouri. He attended the Minor Seminary at Subiaco Abbey and entered the Monastery there in 1952. Ordained in 1958 he attended the University of Arkansas and St. Louis University, earning a M.A. Degree in History.

Most of his life has been spent as a teacher at Subiaco Academy and in various other assignments in the Abbey. He has written the centennial history of Subiaco Abbey: *A Place Called Subiaco,* the histories of St. Joseph's Parish in Paris, Arkansas; the history of *St. Scholastica Parish, Shoal Creek, Arkansas*; and revised and up-dated the history of *St. Edward's Parish, Little Rock,* (at the time of their centennial), and the 25th anniversary of the now-closed Santa Familia Priory in Belize, Central America, a former dependent priory of Subiaco Abbey.

Currently Fr. Hugh is a faculty member and chaplain of Subiaco Academy. He is also organist and choirmaster of Subiaco Abbey. His hobbies are reading—especially local history, exploring the outdoors—in particular old cemeteries and home sites, and working as one of the groundskeepers of Subiaco Abbey.